How to Work for a Japanese Boss

HOW TO WORK FOR A JAPANESE BOSS

by Jina Bacarr

A Birch Lane Press Book
Published by Carol Publishing Group

A Birch Lane Press Book
Published by Carol Publishing Group
Birch Lane Press is a registered trademark of Carol
Communications, Inc.
Editorial Offices: 600 Madison Avenue, New York, N.Y. 10022
Sales & Distribution Offices: 120 Enterprise Avenue, Secaucus,
N.J. 07094
In Canada: Canadian Manda Group, P.O. Box 920, Station U,
    Toronto, Ontario M8Z 5P9
Queries regarding rights and permissions should be addressed to
Carol Publishing Group, 600 Madison Avenue, New York, N.Y. 10022

Carol Publishing Group books are available at special discounts
for bulk purchases, for sales promotions, fund-raising, or
educational purposes. Special editions can be created to specifications.
For details, contact Special Sales Department, Carol Publishing
Group, 120 Enterprise Avenue, Secaucus, N.J. 07094

Manufactured in the United States of America
10 9 8 7 6 5 4 3 2 1

Library of Congress Cataloging-in-Publication Data

Bacarr, Jina.
    How to work for a Japanese boss / Jina Bacarr.
        p.   cm.
    Includes bibliographical references.
    ISBN 1-55972-119-7
    1. Managing your boss.   2. Corporations, Japanese.   3 Corporate
culture—Japan.   4. Industrial management—Japan.   I. Title.
HF5548.83.B33   1992
650.1'3'0952—dc20

92-22909
CIP

To Len LaBrae,
my husband and best friend

Contents

Preface

HARRY WAS LIVING THE AMERICAN DREAM. He had a beautiful wife, two bright kids, a regular place on the Friday night bowling team, and a secure job. Then the Japanese bought the plant. Harry, a middle manager, couldn't adjust to their new work schedule. He continued showing up late for work ("I spend more time at the plant than at home," he would say. "What's a few minutes more or less on the clock?"), he joked about how his new Japanese bosses bowed to each other all the time, and he balked when one of them asked him to copy some documents for him ("What have I got a secretary for?" Harry retorted). He rode his Japanese bosses for not giving him precise answers about what was going on and not letting him have a voice in making decisions. Harry was frustrated. He had gotten ahead in his job by being direct and sometimes brash, so he had never questioned his own tactics. He saw no reason to change just because his bosses had.

Sayōnara, Harry.

A few months later he was looking for a new job. Harry had become another statistic in the current game of corporate musical chairs in which more than 50 percent of American managers are either fired or resign under duress within eighteen months of a foreign takeover. Harry's story is not unusual.

Mary worked in Harry's department and was moving up the management ladder when the Japanese bought the plant. She had been warned of their prejudice toward women and other minorities, but Mary felt secure enough in her job to handle it. How-

ix

ever, every time she made a transpacific phone call to Japan, a male colleague had to place it for her. Mary was told that the Japanese at the home office wouldn't accept her call otherwise. They believed that a call from a woman could only be personal, not business.

Mary is still working for the Japanese, but she firmly believes she's stuck in a dead-end job unless there is a change.

Things *can* change—but only if the increasing number of Americans working for Japanese bosses realize it's a new ball game with brand-new rules. In Japan, for example, a tie game in baseball is the most desirable outcome because no one loses face. Logical? you ask. Maybe not to you—but it's the Japanese way. American workers who can learn to change their way of thinking can come out on top of the game.

Just as the Japanese are curious about us, we have become more aware of the Japanese presence in the global economy. However, before we can learn to work with the Japanese, we must understand them. I believe there is a real need to bridge the cultural gap between America and Japan, so it has been my intention to make *How to Work for a Japanese Boss* an informative and also entertaining book for everyone interested in Japan, its people, and its culture—whether or not they find themselves working for a Japanese boss.

What? you ask, Me work for the Japanese? That's crazy. Sure, they bought Columbia Studios and an interest in Rockefeller Center, as well as the Universal Studios tour, but they're not coming to *my* town.

Think again. They're probably already in your own backyard. From the expansion of the Toyota complex in Georgetown, Kentucky, to Nissan's doubling its production capacity in Smyrna, Tennessee, the number of Japanese bosses in America is increasing. Take the Honda plant in Marysville, Ohio. It employs 10,000 workers—and 400 Japanese bosses. Experts estimate that there are more than 200,000 Japanese managers and their families now living in the United States.

According to the latest available figures from the Japan External Trade Organization (JETRO), there are 9,569 Japanese-affiliated companies with operations in the United States. Nearly

8,000 of these companies are corporate entities (the others are restaurants). From the corn belt of the Midwest to the magnolias of the Deep South, there are 1,043 Japanese manufacturing concerns operating in this country. With the building of a $500-million Isuzu and Subaru plant and a $1-billion joint venture with Nippon Steel, the Japanese have turned what would have been a recession in states like Indiana and Illinois into a boom. A hundred new plants opened in 1991 alone, with additional growth anticipated throughout the 1990s. The Japanese Ministry of International Trade and Industry (MITI) estimates there will be nearly *one million* Americans working for Japanese bosses by the end of the decade—over 600,000 Americans (nearly 400,000 in the manufacturing sector) already work for Japanese companies.

The first Japanese car-manufacturing plants opened in the United States in the 1970s. Now the Japanese are involved in everything from making airliner parts in California to raising cattle in Montana; from meat processing to ceramic production; from banks to ball bearings. Japanese-owned computer companies are also on the increase, as are service-oriented industries. Shiseido, a major Japanese cosmetics firm, established the world's first Cutaneous Biology Research Center with MGH Harvard Medical School in Boston, providing them with an $85 million investment for research on skin care. Even a plumbing and toilet fixture company, Toto Kiki USA, Inc., is bringing its water-saving products to America: they've opened a sales office in Orange, California, and are slated to open a production plant in Atlanta, Georgia, by the summer of 1992.

The Japanese boss is also part of the work force in Great Britain, France, Mexico, Germany, and even Hungary, where Japanese corporations are buying all or part of several major companies. The Japanese were also among the first foreign businessmen on Russian soil after the coup of August 1991. There are currently 900,000 workers in Europe employed at more than 500 Japanese companies or subsidiaries, and by the year 2000, an estimated 16 percent of Britain's work force will be working for Japanese companies. For example, Fujitsu, Ltd., is buying Britain's top computer company, International Computers Ltd., for $1.2 billion, while Mercedes Benz, AG, is holding talks with Mitsubishi Motors Corp. regarding coproducing and jointly selling automobile parts. From Thailand to the Philippines, Toyota is investing $215 million in a project to produce components for their cars.

And what about our adventurous colleagues who ask for overseas duty in Japan? Coca-Cola, Kodak, Nabisco, Mars Inc., even Procter & Gamble, maker of Pampers, all have major concerns there staffed with American workers. But it's not any easier for them. American firms lose an average of $155,000 on each employee who leaves the company before his or her assignment is completed. At the present time, 35 percent leave; not even figured into the loss sheet is the cost of replacing that person.

The main reason that Americans at home or abroad do not succeed with their new Japanese bosses is that they aren't prepared. Companies spend millions of dollars dissecting tiny microbes or taste testing a new cola drink, but most spend little or no money on educating their employees about what to expect on an overseas assignment, or about the foreign boss here at home. For example, a large majority of Japanese companies are located in the South and Midwest, where there is surplus labor and where they are given incentives such as low taxes and cheap land by state governments. Except for what they see on the evening news, workers in these areas are likely to be totally unfamiliar with Japanese culture, customs, and language.

This book answers many of the questions American workers ask ("Why do the Japanese bow, and should I do the same?" "Why don't they ever say no even if that's what they mean?" "Why do they take so long to make a decision?") and addresses the difficulties currently arising in many companies: for example, Japanese managers are being segregated from American managers because of lack of communication. Language is not the only obstacle; it's much deeper than that. Even though many Japanese companies are trying to Americanize their operations, they still haven't solved the problem.

My objective is to teach you how to *think* Japanese. This is more important than speaking the language because often what is *not* said is more powerful than what is. The Japanese call this *haragei*, to speak with the stomach. Americans tend to use logic; the Japanese use a system based on emotions and spiritual values that goes back to feudal times when they were ruled by a class of samurai who had the right to strike down any worker whom they felt was not giving them the proper respect.

Times have changed, but to hear some American workers speak, one wonders. "I can't take the grueling hours—the Japanese expect more than I can give," many executives have been heard to say. Even the Japanese themselves are aware that they are dying at a much earlier age from their rigid and often unbending work discipline. But there is change in the air. A labor shortage in Japan has forced Japanese companies to look to the United States and Europe to fill their employment needs.

The Japanese realize that in order to survive into the coming century, they must raise their level of creativity and also assuage "growing anxiety, even fear, in the international community," according to the Japanese Industrial Structure Council. Famous for its three "visions," which have appeared at ten-year intervals since 1960, the Council presented its latest policy to MITI: "human-oriented international trade and industrial policy" is the focus of the new plan, which also stresses "better harmony with the rest of the world."

Consequently, many Americans have discovered they *can* work with their new Japanese bosses, given the opportunity to understand them better. "They don't expect answers overnight," an American manager said. "Quarterly reports are not as important as building strong personal relationships and exercising your ability for long-range creativity."

Although others disagree, saying that the strenuous work schedules and often standoffish attitude of the Japanese boss can be frustrating, some American workers have proven that with time—and knowledge—a good relationship can be developed. It is often said the less businesslike you are in doing business with the Japanese the better off you are; however, there are several accepted rules of doing business with the Japanese both here and abroad that if not adhered to could produce disastrous results.

Even something as simple as presenting your business card *(meishi)* must be handled correctly. Bowing is another tricky situation. The intricacies of bowing could fill a book by itself (not bowing low enough or even long enough has caused more than a few heads to roll). Saying no or, more to the point, saying yes (*hai*—pronounced "hi") is another Japanese art that has baffled Westerners for centuries. If you interpret *hai* to mean simply, "Yes, I understand," or "Yes, I heard you, but I don't know if I agree with you," you'll be ahead of the game. Remember, the Japanese have been taught since childhood to answer the speaker with what he wishes to hear, not with what they are actually thinking.

This brings up another trait that can frustrate American workers in daily on-the-job contact with the Japanese. The Japanese go out of their way *not* to be precise. Being precise is considered bad manners. But never be so imprecise as to be late for a business appointment. A latecomer is thought of as not performing for the benefit of the group, and this is a breach of Japanese business practice that can finish a career before it's begun.

Don't forget the most important word in the Japanese language: *wa*. It means harmony, and everything from business meetings to the tea ceremony is built around it. The Japanese will go to great lengths to preserve harmony, even if it means disrupting it. It's often been said that harmony is more important than profits. Nothing, however, is more important than "face."

Everything is done so that no one loses face. Knowing when to speak and when not to, when to joke and when to be serious, all of this encompasses face. Inner and outer face cause the most trouble for foreigners, but you can learn to understand the difference.

In *How to Work for a Japanese Boss* I will show you how you can succeed with the Japanese by using my Seven Strategies for Success: (1) The boss must not lose face. (2) Learn Japanese customs and culture. (3) Be aware that the Japanese are a vertical society. (4) Practice team effort. (5) Understand nonverbal communication. (6) Think Japanese. (7) Do not try to become Japanese.

With over 600,000 Americans now working for the Japanese and a prediction of nearly *one million* Americans working for them by the end of the decade—as well as the 900,000 Europeans now working for Japanese companies—now is the time for many of us to learn how to work for a Japanese boss.

Acknowledgments

UNDERSTANDING THE JAPANESE, their culture, and their way of doing business has been a lifelong endeavor that has taken me to many interesting places around the world. Over the years I have met numerous Japanese and Americans in the business world and in the classes that I have attended, who added to my knowledge and understanding of the Land of the Rising Sun. Some I met only in passing, but they all graciously told me their personal stories about the Japanese, their culture, and their history, and requested only that I "get it right" in my book. To them I say, *domō arigatō gozaimashita,* thank you.

In preparing this book, there are several people who were instrumental, not only because they told me their personal stories, but because they shared their observations and knowledge of the Japanese in the business world. Thank you to John R. Fuller, Kathryn Brockman, Steve Shu, and Tony Conrado.

There are also several other people whose belief in me and my project was crucial in seeing it through to its production. Thank you to Hillel Black for acquiring my book and looking into the future to see the need for such a book. Thank you also to Bruce Shostak for his suggestions and constructive critique in helping me to put this book together. I would especially like to thank my agent, Richard Curtis, for his belief in me and in my project.

Finally, I would like to thank Len LaBrae, whose valuable insight, critical observations, and ongoing research helped to make this book a reality.

How to Work for a Japanese Boss

1

Why the Japanese Are Different From Us

For if there is one single truth about Asia,
it is that while each country there is totally
different from every other country, Japan is
the most different of them all.
　　　　　—Pearl Buck
　　　　　　The People of Japan

Introduction to the Japanese Culture and Psyche

The world-famous film actor was perspiring under the hot lights on the soundstage as a group of Japanese businessmen silently watched the crew set up for the jeans commercial. Everyone was nervous: the actor, whose yearly salary was reputed to be over $30 million, was concerned about his timing; the director was worried about getting the special effects right on the first take; and the producer was sweating over the exorbitant budget. But no one was more apprehensive than Robert, the American advertising representative. He had put together the deal between the American

1

actor and the Japanese company that was paying him a million-dollar salary to advertise its product. He prayed nothing would go wrong, but he didn't know the Japanese.

The cameras started rolling. As the actor took off his shirt and revealed his muscular physique, the entire entourage of Japanese businessmen broke into continuous, loud applause to show their approval. Surprised, the director yelled "Cut!" The actor turned red and the producer scowled at Robert, who couldn't understand why the Japanese had started clapping wildly. At the meeting earlier that morning they had been serious and reserved; now they were acting like kids at a birthday party. Robert didn't know that Japan has long been called the land of twelve-year-olds. He was working for the Japanese, but he didn't understand them.

Robert had fallen into the trap of thinking that working for a Japanese boss required learning only how to bow and use the right end of the chopsticks. But the Japanese are really different, and working for them without any preparation is like trying to put together a jigsaw puzzle without knowing what the entire picture looks like. The more you try to put it together, the more the pieces don't seem to fit. Yet you *can* learn to understand your Japanese boss. All it takes is time and knowledge.

A History of the Mysterious Japanese

Modern Japan evolved through a series of dynasties ruled over by feudal lords. Historical writings from 807 A.D. record the founding of the first dynasty by Emperor Jinmu in 660 B.C. Since then Japan has always kept an eye on the outside world, although it was never a part of it. Its protected viewpoint was like that of a child peeping through a keyhole. The first actual contact between the Japanese and the Europeans came with the landing of a Portuguese ship in 1543, but by 1639 Japan had decided to adopt an isolation policy and maintained a self-imposed seclusion from the rest of the world for over two hundred years, during which time the *shōgun* ruled by the edge of the sword, forming the beliefs and values of hard work, discipline, obedience, and sacrifice that penetrated the Japanese psyche and still dominate their perception of the workplace today.

During this period, they allowed only the slightest contact with the outside. For example, a Dutch ship could put into port only once a year at a man-made island called *Dejima* (Exit Island) off the coast of Nagasaki. Through the Dutch traders the Japanese were introduced to guns, venereal disease, and tobacco. It's no wonder they didn't open the door any wider.

When the Japanese finally did reopen their doors to the West, they didn't hesitate to explore the opportunities on the outside. The first boat sent to meet Commodore Perry when he anchored his ship in Yokohama Bay in 1853 was not filled with serious-looking officials, but with curious artists, sketching in great detail the Western "barbarians," with their hairy faces and ponderous clothing. Peculiarly Japanese, they were more interested in silently copying what they saw than in trying to communicate with the foreigners, and wasted no time in getting started. These artist-reporters captured the foreigner's habits and customs on woodblock prints that served as photographs for Japanese officials. They scrutinized everything from steam engines to bustles.

Even today the Japanese have been known to follow a similar procedure in business. They often buy an American company to learn how to make a specific product; then, once they've copied it, they perfect it and buy the license to manufacture it in Japan. To keep a pipeline open to American technology, they may continue to operate the U.S. plant as well—but only if it is profitable. Otherwise they will close the U.S. plant and continue to manufacture that product only in Japan.

The practice of copying often frustrates American workers. Sharon was a talented graphic artist who answered an ad to work in Tokyo. As part of her training, she attended a series of classes at a cultural center focusing on Japanese art. Sharon enrolled in a "paper tearing" class where the students were required to copy a collage of paper forms arranged in a specific design. Hoping to impress her *sensei,* or teacher, Sharon felt she could improve upon the design and so she rearranged it. Her teacher, however, severely reprimanded her, and made her do it over and over again until she copied it exactly. Sharon learned from a friend that the Japanese pride themselves on being able to copy things exactly before taking any steps on improvement. Their apprenticeship system is based on this art of copying, and only after mastering it can one become an innovator.

World War II: Who Really Won?

Less than a hundred years after the Japanese began copying the technology of Perry and those who arrived after him, they decided it was time to make that technology theirs alone. When the Japanese invaded Manchuria in 1931, historians warned that this was a step in their strategy of *hakko ichiu,* their plan to cover the world under one Japanese roof. The United States expressed disapproval as they continued their full-scale assault on China, but Americans remained isolationists until a Hawaiian Sunday morning, December 7, 1941, when the United States became a victim of Japanese aggression and entered World War II. The Japanese saw their plan come to a devastating end less than four years later, in part because of their own lack of cultural flexibility.

One of the most important U.S. strategies in winning World War II was cracking the Japanese secret code. Messages from the Purple Machine, as it was labeled, were deciphered and broken only when the Japanese made the fatal mistake of adhering to their unvarying code of rank and ethics and transmitted the same message on two different machines (the Purple Machine was used to send messages to high ranking officials and the Red Machine to embassy personnel). We had already cracked the Red Machine, and when they sent out their duplicate messages, a simple comparison between the two machines assisted American cryptic experts in deciphering their elaborate code. The Japanese were dumbfounded—all the way to their surrender on the USS *Missouri* on September 2, 1945.

When the Allied forces entered Tokyo after the bombing of Nagasaki, Hirohito's hand trembled in fear when he met Gen. Douglas MacArthur for the first time. But the Japanese people found a friend in General MacArthur and in the Truman administration. When the Korean War broke out in 1950, Japan had her first chance to begin on the road back to economic recovery. The war machinery was turned on again as Japanese industry supplied American troops with transports and other war weapons, but this time the big *keiretsu,* or business conglomerates, were running the show, not the military. In the late 1940s when American statistician W. Edwards Deming taught his management theory of planning, implementation, check, and action to the Japanese, he predicted that Japan would bounce back economically in five years. He was surprised when it took only four. Even though not everyone agreed with Dr. Deming's ideas, the Japanese knew that their economy was in a shambles and that they had to change. By 1956, Japan had doubled its prewar industrial output. The Japanese had been quick to realize that the United States had decided not to place any limitations on peaceful production in Japan as long as the people agreed never to take up arms again. (They didn't have much choice. After World War II, the Allied forces even made Japanese schoolchildren cross out any references to "militarism" in their textbooks.)

Japanese industrial output continued to mount during the cold war, fueled by the U.S. strategy of keeping bases in Japan to secure a strong military presence in northern Asia that countered the Soviet Union and the Chinese communists. In return, Japan gained access to the expanding U.S. market and, more important, to the American technology that it needed to keep growing. By 1985, Japan's trade surplus was $39.5 billion. The United States decided that the Japanese were getting *too* rich, too fast. Following a meeting of the top financial officials and central bankers from the group of seven (G-7) major industrial countries (Britain, Canada, Germany, France, Italy, Japan, and the United States) at the Plaza Hotel in New York City, the yen was slowly revalued over two years from 238 to the dollar to around 144. But with Japan's strict import rules, unfair trade practices toward American businesses, and the voracious appetite of Americans for Japanese cars, stereos, and Walkmen, and in spite of the doubling of the yen's value, Japan's trade surplus continued to grow—from $47.6 billion in 1988 to $49 billion in 1989. It declined slightly in 1990, to around $41.1 billion, due to the U.S. recession and Japan's monetary contribution to the Gulf War, but it went up again in 1991 to $44.1 billion. According to an Associated Press poll taken in 1991, three out of four Americans believe the United States is losing the economic war with Japan, and a Times Mirror poll in 1992 concluded that 31 percent of Americans perceive Japan as the new enemy since the cold war ended.

Now it is Uncle Sam's hand that trembles in fear as Americans meet their Japanese bosses. Like those early Japanese artists eager to learn the secrets of Perry's ships, we meet the landing fleets of Japanese businessmen with a mixture of curiosity, awe, and, sometimes, distrust. Take the case of Andrew, a middle manager for a chemical company whose faltering business was recently revived with a large infusion of yen. Andrew was unsure of what would happen to him. After all, he didn't know what to expect from the Japanese. He considered looking for a different job, although he had been in line for a promotion when the Japanese took over. When his Japanese boss did not lay everything about himself on the line, Andrew thought he was being distrustful. Andrew became discouraged and withdrew into himself because his new Japanese boss didn't communicate in a way familiar to him. Other workers began to label Andrew unfriendly, hurting his chances for promotion. If Andrew had learned that the Japanese have a self-effacing reluctance to speak about themselves, he might have been able to change his attitude.

How *do* we get to know the Japanese better? Let's start with the outer layer.

The Physical Makeup of the Japanese

Take something as simple as a driver's license. In the U.S., a license includes your date and place of birth, hair color, eye color, height, and weight. Pretty conclusive. But a Japanese driver's license has no place for hair or eye color. In a country that prides itself on its homogeneity, everyone has the same hair and eye color. Height and weight vary somewhat—the height for the average Japanese has increased significantly over the past century since it opened up to the West. Japanese men grew from an average five feet three inches in the late nineteenth century to five feet nine inches today, while Japanese women increased in average height from four feet ten inches to five feet three inches.

Yet the Japanese are still conscious of the difference in ·their body shape in relationship to Westerners. Mike discovered this when his agent booked him for a commercial in Japan. After seeing his photos, the Japanese advertiser requested him exclusively. Mike was flattered. American actors make big money in Japan, from Steve McQueen, who was one of the first celebrities to do commercials, to Madonna's recent commercial entry where she appears on an elephant. What Mike didn't know at first was that only his hands would be seen on camera. When he asked why, the Japanese ad man replied that Japanese hands were not big enough to be effective in the ad.

Diet plays an important part in Japanese physical makeup. According to the World Bank, the average Japanese eats the leanest diet in the industrialized world: 2,850 calories a day compared to 3,670 calories a day for the average American. There is less protein and more carbohydrate in the Japanese diet than in Western diets, although, according to the Japanese Health Ministry, the average percentage of fat in their diet has risen to 25.7 percent, up from 25.5 percent in 1990. Americans consume more than 37 percent of fat in their daily diets.

According to the latest figures, Japanese life expectancy is the longest in the world, averaging eighty-two years for women and seventy-six years for men. The Health Ministry attributes their longevity not just to medical breakthroughs in combatting disease, but to the healthy Japanese diet consisting mainly of rice, fish, and vegetables. (According to the *Guinness Book of World Records,* the oldest authenticated age was that of a Japanese man: Shigechiyo Izumi was 120 years and 237 days when he died in 1986.) But the United States is catching up: the average life expectancy here is now eighty years for women and seventy-three years for men.

The Japanese diet may also have something to do with their high energy level. In a survey done by an American national health organization, the Japanese led the pace in walking the fastest, and their postal clerks took the least time in selling stamps. Even blood types have come under scrutiny as affecting ability in the workplace.

According to a study done in Japan in 1927, blood types (A, AB, B, and O) can categorize personalities. In the 1980s Mitsubishi Electronics decided to implement this theory by dividing their employees into departments according to blood type. They put together a product-development team with only AB-type person-alities (supreme planning ability and coming up with new ideas are supposed to be AB-blood-type characteristics), while managers were promoted from workers with A-type blood.

Mitsubishi employees reacted favorably to the blood-type exper-iment, and other companies are considering following the same course. This phenomenon of blood-type stereotyping can also be found in some nursery schools, and is included as part of the vital statistics of the employees of an escort service. In the United States it is not unusual for someone to ask, "What is your sign?" In Japan the question is more commonly, "What is your blood type?"

The Inner Sanctum of the Japanese Mind

When Paul went to work for a major Japanese automaker, he brought with him his old gripes about coworkers. He tended to see everything as a bilateral problem—Paul versus everyone else in the office. He never asked for any assistance, but lamented that he had to do all the work alone. His attitude didn't change when he was asked to write a financial report for an administrative meeting. He began complaining right away that he wasn't getting any help from the other people in his office. He spent so much time moaning about his problems he didn't realize that his Japanese coworkers were waiting for him to start the ball rolling. Instead of trying to communicate with them, Paul continued complaining. His report was late, resulting in a lost account. He quit and took his gripes to another company.

Paul didn't realize that Japanese workers perform best in coor-dination with others and often wait for somebody else to point out what to do. Their objective is to remain hidden in the group con-sciousness, so they wait to see what someone else is doing first before they act. They are slow to get moving, but once they move they don't stop.

Studying judo can give you an inside track to understanding the Japanese mind. Meaning "gentle way," judo deals with the idea that reality does not exist by itself, but only in relationship of some-thing to something else. Much of the time in judo is spent waiting for your rival to make a mistake. That requires patience, and patience is learned through meditation. The Japanese have learned to perfect these virtues with their study of Zen—the contemplation of the void. This study of nothingness, known as *mu*, is the root of much of their success.

Mu is the ability to look into the great void and see the possibilities invisible to the naked eye. It does not represent a negative notion as we know it in the Western world; instead, it is a largely unconscious but powerful idea that permeates the Japanese culture. It takes on a similar form in language—in Japanese literature the "words in between the lines" are often the most beautiful because they come from the reader's own interpretation. Japanese artists are famous for their empty spaces on canvas, and Japanese businessmen are even more famous for their silent speeches in American boardrooms.

Mu has enabled the Japanese to rise up from the rubble after World War II, when they had nothing, to a strong economy by believing in the possibilities of building up their country from that nothingness. But what causes the most confusion for American businessmen in everyday communications is the language of *ma*. It's something your mother never taught you.

Timing Is Everything—Especially in What You *Don't* Say

Ma, "space," with the additional meaning of "interval" or "pause," is often the least understood concept of Japanese communication and the one most experienced by Americans working for the Japanese. It is based on the concept of expressing your true feelings through words that may or may not convey your meaning with what is actually said. What *isn't* said, but merely implied, is known as *ma*.

Ross was a quality control manager who prided himself on getting along with his company's Japanese engineers. He went to night school to learn Japanese and felt very honored when they asked him to join them for lunch. They rarely mixed with the Americans, preferring to relax and converse in their own language during their breaks. Ross enjoyed practicing his Japanese, but he almost ran into trouble when one of his co-workers asked him if he liked sea urchin. Ross hated sea urchin, but if he were to say that directly, it would offend his fellow workers. Even if he were to answer that he didn't like it, that might also be considered too direct. Instead, he answered in Japanese that he liked it a little and gained respect in their eyes by giving a proper answer. By giving an answer that would not offend anyone, he correctly used *ma* in order to maintain the calm surface so desired by the Japanese.

"Don't make waves" is the undercurrent that runs throughout the Japanese culture enabling them to maintain their outer calm. The Japanese sometimes respond to your *intention* rather than to what you actually say. Giving a blunt refusal can startle the listener to such a degree that you don't get your point across at all. The Japanese language is structured in a way that you never have to give an overtly negative answer. Even when you use the word for "no" (*iie*, pronounced ee-ay, or iya by men), it is used most of the time as a way to show consideration for others (as in making a choice of what you want) and doesn't really mean no. You can achieve a negative response by what you *don't* say through nuances and timing, which are felt more than learned. The Japanese have devised these methods of communication to convey their feelings in such a way that no one is offended. To the Japanese, the center of those feelings is the stomach.

The Stomach: The Center of the Japanese Soul

In Japanese you don't make up your mind; your stomach, *hara,* decides the course of action. In the West, we employ logic and directness to express our needs—the mind. The Japanese often rely on feeling or intuition—the stomach. For example, if someone wants a favor from you, they merely drop suggestions; consequently the greater the favor, the more elusive the suggestions. The Japanese mind thrives on ambivalence, and this can often be confusing in the workplace.

Dean was assigned to work with a technician newly arrived from Japan. Hideo didn't have his own office yet, so the two men shared a space in the department. It took Dean several days to realize that every time Hideo wanted to use the telephone, he would merely smile, stare at the telephone and mutter, "Excuse me, but . . ." Soon Dean could anticipate Hideo's wants without his saying more than the few English words he knew. Dean learned how important it is to be intuitive in the workplace.

Hara o gaguru means the Japanese businessman is probing your real motives by looking you in the stomach, not in the eye. *Hara ga ōkii* (directly translated: big stomach) means that someone is big-hearted, or magnanimous, not pot-bellied, and *haragei*, words from the stomach, refers to the art of communicating by simply suggesting your meaning in the fewest possible words.

The Japanese maintain this ambiguous outer image of merely suggesting their inner desires to prevent them from being swept away by their emotions. They believe that if their emotions took over they would lose the inner war with themselves and not be able to bounce back strong and powerful, like the resilient *take*, bamboo.

The Bamboo Curtain

Bamboo is strong and, at the same time, extremely flexible. There are 118 varieties of bamboo available in Japan, and it can be bent, stretched, and pushed into almost any shape imaginable—more than 1,400 uses have been listed, everything from chopsticks to water pipes to fans. Bamboo represents eternal life because it remains green all year round. What makes it so special to the Japanese people is its ability to snap back to its original form and continue to grow tall and strong, even after it has been completely bent out of shape.

This notion certainly appeals to the Japanese people, who rose from poverty and devastation to become a dominant power in the world marketplace today. Even though they have achieved that position with the help of Western technology, they continue to reject the Western way of doing things—where individualism is often called in to save the day. Instead, they point to their current success as proof that the way they organize and carry out their ideas is right. After all, they argue, all of their products (which rarely need servicing) are produced by committees and assembled by hierarchical teams.

Let's examine some of those behind-the-scenes work procedures.

It's Off to Work We Go

Cindy enjoyed her job as a tour guide at a world-famous amusement park, especially when she was assigned to escort international travelers. Imagine her surprise when an entire tour group of Japanese engineers asked to spend the day in the huge parking lot. Cindy stared in amazement as the Japanese watched visitors arriving at the park, then carefully recorded how people got in and out of the cars, how many people were in each car, their ages, what they were carrying, and anything else they deemed significant. What Cindy didn't know was that the Japanese engineers were engaged in observational research. After making a careful analysis of their data, they would change their cars to better serve the customer.

Observational research is an important part of the Japanese success story. While American businesses generally spend around 3 percent of profits on research and development, in Japan the figure is more like 25 percent. This works to everyone's advantage because in Japan the results of a project belong to everyone involved. In the United States, if a company develops technology for the government, the contractor retains sole access to that technology. This often results in delays and political bickering. In Japan the race is to see who gets the technology to market first, not who owns it, thereby speeding up the process by a number of years. Japanese companies in the United States, however, lead the list of foreigners who won nearly half of all U.S. patents in fiscal 1991 (ending September 1991); four Japanese firms were among the top five foreign concerns granted patents. (Japanese companies were granted a total of 21,464 patents through August 1991, according to the U.S. Commerce Department.) This is even more amazing considering the fact it still takes a Japanese worker an hour to produce what an American can produce in thirty-one minutes. Overtime in Japan is so common it is considered to be a part of a worker's normal salary—two thirds of Japanese workers continue to put in six-day weeks, even though there have recently been efforts to reduce the number of hours worked.

As the Japanese economy continues to expand, with exports up

9.6 percent in 1991 and imports up only 0.7 percent, many Americans have discovered that the rules of the game aren't always the same on both sides of the Pacific.

Do the Japanese Play by the Golden Rule?

Kurt, an account executive for a food products company, had been working for years to break into the Japanese market. Import quotas had kept his company from competing successfully in Japanese stores, so Kurt was overjoyed when the quotas came off his products. However, although the quotas were lifted, the tariffs went up, and the prices on his products in the stores remained unchanged and were even slightly higher in some cases.

The directors of Kurt's company accused the Japanese of cheating, but Kurt was determined to succeed in the Japanese market. He thoroughly researched their management style and came to the conclusion that the Japanese were simply playing by different rules. He discovered that economic policy drives the Japanese machine and it's almost impossible to know where government ends and the private sector begins.

To compete successfully in their market, Kurt changed the strategy of marketing his products. First, he created a need for his products by providing classes to housewives to show them new ways to use them. The turning point came for Kurt when he changed the packaging and altered the sales campaign to appeal to Japanese taste and the way they live at home. Kurt had learned that the Japanese market appeals to the wants of the consumers as well as the needs. It didn't matter what the cost of the product was once the market had been created.

At Home With a Salaryman

Tatsuo leaned back in his cypress-wood tub and closed his eyes as his wife scrubbed his back with long, caring strokes. Fumiko also enjoyed the ritual. It was the only time they had together to share their thoughts at the end of the salaryman's long day. It was close to 11:00 P.M. and this was the first time Tatsuo had relaxed since leaving home that morning at 6:30 for his long commute to the city. He wasn't alone. The average worker in Japan labors 2,044 hours a year compared to 1,800 hours for American workers.

But the Japanese also enjoy the highest average salary in the world—approximately $32,400 per year (including bonuses, overtime, and housing and other allowances)—and they spend the most money when they go on vacation to the United States: $7.5 billion, or $3,400 per person, per trip. Nearly ten million Japanese traveled abroad in 1990, but Fumiko was not wondering if the family was going to spend her husband's yearly bonus on a vacation. Her conversation centered on the children and their teacher's visit to their home (a common occurrence in Japan). She never asked her husband what went on at work. Many Japanese wives are now trying to change that. They realize that the stress of long commutes and grueling hours is taking its toll. Recent studies support this notion and have coined a new phrase, *karoshi*, or death from overwork.

The Cleansing of the Japanese Mind and Body

The Japanese not only love their baths, but believe that the bath comes straight from the gods (according to creation myths, the gods bathed both during and after producing the universe). Bathing remains a national pastime for them, whether in the privacy of their own homes (83 percent of Japanese households have tubs) or in one of the remaining public bathhouses. In Tokyo's Shirogane district, for example, the Horaiyu bathhouse provides bathing services, but you have to bring your own soap or buy it out of a vending machine. (You can get a coin shower at one-third the price down the street or visit one of the neon-lit *Health Lands* that features everything from billiards to video games.) Today the bathhouse is supervised by a cashier sitting in the waiting room, but in the old days, the job description was far more interesting. Then, the cashier (usually a man) would sit in a perch where he could monitor the activities in both the men's and the women's baths. So much for progress.

The Japanese *are* making progress in toilets. They are currently perfecting an "intelligent toilet" that will analyze urine and sugar levels, proteins and other substances that may signal disease. The results are displayed on a computer screen near the toilet. This may be especially confusing to Westerners because Japanese toilets are confusing in the first place. The toilet you find in Japan has no seat; instead, you simply squat astride the open porcelain bowl and face what we would consider the opposite direction (toward the rear—the better to read your computer printout). However, the Japanese are also fond of eliminating the need for the toilet altogether. *Tachishōben,* the act of urinating in public, is especially confusing to uninitiated foreigners. It's not unusual to see a tipsy salaryman relieving himself against a wall after a night of robust drinking. The Japanese believe it's okay to practice *tachishōben* on the street, but not in a private garden. We know the people who own the garden, they argue, but the people we encounter on the street are merely nameless strangers, and therefore not important. What *is* important in Japan is your *koseki* or official family register.

What's in a Family Name?

When the nineteenth-century writer Lafcadio Hearn decided to make Japan his permanent home, he had to fulfill two requirements for citizenship: first, he adopted a Japanese name (Koizumi Yakumo); then he established a family register, or *koseki*. No Japanese citizen is without one. It is your official identity, your entrée into society. Even though no photo is attached, it is accepted without doubt as positive evidence of your identity. However, it is considered to be the *family* registry (even if the family has only one member) and lists the home address according to the family name, even if you have never been there. It is accessible to any employer or even prospective in-laws who may want to check into your family history.

The *koseki* is also the only legal requirement for marriage in Japan. You and your partner must open up a new joint register at the local Legal Affairs Bureau Office in your city (the wife's name is removed from her family register at this time as if she never existed) or you are considered to be living in sin by the state, no matter how many wedding ceremonies are conducted. (A recent ruling by the Tokyo District Court upheld this law when a couple who did not register their marriage lost their appeal to have their daughter declared their legitimate issue.) After you *are* legally wedded, next comes the pitter patter of little *tabi,* or stocking feet.

School Daze

Children are revered in Japan—there's even a special day on May 5 called Children's Day (*kodomo no hi*)—but even childhood has its pressures in Japan.

Koji was only four years old when his mother enrolled him in a private kindergarten. He wasn't alone—92 percent of all Japanese children start school between four and five years of age, and half of them begin at three. The cost for Koji's school was over two thousand dollars a year, but his playmate, Sanae, was sent to a kindergarten that cost his family nearly ten thousand dollars a year. By the time Koji entered first grade, at age six, he could already write the fifty-one characters of the Japanese alphabet (*hiragana*) and do simple addition. As Koji continued his schooling, he attended extra classes on Saturdays, and later crammed for high school exams on Sundays as well. Once he was accepted into a university (it is often said that it's hard to get in, but easy to graduate), he couldn't change his major or combine independent studies and honors classes to graduate early, but had to follow the course his family had planned out for him.

After kindergarten, the parents of his friend, Sanae, chose the *Jiyu Gakuen,* or Freedom School, for him. There are more than 1,200 students in the school, from kindergarten through college. Here the students learned self-expression, a direct contrast to their traditional system. The students volunteered for activities, asserted themselves in open debates, and often expressed their real thinking. These are traits Americans hold in high esteem, but the majority of Japanese workers you will encounter in the workplace are products of the traditional system where the group-think, group-act approach is the answer to all problems and projects. Remember, the basic unit in Japanese culture is the group rather than the individual. Once you learn to understand this and other cultural differences, you can then apply them to working for a Japanese boss.

2

The New Financial Giants of the Twentieth Century

If you don't want Japan to buy it, then don't
sell it.
        —Akio Morita
        Chairman, Sony Corporation

The Rising Sum of Japanese Investment

Everyone in the office speculated about what the Japanese businessman was carrying in his leather briefcase as he and the other
executives got off the elevator at the penthouse suite. Could it be
cold, hard cash? Everyone had heard stories about cash-rich Japanese buying entire buildings with hundred-dollar bills. Was their
building going to be next? The only man who knew smiled silently
as he ushered his clients into his private office. Stuart was a real-
estate lawyer who specialized in linking local start-up companies
and builders with venture capital. The Japanese businessmen were
his first opportunity to tap the Pacific Rim market. As his secretary
served tea to his clients, Stuart continued to smile—but not for

17

long. He had a lot to learn about managing the fine art of Japanese investment.

First, he had to clear up a couple of lost deposits on some property the Japanese had made an offer on, then reneged on soon afterward when they had tried to negotiate the deal themselves with disastrous results. Culturally, the Japanese have an aversion to dissension on a business level, thereby excluding the use of lawyers because of the very nature of their function. Now they had decided to come to a professional consultant like Stuart, but even then they followed their own rules. They drove Stuart and his staff crazy as they rushed him to draft a purchase and sale agreement, and then continued to review it in painstaking and excruciating detail right up to the scheduled closing date. Even after they had signed the papers, Stuart wasn't certain the deal would go through. Much to the disappointment of his staff, the Japanese didn't pay in cash—the funds were cabled from their Tokyo bank to the firm's local banking institution—but the deal finally went through.

Stuart's story is becoming more common as we speed into the changing economic stratosphere of the 1990s. The Japanese are continuing to invest in the United States (as of 1990 they'd invested more than $200 billion offshore—$130 billion in the United States alone). Although Japanese direct overseas investment retained its number-one spot in the world in 1990 ($48 billion, up 8.8 percent from 1989), it fell 28.7 percent in the first half of fiscal 1991. According to the *Japan Times* they will still commit between $650 billion and $700 billion to direct foreign investment over the next ten years, although at a much slower speed since their highly visible trophy purchases in the late 1980s and early 1990s. American businesses are no longer turning up their noses at Japanese investment. They have little choice. U.S. venture capital has seen its money supply shrink considerably since the mid-1980s, with American venture-capital commitments falling nearly 50 percent since 1988. American financial institutions are no longer lending money for real-estate building, but some Japanese investors are willing to bankroll single-home developments. Only 13 percent of venture-capital investment now comes from foreign sources and that figure will probably decrease as Japanese investors rethink their strategies and invest in the United States at a slower and less conspicuous rate. (The Ministry of Finance has instructed Japanese banks to curtail financial speculations and no longer lend money based on collateral in Japan, but on American investments.)

Although the Japanese economy has slowed down since the speedy growth of the 1980s, it expanded by 5.7 percent in 1990 (compared to 0.9 percent in the United States) and grew at an annual rate of 11.2 percent in the first quarter of 1991 (the United States decreased by 0.1 percent), the highest rate in eighteen years, according to the Economic Planning Agency. It continued to expand in 1991 and surpassed the record fifty-seven-month economic boom that began in October 1965. And it seems like only yesterday when the United States was actually exporting more to Japan than they were exporting to us.

Japan: The Little Country That Could and Did

The year was 1937 when Bert and his girlfriend sat in a darkened movie theater and watched a newsreel about cherry blossom viewing in Japan. They were more interested in holding hands than in watching the screen as the announcer's voice told them about the strengthening economy of the Land of the Rising Sun and its emerging steel industry. Bert and his gal didn't realize that Japan was coming into its own in the early part of the twentieth century and we were helping to put it there.

In 1937 Japan exported $213,142,666 worth of toys, pottery, vegetable oil, and raw silk to the United States, while we exported nearly twice that amount—$423,180,666 worth of lumber, copper, machines, tools, steel, and iron, as well as raw cotton—to them. Hard to believe that half a century later the positions would be reversed with the American trade deficit peaking at a record $57 billion in 1987.

How did this happen? From 1975 to 1989 mortgage rates in Japan remained steady at around 6 percent, while the price of land increased four times. While Japan built factories and expanded the economy, land became their most precious trading asset. Suddenly, many Japanese found themselves with huge equities in real estate. This enabled them to use that equity as collateral to secure bank loans. The Japanese were now suddenly cash rich with no place to invest it. But not for long. With a stable political environment, familiar culture, and a government that welcomed foreign investment, the Japanese played their own version of Monopoly on the game board of the United States.

We welcomed their investment, especially in the factories and electronics industries. After all, we had spent most of the 1980s grooming ourselves for a service economy (now expected to grow at the rate of 1.5 percent annually over the next ten years because of competitive global pressures). Our engineering schools were filled with foreigners who did not speak English, but did speak math, while graduates of American business schools didn't want to dirty their hands in manufacturing. Who could blame them? The U.S. system placed more importance on short-term results, rather than on years of research and development.

We kept the doors open to Japan—until they began buying our national heritage: 51 percent of Rockefeller Center for $846 million and Columbia Pictures for $3.4 billion in 1989, then MCA/Universal Studios for $6.13 billion in 1990. Our gross national product was nearly twice that of Japan's in 1991: $5.5 trillion compared to about $3 trillion. People began wondering, where was our money going? We spend around 12 percent of our gross national product, or $650 billion, each year on health care. In turn, the Japanese spend $675 billion each year on direct investment, consisting mostly of factories, companies, and real estate. Since 1988, about 60 percent of Japanese capital investment has been devoted to research and development of new products and services, as well as to creating new designs and development. Back in 1987, their direct investment made up only 14 percent of their outflow of capital, while in 1990 that figure had risen to 70 percent. By the end of 1990, the overseas assets of the Japanese government, companies, and individuals were $1.858 trillion, up 4.9 percent from a year earlier. Japanese overseas investment is now bigger than the entire output of Canada. Japanese investors are also pouring their money into Europe. Japanese European investments rose from $6.6 billion in 1990 to $54 billion as of April 1991. Their presence is being felt everywhere in the European Community, from Fujitsu's purchase of ICL, Britain's computer maker, to Mitsubishi's teaming up with Volvo in Holland.

When will this seemingly endless river of cash dry up? It's difficult to predict. Although Japan's trade surplus fell in 1990, by 1991 it started to rise again sharply. In August 1991 alone, weaker imports pushed it up nearly 70 percent, to $5.76 billion (it was $3.42 billion for the same month a year earlier), and rose to an historic single month high of $13.58 billion in March 1992, according to the Finance Ministry. The trade surplus is determined by what is in the current account, which measures trade in goods and services. Exports in April 1992 rose 13 percent to $26.58 billion. The Japanese surplus jumped 51 percent in May 1992, with the United States and 25 percent with the European Community. Some analysts argue that we're too concerned with Japanese investment. Great Britain is still the number-one investor in the United States: $400 billion in 1989 and 1990, compared to Japan's number-two $250 billion. However, the Japanese only recently took that position away from the Dutch—most experts predict they will take over the number-one spot before the end of the decade.

What can we do to balance this shift in economic power?

Balancing Act

With few exceptions, in the United States the Japanese have created jobs, improved productivity, provided new capital, and kept flagging markets from disappearing altogether. In addition, Japanese bank assets in the United States account for 11 percent of the total sum of deposits, and Japanese investors generate up to 25 percent of the trading volume on the New York Stock Exchange.

The Japanese are aware of how influential their financial presence is in the United States, but they are now more sensitive to our national pride in their acquisitions. They have learned how to portray their purchases as ones invited by their American hosts, emphasizing long-term market share through limited equity investment. This not only keeps their investments low profile, but they can continue to create new jobs without the political complications of corporate takeovers. More than thirty states maintain offices in Tokyo to vie for such investments, bringing about criticism from local detractors who say that profits and control of vital industries should stay within our borders. The Japanese counter that they are saving many American companies by providing capital the companies can't get at home. They believe U.S. companies have nothing to lose, but a lot to gain. They want us to see their investment as a relationship between the two countries, not as a race to the finish line.

Showdown at Detroit City

Fred peered out the showroom window, surveying his stock of new Chrysler cars. It was raining and there were no customers. Even if the sun had been shining, there wouldn't have been more than a few tire-kickers strolling through the lot. Fred remembered the old days when GM held over 50 percent of the car market, before people like the Honda dealer moved in down the street. Now General Motors could claim only 36 percent of American auto sales, while during the past nine years Japan had gained 29 percent of new-car sales, and this percentage was continuing to rise. Recent figures even put the number as high as 30.3 percent. The Japanese expect to repeat this success in Europe when trade restraints there are eased. They hope to increase their European market share to 16 percent by 1999—beginning in the year 2000 there will be no limit imposed on them. Even the tire-kickers had only one American brand of tire to choose from these days: Goodyear. The other four tire producers were bought by the Japanese, and the number of American auto-part suppliers had been cut in half, from four thousand to two thousand.

Fred gulped down his cup of cold coffee and closed the shades. Along with other Big Three dealers (who formed a manufacturing business called New Venture Gear to combat Japanese automakers) he was reporting huge losses, while autos built at Japanese transplants (Japanese-owned auto plants on American soil) in the Midwest were selling like hotcakes.

When the phone rang, Fred picked it up quickly, hoping it was a customer. It wasn't. Fred couldn't believe his ears when he heard that Mitsubishi Motors Corporation was working on a $100-million-buyout deal of Chrysler's 50 percent share of Diamond Star Motors. Fred didn't know whether to laugh or cry. In an indirect way he too would be working for the Japanese.

More and more Americans are now working in Japanese transplants, adding to the already eroding market for Detroit's products. In 1990 these transplants captured 8.5 percent of the auto sales, and since more plants are being put into operation their share will probably rise to 19 percent by 1993, according to the Industrial Technology Institute in Ann Arbor, Michigan. Nissan plans to open a $500-million car engine plant in 1996. This is their second U.S. facility outside Decherd, Tennessee, and it will initially employ five hundred people, with total employment in the one-million-square-foot plant expected to reach one thousand. Also, Toyota is expanding its Georgetown, Kentucky, plant to boost its U.S. sales to $1.5 million by the mid-1990s, while Subaru and Isuzu have spent $500 million on new assembly plants that employ 2,200 workers to make cars for the American market.

These now join several Japanese-owned assembly plants that have transformed the landscape of America's heartland—Ohio, Kentucky, Tennessee, Indiana, and Illinois. America's Rust Belt fared better than most regions through the recession of 1991, thanks to the economic stability of the Japanese corporations. For example, the Illinois jobless rate averaged just around 5.9 percent in 1989, while during the last recession in the early 1980s it peaked at nearly 11.5 percent. At the early signs of the recession in the winter of 1990, the Indiana unemployment rate dipped below 5 percent. It was in the double digits from 1981 to 1983. In Ohio, the Honda plant alone accounts for more than ten thousand workers, while GM closed down one assembly plant in Cincinnati and threatened to shut down another one in Youngstown.

Americans have jobs, GM says, but at what cost? These transplants will most likely cause the U.S. auto deficit with Japan to jump 47 percent to $45.7 billion by 1994. In the meantime, GM has laid off more than 40,000 workers. There are even cries of foul play in the transplants themselves. Michael Armacost, the U.S. ambassador to Japan, has urged Japanese automakers to increase purchases of U.S. auto parts, claiming that the imbalance of the automotive trade industry is responsible for three-fourths of the

U.S. trade deficit with Japan. (The auto-parts deficit alone could double to $22 billion by 1994, according to the Auto Parts Advisory Committee.) Honda, for example, imports on the average $8,445 worth of parts from Japan for each vehicle; U.S. parts makers account for only $1,585, or 16 percent of the total package. This has caused friction between American management and Japanese owners: The Japanese argue that they have invested $13 billion to build 250 U.S. automobile assembly and parts facilities and employ 78,000 workers. However, according to a study by the Economic Policy Institute in Washington, D.C., they will have eliminated 158,000 more U.S. jobs than they have created. The Japanese insist that they have created jobs where jobs never existed before. To prove their point, Honda, Nissan, and Mazda are encouraging the start-up of major research and development ventures to create even more jobs in the future. Toyota has already opened a new $46-million research and development headquarters in Torrance, California. This is only part of a $220-million investment to strengthen their U.S. research and development capability.

Tom and Ryan are two of four hundred engineers jammed into the temporary offices of an R and D division of a Japanese automaker in the Detroit area. They were both hired away from the Big Three, and Tom expects to return someday, but the two men agree that working for the Japanese is the best of both worlds at this time. Ryan likes the slower pace and time given to produce results, while Tom enjoys the increase in salary.

Both engineers concur that the Japanese are committed to continued development in the auto market, as evidenced by the overwhelming success of two new luxury cars. According to Nissan, over half the owners who purchased the $39,000 Infiniti Q45 sedan traded in foreign cars that cost thousands of dollars more (Mercedes-Benz was the number-one trade-in), while Toyota reported a similar trend with 80 percent of Lexus LS 400 (around $38,000) buyers trading in either American or European cars (Mercedes-Benz, again, was the number-one trade-in).

But the Japanese haven't stopped there. After World War II Japan was known as the "factory to the world," but that is changing as we approach the twenty-first century. Their emphasis is now on taking the miracle of those factories and developing new products before launching them on a global network. We will see a new dawn of auto production pioneered by the Japanese as they strive to develop systems to speed up the manufacturing time to produce cars (from inception on the R and D drawing boards to production) from the current five years in the United States to two years. Their scientists are currently working on mass-customized modular cars that contain a few hundred parts instead of 30,000. It's similar to ordering from the Sears catalog—you pick out the features and accessories you want using mass-customized modular parts. Such advances mirror what the Japanese have been accomplishing in the electronics industry.

Made in Japan, But Invented in the USA

Hugging the pocket in his Roosevelt High letterman's jacket, Bruce couldn't get to school fast enough. His dad had just given him his birthday present, and he couldn't wait to show the guys. As he threw open the locker-room door, he pulled out his new transistor radio and turned up the sound. The year was 1958, a Chuck Berry tune blasted through the locker-room, and a surprised bunch of teenagers heard rock 'n' roll on a transistor radio for the first time. No one knew that while the radio had been made in Japan by a little-known company called Sony, the transistor had actually been invented by American scientists who had won a Nobel Prize for their invention. As soon as America opened her knowledge to the world, Japan took advantage of it. When the Japanese announced they were going to use the transistor to make small radios, the Americans scoffed. That's crazy! they said, and went back to their labs.

During the 1960s and 1970s the Japanese again took advantage of American technology when they picked up an idea that had remained untouched in the public domain for decades: flat-panel displays. Most of the basic technologies for these were invented in the United States, and there were several American companies producing the displays, but the companies had either been sold or closed by the end of the 1980s. Meanwhile, the Japanese recognized the future significance of these flat screens (little flip-up screens that double as dust covers on notebook-sized personal computers) and invested money and engineering talent into turning the concepts pioneered by American engineers into workable products. The Japanese now plan to invest more than $2 billion from 1990 to 1993 in further development. Once again, U.S. companies could find themselves out in the cold (as they have with VCRs) with no stake in what promises to be an $8.4-billion-a-year industry by 1997. For example, Toshiba's portable laptop computer, which fits into a briefcase, is designed to replace the desktop computer.

Sharp was one of the first companies to come on line with a $30-million investment over two years in the building of a plant to make laptop screens in Camas, Washington, that will employ 250 workers. Also, Sony Corporation and Apple Computers are discussing the expansion of their business ties in the laptop market. This is one area lacking in Apple's product line. It makes you wonder what the Apple engineers were doing when Sony's people were developing what Americans had invented in the first place. Now we have to pay for something we once owned.

What do Japanese companies have in store next for the United States?

Computer Chips off the Old Block

When two Japanese businessmen ran into each other at the World Trade Center in New York, they bowed slightly and asked: *"Genki desu ka?"* "How are you?" However, when a third Japanese businessman joined them, his greeting was quite different. *"Moh kete imasu ka?"* the gentleman from Osaka asked his fellow countrymen. "Are you making any money?"

Matsushita Electric is based in Osaka, the most business-oriented city in Japan. Matsushita is one of the most powerful *keiretsu*, or conglomerates, and is made up of a complicated web of interlocking corporate shareholdings in Japan. The conglomerate is proud of its seventy-three-year-old history that has stressed a hard-nosed, old-fashioned approach to business. Yet most Americans said they had never heard of Matsushita when it bought MCA/Universal in 1990—even the newscasters couldn't pronounce it. But how many Americans have Quasar microwaves or Panasonic VCRs? These are Matsushita brand names, as is Technics. Matsushita has eighteen plants operating in the United States, Mexico, Canada, and Puerto Rico, and employs 14,000 workers in these plants (Matsushita has 240,000 employees worldwide).

Now Matsushita is doing more than cooking our frozen dinners: it's buying a giant American computer-chip plant. National Semiconductor Corporation has signed a letter of intent to sell its Puyallup, Washington, chip-making plant to Matsushita for $86 million plus debt. What's startling about this is that when Fujitsu tried to acquire Fairchild Semiconductor in 1986, there was such a political uproar about selling out our technology that they backed out. But when Matsushita announced their impending deal with National, not a whimper was heard.

Why not? Because the United States has already given up too much of its manufacturing capability and we've virtually abandoned the production of consumer electronics altogether. We're no longer in a position to compete with a company like Matsushita. Consider Zenith, the only American company still making television sets. They're pursuing HDTV (high definition television), but they lack the programming resources to make it profitable. General Instrument Corp. and the Massachusetts Institute of Technology (MIT) are one of four American groups proposing a design for an American version of HDTV, but the Federal Communications Commission won't make a decision as to which system of HDTV to adopt until 1993. In the meantime, Sony Corp., Toshiba Corp., and Matsushita Electrical Industrial Co. already operate HDTV research centers in the United States (Hitachi is in the process of opening a HDTV lab in Princeton, New Jersey). The Japanese system costs around $30,000 and features a wide-screen format and 1,125 horizontal picture lines rather than the 525 in traditional television systems. It is difficult to say whether this will continue to be the standard for the industry, although Sharp Corp. introduced a cheaper, simpler HDTV set for $7,580, referred to as "Home" High Vision, in April 1992 and Sony introduced their cheaper version in July 1992.

Matsushita, also slated to introduce a cheaper version of HDTV in summer 1992, is a prime strategist in putting software and hardware together for a total package—that's why they bought a piece of Hollywood along with a semiconductor plant. (Semiconductors are the integrated circuits that are the basic building blocks of computers, wristwatches, telephones, and other electronic equipment.)

Back in Tokyo, the semiconductor business is even better. NMB Semiconductor has the most modern and lowest cost chip-producing operation in the world. They earned $61 million on $260 million in sales in recent years, helping Japan keep its 51 percent of the world semiconductor market (the United States holds 37 percent of the market). It's doubtful that the United States will be able to catch up. It takes two years to build a chip plant here, while in Japan it takes only half as long due to its numerous *keiretsu.* These interlocking conglomerates (like Mitsubishi, whose company officials have met every Friday for over forty years to map out their strategy) produce a steady supply of production engineers and abundant, low-cost capital. In a recent survey by the American Chamber of Commerce in Japan (ACCJ), one-third of the 340 American companies surveyed said that the *keiretsu* have had a positive effect on their business, but with technology changing rapidly, being the first to the market is still the key to being number one in this critical industry. However, critics claim the United States is behind because American semiconductor and computer makers must rely on Japanese suppliers for their technology. If a Japanese company is slow getting that information to American firms, then the U.S. company is late getting their product to the market and is usually left out altogether.

There was a breakthrough, however, in 1991 when the Japanese signed the U.S.-Japan Semiconductor Agreement, a five-year agreement that will give the United States and other foreign countries at least 20 percent of Japan's domestic chip market by the end of 1992. There were some problems when both Toshiba and NEC expressed less than positive views of the agreement, and U.S. officials complained that the agreement was so ambiguous it might sow the seeds of new friction over trade. (As of June 1992, the share of foreign-made chips in Japan is only around 15 percent.)

The playing field may get better for the United States now, but the Japanese continue to acquire the chip designs so they can get to the market first. So how does this happen? The answer is simple:

Several Japanese semiconductor companies continue to buy designs from small U.S. chip-design firms, or even to buy the American companies and the licensing to go with them. But even that doesn't satisfy their demand for new technology. There's a new trend in the works—the idea of Japanese-funded labs run by American scientists on American soil. It sounds like a good idea, but who owns the store?

Welcome to My Laboratory

Parker was very excited about working in a new lab run by a Japanese computer corporation. He had struggled for years to get funding that would allow him to work on his new theories, and now the Japanese were not only giving him more money than he needed, they were also allowing him the freedom to take the time to pursue his research at his own pace. What he wasn't prepared for was his first day at work. He was told by his Japanese boss that he would not be given any technicians to do the lab work, and that he was expected to participate in frequent meetings with customers. Parker was stunned. In his American lab, his work had consisted mostly of individual "think" time to explore lab results, and he had never met with a customer in his entire career. But Parker decided to give it a try. With over 52,000 Japanese scientists working in U.S. labs and fewer than 5,000 Americans working in Japan in 1990, America is experiencing a different kind of trade gap that cannot be ignored.

The Japanese are spending hundreds of millions of dollars to advance their creative IQ and are willing to take a chance. For example, MITI is encouraging Japanese companies to pursue a concept close to nanotechnology (building complex objects on a molecular scale atom by atom), which they believe will be a critical technology in the twenty-first century. NEC, Matsushita, Canon, Hitachi, and Mitsubishi are all participating in opening labs in the United States, with Fujitsu and Ricoh not far behind. Even the U.S. government is trying to attract Japanese funding for a $8.2-billion atom smasher to be built in Texas.

Many American scientists applaud the infusion of Japanese investment in U.S. general research labs, but they may still have their noses stuck in a textbook when the final results are tabulated. Although the Japanese say that the results of their work will be published in scientific journals, the Japanese will also claim the patents on the researchers' best ideas. Where does that leave the United States in the long run? We could end up helping Japanese companies to compete economically against ourselves.

The thought of Japan owning American ideas even before the pencil leaves the drawing board has opened up a few eyes in Washington—the U.S. government has included money in the 1992 budget for the first portion of a $19-billion five-year plan to sponsor research at university and government labs. The only question is: Will it become more than a deal on paper before it's too late?

It's already too late for the steel industry.

Men of Steel

Until 1959, when a 116-day nationwide strike opened American ports to steel imported from Japan, the great steel companies in the United States bore names like Carnegie and Inland and U.S. Steel. Today these names are more likely to be Daido and Nippon. Only twenty years after their plants were burned to rubble during World War II, Japan was exporting better and cheaper steel to its markets than the United States or Europe could manufacture, and by 1980 they were producing more than 110 million tons annually. This arose partly from their huge investment of approximately 30 percent of their annual income in new plants, compared to 16 percent in the United States, as well as their foresight, which envisioned future dominance of the auto industry. Now that dream has come full circle. The Japanese investment in American steel—valued at $7 billion in sixty-six Japanese-owned or joint ventures in U.S. steel plants—today employs 30,000 workers. Big players like Nippon Kokan Steel of Japan have united with Pittsburgh's National Intergroup in a joint venture (Nippon owns a 70 percent stake) to modernize the Great Lakes Steel operation in Michigan to supply steel for the growing number of Japanese transplants. Nippon Steel is also teaming up with Chicago-based Inland Steel in a $1-billion joint venture to produce high-quality steel at a new mill in Indiana.

The world's largest special steel maker, Daido Steel Company of

Japan, bought a 17 percent equity stake in CSC Industries, the U.S.-based parent of Copperweld Steel Company, for approximately $2.7 million. Yet American steel companies, even with Japanese partners, are suffering. Kawasaki Steel and Armco Steel have postponed scheduled construction of a new galvanizing line in Middletown, Ohio.

With American companies losing as much as $1.3 billion in 1991, one U.S. steel company is fighting back. Nucor Corporation is known for its maverick management style and for its continuous casting machine (only 66 percent of U.S. raw-steel processing is done this way, compared to 93 percent in Japan). Nucor continues to figure out how to undercut the Japanese in a field that has all but disappeared from the American landscape. But the corporation may be fighting a losing battle: experts predict that most of the U.S. steel industry will be in Japanese hands by the year 2000.

The Japanese are also buying the ground from under our feet.

This Land *Was* My Land

Pam and Keith fell in love with the house the minute they saw it. It was part of a new housing development, based outside Los Angeles in Orange County, that consisted of low-priced homes and condos, and that offered them the kind of planned community where they could raise a family. It was their part of the American dream.

What Keith and Pam didn't know was that the major residential-development company, Birtcher Homes, that was building the project was 50 percent owned by a Japanese trading company, and along with its new American partners, it expected to build as many as one thousand such homes and condos annually by 1996. Even when Keith and Pam applied for their home mortgage, their note was held by a Japanese investor who had bought mortgage-backed securities. Ten percent of new home mortgages in America now flow into the hands of the Japanese. One company, Blackstone Group, sold out a special $570-million mortgage securities package it had created especially for Japanese investors. Tens of billions of such dollars are expected to enter the home-mortgage market in the future.

Why are the Japanese suddenly turning to the home market?

Don't they already own enough American real estate? (They control 60 percent of prime real estate in the downtown Los Angeles financial district.) New tax laws, however, make it more difficult for them to invest in U.S. real estate, and they're still reeling from the big losses they suffered in office development in the 1980s. Although the strong yen allowed the Japanese to pick up U.S. real estate at half price, they've discovered that homebuilding offers a quicker financial return than buying and holding large office buildings that often have big vacancy ratios. One prominent American real-estate developer said that Japanese investment has become very important in a period when domestic financing for developers has practically dried up.

There's even talk from some American builders about extending their partnership to the home-building industry in Japan when the Japanese lift a ban on wood-frame apartment buildings in 1993. If this happens it will help smooth over bad feelings between American builders and Japanese businessmen. While both countries receive approximately the same amount in contracts from each other's government ($100 million), Japanese construction firms won about $3.3 billion worth of new work from private U.S. businesses, while U.S. firms have received only about $440 million in construction contracts (including architectural and design work) from the private sector in Japan as of April 1991. An agreement in the summer of 1991, however, opened up an additional $6.4 billion worth of seventeen new construction projects available to American and other foreign firms. This helped ease tensions between the United States and Japan, but it's not the final answer.

Although the United States does own property in Japan, it didn't come cheap. The cost of land in Japan rose an average of 38.1 percent in 1990. According to Colliers International, at an average of $214 a square foot, Tokyo tops the market for the most expensive office space in the world. A square yard of land in Tokyo's Ginza shopping district goes for $252,000, or up around 17.5 percent from $215,000.

It's no wonder that *Forbes* magazine reported in 1991 that four of the ten richest men (excluding royalty and heads of state) in the world are Japanese. Number one is Taikichiro Mori, a Japanese economics professor who owns seventy-eight office buildings worth $15 billion.

According to experts, the Japanese will continue to invest in U.S. real estate, although at a slower pace (around $5.1 billion in 1991, compared to $14.8 billion in 1989 and the peak in 1988 of $16.5 billion). According to a recent survey of Japanese executives by Mead Ventures Inc. of Phoenix, Arizona, 43 percent of those executives polled said they expect their firms' real estate-related business to decline in 1992, compared with 1991. The Japanese are a land-poor nation and traditionally cultivate what they don't have—especially American movies.

The Japanese Take Over Hollywood

The magazine stand on Hollywood Boulevard was packed with actors, cameramen, makeup people, soundmen, and wardrobe ladies grabbing every copy of *Variety* from the stands. None of them could believe the headline, SONY TSUNAMI TAKES COLUMBIA, but it was true. The Japanese corporation had finally made public what had been just a rumor: In September 1989 it purchased Columbia Studios for $3.4 billion. The biggest question on everyone's mind was: would it change the way movies were made?

Meanwhile, Matsushita Electric was getting in on the action when they agreed to buy MCA/Universal in November 1990 for $6.13 billion, making it the fourth of the nation's seven major studios in foreign hands. MCA controls many properties, including Universal Pictures, Universal Studios Tour (in Universal City, California, and a similar theme park in Florida), a publishing house (G. P. Putnam's), record labels, and interests in cable television and movie theaters.

In March 1990, *Variety* reported that Japanese enthusiasm for show biz was running high, even going so far as to say that "hundreds of millions are bubbling everywhere and new transactions seem to pop up daily." "Hollywood people are learning Japanese," the trade paper touted, as if that was as easy as naming a new dish in the studio commissary.

A year later, in April 1991, the bubble burst, as *Variety* reported

JAPANESE ARDOR FOR H'WOOD DIMS in connection with the overaggressive deal Yamaichi General Finance Company had orchestrated with Disney, in which the Japanese securities firm received only 6 percent on their $600-million investment, while U.S. investors were receiving 15 percent—and the Japanese didn't even know the titles of the films they were backing. Things didn't improve when a memo written by Disney boss Jeffrey Katzenberg began circulating around Hollywood, stating that the Japanese were getting into a business outside their cultural ambit. The Japanese responded by saying they wanted to make money, not movies (in Japan, investors can write off 90 percent of their investment in a film in just two years—that's almost twice as fast as the IRS allows U.S. film investors).

Meanwhile Japan's Nissho Iwai Corporation has developed a $150-million motion picture investment fund with Mount Film Group of Los Angeles with distribution by Universal, which just happens to be owned by Matsushita, which also has an interest in the Cineplex Odeon theaters. Could this be the beginning of a *keiretsu* on American shores? How about Sony? That Japanese corporation owns the Loews theater chain and has already formed Sony Electronic Publishing to cash in on the video game business, which has $5 billion in retail sales annually. Using video and computer technology, Sony is working on incorporating clips from movies into video games—and they have a lot to choose from. When they bought Columbia, they received a library of 2700 films and 23,000 television episodes. They are also leading the pack with HDTV research and have recently introduced the new Data Discman in the United States in November 1991 (the Data Discman is a personal information machine the size of a pocket dictionary, connected to a nineteen-inch color television). It contains travel guides, dictionaries, even golf guides.

But the Japanese are not confining themselves only to the American media. Japan is already producing a sort of HBO of Asia, called "WOWOW: World's Worth of Wonder" (Home Theater Channel), that went on the air in April 1991 from Japan Satellite Broadcasting, Inc. (They also have a $2 million stake in the Tony Award-winning show *The Will Rogers Follies* and they recently signed a deal with Sony to license feature films.)

Surprising Acquisitions of the Japanese in the United States

As Millie rang up the customer's snack cakes and soda pop on her old cash register, she couldn't help but notice the paint peeling off the walls and the cracked formica counter. Thank goodness the Japanese had pulled her store out of bankruptcy, she thought. Now they would be able to make all the repairs they had been putting off for years. The Japanese like things *just so,* she reflected, handing the customer his purchases. Everything was going to be all right now. "Thank you for shopping at 7-Eleven," she said with a big smile.

The 7-Eleven chain, which started out in 1927 as an ice shop in Dallas, is now 70 percent owned by Ito-Yokado Company of Japan. When Southland Corporation filed the second-biggest retailing bankruptcy case in U.S. history, they weren't sure whether the Japanese would pump the $430 million they needed into the company, but they succeeded in overcoming the Japanese aversion to bankruptcy and closed the deal.

Other American companies have also looked to the Japanese for investment in recent years—many of them are old favorites. Thermos Company was bought by Nippon Sanso K.K.; Steinway Pianos, founded in 1853, was sold to Kawai; Daiohs Company, Ltd. bought both Secretary Coffee Service, Inc. and Almar Service of California; Heavenly Valley Ski Resort in South Lake Tahoe was sold to Kamori Kanko Company; the company that makes Fender guitars was sold for $12.5 million to a group of Japanese investors; even trees in Alaska were sold to a mill owned by a consortium of Japanese investors; and, finally, Yamanouchi Pharmaceutical Company bought the Shaklee Corporation for $395 million.

Putting a Japanese Investor on *Your* Shopping List

How do you interest a Japanese partner or buyer? Here are a few tips: (1) Know the strengths of your company before you seek out a partner/buyer—the technology you have to offer, new products, services, etc. (2) Develop a slow but steady relationship with a comparable company in Japan. If you are a small company, working with a young Japanese entrepreneur can be advantageous for both of you, but if you need major contacts, working with a top-ten company would be more beneficial. (3) Network with other Americans who have been successful in working with Japanese investors. You can learn from their mistakes as well as pick up new leads. (4) Find a good adviser who speaks Japanese and understands your market. You can never fully negotiate by yourself, and you need someone to keep you apprised of any negotiating nuances you don't understand. (5) Finally, even after you've found an investor, nothing is guaranteed. Although as a rule Japanese companies prefer joint real-estate ventures with Americans because of the flexibility, this does not guarantee that they will always be in agreement with you. They will pass or back a deal according to their needs. Follow through on every point as carefully as your Japanese partner does. Although the Japanese believe that a handshake is as good as a contract, you will experience many group meetings before all the details are worked out.

Japanese investment in the United States was at an all-time high in the 1980s before taking a downturn in the early 1990s, but it will continue to be part of the American landscape as we head toward the twenty-first century.

3

The Japan of 1001 Faces

Face is more powerful than money.
                    —Japanese proverb

What Face Is and How Not to Lose It

Face exists everywhere in Japan and can sneak up on you when you least expect it, even at a baseball game.

As the crowd of Japanese *bēsu-bōru* enthusiasts anxiously waited for the next player to step up to bat, Dave (an importer for a medium-sized company) looked at the smiling Japanese businessman sitting next to him. The American was pleased. Since his arrival in Japan, everything had been going according to schedule. He had been working on building a personal relationship with Mr. Yamato for several weeks, and today promised to be the highlight of his trip. He was certain Mr. Yamato would be ready to discuss business after the game. Dave could already envision his company's products being loaded for delivery to Japan.

As the batter made contact with the ball, Dave looked up to see a foul ball heading straight toward him. He caught it with his bare hand, then showed it proudly to his client. Mr. Yamato said nothing. He merely smiled. Dave smiled back as he put the ball into his pocket. What a souvenir this will make, he thought, not realizing that Mr. Yamato seemed to be waiting for him to do something. Dave had no idea he had missed an opportunity to gain face in the eyes of his client by following the Japanese custom of returning the foul ball to the park usher. He would still get the account, but he would have to wait longer than he expected.

And so it is in the Japan of 1001 faces.

Defining Face

Face is the image you show to others through your actions or your nonactions. It is your silent partner at meetings with your Japanese boss or clients, where politeness is considered to be more important than accuracy. This often confuses Americans. We are used to saying what we mean. We like direct eye contact and believe it is essential to establishing our good intentions in business. The Japanese, however, consider direct eye contact discourteous and disrespectful. They go out of their way to avoid it.

Face has also been defined as an intuitive ability to know when to speak and when to be silent; when to say yes and when to say nothing at all; when to talk business and when to joke; when to take your shoes off and when to leave them on. Japan is a culture that fears failure, and it is this fear that constitutes the underlying purpose of the safety valve we've come to know as "face."

Your Japanese boss or co-workers will more often than not say what they think you want to hear, implying that by not saying anything negative they are saying something positive and keeping face. They have a deep-seated desire to protect *wa*, harmony, at all costs. *Wa* comes from the ancient word meaning "circle." A circle has no beginning or end, no way in or out. The Japanese not only accept this concept in their work ethic, but embrace it with reverence and deep emotion and work hard to keep their circle intact. This way of thinking has a long history.

A History of Face

The concept of face originated in Japanese mythology, which maintains that Japan was created by two divine beings, or *kami*.

This belief long ago instilled in the Japanese a sense of superiority, but they've also harbored feelings of inferiority since the third century, stemming from their own inadequacies at that time in comparison to the rich culture of China.

Throughout Japanese history, face has been more important than anything else. During feudal times the samurai considered it their duty to commit suicide if they failed in a mission rather than lose face. Even though they held the purse strings, the merchants and bankers were subjected to losing their heads if they threatened the "face" of any samurai. They ranked below the samurai in society, and their place was clearly established by the shabby clothes they were mandated to wear by the ruling class. The merchants, however, gained face among themselves by lining their worn outer garments with expensive silks and furs.

From everyday situations to the most formal events, everything was regulated. Every manner or action was either right or wrong. Etiquette even went so far as to require a person riding in a vehicle to stop, get out, then bow to a senior person walking on foot. Face would be lost to those who did not follow the rules. This is an example of *shikata*, or the way of doing things. It became more important to do things the right way rather than to do the right thing. Because of this the Japanese have developed a unique perception of the world known as inner and outer face.

Inner Versus Outer Face

The Japanese have long been accused of being "two-faced," but what we are really dealing with is the emotional quality of an action versus what is being said. Form, the accepted way of doing things, is more important than words to the Japanese. Words are merely a verbal interpretation of the situation (the words may or may not convey what is going on) so that social harmony can be maintained at all times. The Japanese call this *tatemae*, face or façade. *Honne*, honest voice or real intentions, is what is not being said. Politeness versus honesty. Although we do it too (but not to the extent of the Japanese), it often causes misunderstanding between Americans and their Japanese bosses and co-workers. Once *tatemae* and *honne* are understood, however, we can learn to work along with the custom.

Julie worked in a large Japanese company on the West Coast that had brought over several Japanese secretaries to handle the heavy correspondence load. She became friendly with Tamiko and decided to drop by her house one day to deliver some paperwork. Tamiko politely told her she was about to make some lunch and invited Julie to stay. At first, Julie thought this might be a way to develop her personal relationship with Tamiko and asked her if she could help in the kitchen. Tamiko looked at her strangely. Luckily Julie remembered it was considered impolite to look into a Japanese kitchen of a home you are visiting. She realized her mistake. Tamiko was actually asking her to leave in her tactful, Japanese way. Julie thanked her for the offer and left. After that Julie noticed Tamiko went out of her way to help her at the office. She had gained great face in the eyes of the Japanese secretary.

Face in Today's Workplace

Today's Japanese businessmen follow a modern code of *Bushidō*, or Way of the Warrior, where face is more important than meeting a deadline, being frank or consistent, or, in extreme cases, even life itself.

This was evident when Mazda executives voluntarily took temporary 5–10 percent pay cuts because of the mishandling of safety problems in some of their passenger cars. It also is the reason the president of Japan Air Lines resigned when a plane crashed and killed 520 people, and why, during a recent political scandal, a member of the Japanese Diet hanged himself. Yet many argue that scandal is an integral part of the Japanese financial system and is almost impossible to prevent—especially when the only form of punishment is *hansei* (when Japanese executives promise to reconsider their plan of action and presumably reform). New rules to curb paybacks by brokerage houses to clients, however, are being issued by the Finance Ministry—all in the name of saving face.

Typically, Americans wouldn't resign from a job, take a pay cut, or commit suicide if they shamed or embarrassed others. (In a survey by the *Los Angeles Times* of tens of thousands of newspaper and magazine articles over the last five years, only a handful of stories could be found where American executives openly acknowledged their own responsibility for organizational failures.) Americans working for the Japanese find it difficult to understand this kind of face where, according to an old proverb, "the emperor suffers first and takes his pleasure last." We are more concerned with personal or individual advancement in our jobs (although several American companies are now adopting the idea of using work teams who supervise themselves). We are more accustomed to having lawyers and public relations firms eliminate responsibility for mistakes with lawsuits and form letters. For example, when Ford Motor Company falsified emissions tests, no resignations or apologies were made. Ford merely paid off the $7-million lawsuit and continued doing business.

The Japanese way of thinking, however, encompasses a deeper feeling of loss, especially if they have lost face in front of others. Whether on a national level or in a small business, they will feel the pain of that loss for a very long time.

Face Is More Than Skin Deep

Learning how to acquire face is not new to Americans embarking on business ventures in Japan. Commodore Perry spent many hours in his cabin poring over his options when he anchored his ship in Yokohama harbor in 1853. He knew that he had to "confer personally with no one but a functionary of the highest rank of the empire" to be granted respect, or face.

Perry was aware that the Japanese do business based on your level of face. This includes your rank, your importance within the company structure, even the way you conduct yourself socially. Finally, your humility and manners also determine your level of face. According to the Japanese way of thinking, you are not only representing yourself and your company, but also your ancestors as well as future descendants.

This type of face has its roots in a very complicated system of rules and obligations that still exists today, beginning with the basic *on*, or debt, received from one's family, teacher, emperor, or anyone else imparting an obligation to be fulfilled (receiving a gift, for example). There is also *gimu*, which is a required debt from one's emperor, parents, and ancestors. And finally, *giri*, duty to one's name, which is the Japanese way of making payment to an *on* incurred outside one's circle. To lose face means more than simply being embarrassed or insulted—the national character is at stake. This deep sense of duty compels them to act in a way we may not understand, or at times appreciate.

Randy and Kaiho worked together in quality control in a computer company. When some defective parts were shipped to a customer, Randy called the store and assured them a new shipment was on the way. Kaiho said nothing, but he felt obligated to hand in his resignation and return to Japan. Randy called him and sent letters, but he received no response. Because of the mistake with the parts, Kaiho believed he had lost face, and acted accordingly. Kaiho assumed that Randy would understand his actions and accept them. It is a cultural trait of the Japanese not to express themselves clearly, even in a business situation.

In working for a Japanese boss, it is necessary to understand the meaning of *on* and be prepared to act when a debt is incurred. Repaying a debt, however, is a difficult art to master with finesse.

Kenneth was a private real-estate investor with many Japanese clients. On a trip to Japan, one of his clients gave a lavish banquet in his honor. Kenneth reciprocated by throwing a bigger and more expensive party for his client. When he noticed his phone calls were not being returned, Kenneth discovered that he had made his customer lose face by outdoing him. Only after several months of casual visits to his client's office to display his friendliness and trust did Kenneth regain face. The Japanese call this "selling face," and it can also be used as a way of reminding a Japanese businessman about a pending deal without appearing to be too brash or bold.

Face Taboos

Embarrassing moments caused by cultural differences can be handled without losing face if you are aware of those differences.

Brittany worked for an American firm recently bought by the Japanese. She had been at the company for more than ten years and was surprised when her new Japanese boss asked her age. She didn't know how to answer. She was nearly forty, but she had never told anyone in her office. She told him the truth, but she was curi-

ous to find out if this was a common question in Japanese companies. She did some research and discovered that the Japanese are
not sensitive about personal information. However, to gain face,
Brittany could have also assured her boss that if he was asking
about her experience and loyalty to the company, her work record
was proof of that.

Age to the Japanese mind is a matter of respect, not a subject to
be ridiculed. In the American workplace inquiries about age are
illegal questions. (However, according to a Supreme Court decision in May 1991, some employees may not be able to sue for
alleged age discrimination if they have signed a previous agreement with their employer that they will submit any claims to arbi-
tration.) Many male and female American workers dread the
stigma that is often applied to approaching age, and younger men
are often insulted when it is implied they are too young for a position with responsibility. In Japan a man's opinions and thoughts
don't become important until he reaches the age of forty-one. The
middle years, when a man tries to find his place in the world and is
making a living, are not given much respect in Japan. Forty-one is
the turning point as a man heads toward *beiju*, the age of rice, or
eighty-eight years of age. (Celebrations of old age begin at sixty.)
And a senior manager does not attain full senior status until he has
worked thirty-five years with the same company and shows *gaman-
zuyoi*, strong perseverance.

The Japanese are not only open-minded about age, but are open
as well about religion, education, and income level. In fact, when
Japanese salarymen get together for a game of golf, they tee off
according to their salary levels.

How Not to Lose Face With Gift Giving

We do it frequently, but the Japanese do it all the time: give gifts.
There are strict rules of etiquette regarding the giving and receiving of gifts that can make you gain or lose face in the eyes of your
Japanese boss. Some Japanese can calculate the expense of a gift
down to the last yen and return one with the same value. Recip-
rocating with a gift is not expected by your Japanese boss, but it is
important to follow some simple rules in giving and receiving gifts.

Alanna worked as an assistant for a manager in a Japanese company with a branch in the United States. When her boss gave her a gift after he returned from a trip to the home office in Osaka, she was so enthusiastic she opened it immediately in front of everyone in the office. It was an expensive bottle of French perfume. Alanna apologetically told her boss she couldn't wear heavy perfume because of a skin allergy. She learned later that she had lost face—not because of her comment about the perfume, but because she had opened the present in front of her boss and everyone in the office. This gesture had caused everyone to lose face.

If you receive a gift from your Japanese boss or co-worker, be certain to accept it with great pride and open it later in private. Thus, if the gift is not appropriate or if the receiver doesn't understand what it is, no one loses face. You could also lose face by leaving the gift in a corner of the room or by putting it by the side of your desk, as if it were forgotten. Another business strategy that can backfire is giving surprise gifts. If the recipient doesn't have one to give in return, at least the same value or a more expensive one, it can mean loss of face for that person.

When you give a gift for a job well done or at the times of year when gifts are given in Japan, be certain to give them privately so that no one is singled out for special attention. (*Seibo* are given out from about December 10 to the end of the month; *chūgen* are given out on the last day of the Lantern Festival, July or mid-August.) Furthermore, wrapping gifts is such a complicated process, have yours wrapped by a professional gift wrapper who knows the subtleties of gift-giving, especially if the gift is for a section chief or company head. (In the United States, go to a Japanese gift shop, if possible.) Finally, be aware that the Japanese often give gifts as a way to incur *on*, debt or obligation, in the workplace. This is an unspoken means of communication used as a reminder of the interdependence of the group.

In choosing gifts, the Japanese put a face value on status. Knowing this could result in gaining face in the right situations.

Doug thought he understood his Japanese bosses, but on a trip to Japan he found out differently. He enjoyed the after-hours time he spent with his colleagues at the *ofuro*, bath, but he couldn't understand why he would catch them sneaking glances at his clothes as the men disrobed before going to the baths. The Japanese were merely checking out the labels on his clothes. The Japanese love designer labels on everything. What we often consider ostentation, they consider status.

Certain labels, such as Bally, Gucci, and Valentino, rate very high and give the wearer great face (occasionally, Japanese businessmen even wear their designer ties turned over so that the labels show). Swiss watches are considered to be first class (*itto*), so are Louis Vuitton goods.

Female Face

Women encounter unique difficulties regarding face in Japan. Even the way a woman dresses is important in maintaining face: a woman's neck is considered to be the most sensuous part of her body and should always be covered in the workplace (geisha are notorious for wearing their kimonos pulled low in the back, revealing more neck and back than a proper lady would ever dream of doing).

Most women stay in the workplace for a maximum of five years, during which time they are supposed to be looking for a husband to keep face.

Face often requires understanding the unique perspective the Japanese have of the world. This includes more of what isn't said but merely implied. Many times losing face has its roots in a long history of form and custom totally foreign to our way of thinking, as in the case of Didi.

Didi was very excited when she was invited to attend a flower show with the wife of her Japanese boss. She knew she was being given a rare opportunity to socialize with a Japanese wife and this could strengthen her relationship with her boss. She wanted to make a good impression so she dipped into her savings and bought an expensive outfit in bright, pretty colors. She didn't understand the guarded looks of her hostess and the other women when they stared at her dress. The other women were all dressed in soft, pastel colors so they wouldn't lose face by taking away from the beauty of the flowers. Didi was unaware that her bright clothes made her lose face. It took many months before any future invitations came her way.

Women have long been the victims when it comes to losing face in the masculine-driven Japanese society. In fact, the Japanese character for woman also means noise, which is something they find unpleasant and determine to be a loss of face in excessive amounts.

But the biggest problem comes from Japanese men who are known for shifting the blame of losing face onto someone else. During the notorious Recruit Scandal in 1988 when several businessmen and members of the Japanese Diet could have suffered loss of face, the responsibility was often transferred to their secretaries or wives. But some women are fighting back.

When a Japanese woman lost face because her husband died during a routine operation for appendicitis, she refused to take the blame. She had been criticized for taking a job, which in the eyes of Japanese society caused her to neglect her husband and was considered the underlying reason that the operation was not a success. The woman, however, gained face when she sued the doctor for malpractice.

Japanese women are also changing the way they approach the challenges of entering the workplace. Many young Japanese women continue to have plastic surgery on their faces (doubling eyelids and heightening noses are the most popular surgeries performed) to appeal more positively to male recruiters in Japanese companies.

Gaining Face With a Song

Gaijin, foreigners, can gain face in the eyes of their Japanese bosses outside the workplace as well. Howard and Stacy both worked for a large Japanese company. When they were invited to the annual office party, Howard arrived ready to have a good time and forget the pressure of the daily grind of trying to understand his Japanese bosses. This was a "let-your-hair-down," or *bōnenkai,* party. What Howard didn't realize was that it didn't mean "let down your face." While his Japanese co-workers took turns performing in front of the group (singing, playing a musical instrument, giving a recitation, even doing a traditional dance with fans), Howard merely shook his head when it was his turn. He wasn't going to make a fool out of himself with some silly fans or singing in front of a tape machine. Stacy, however, grabbed the mike and warbled her way through numerous choruses of "My Way." She was the hit of the evening and gained great face in the eyes of her Japanese boss and co-workers. Howard not only lost face for himself, but for his host as well.

The Japanese expect everyone to have a *kakushi gei,* a hidden talent, that is displayed only at parties or social gatherings. Singalong machines and tapes called *karaoke,* meaning "empty orchestra," have become the most popular way of performing at parties.

Entertaining at parties is not the only way to gain face socially with your Japanese boss. Chad was a manager at a Japanese securities company and often took his clients to dinner at fancy continental restaurants. Although he spoke the language reasonably well and was knowledgeable about the culture, he felt something was missing in his relationships with his Japanese clients.

One day after work he wandered into a small Japanese restaurant hidden away in the corner of a mini-mall and was surprised to see many of his clients dining there. He had never seen them so open and friendly, laughing and joking together. He found out the reason they were so relaxed was because they were well-known, that is, they had face at the restaurant. Chad made a point of frequenting a special Japanese restaurant several times a week until he gained face with the owner and servers. Afterward, he began taking his clients there, impressing them and gaining face. Chad's business increased dramatically; he had learned that face is more important to the Japanese than business acumen.

Smiling Faces

Aiso, the art of smiling and being courteous, is as much a part of the Japanese character as bowing—and often a source of irritation to Westerners. We often interpret constant smiling to be a sign of deception or nervousness, while the Japanese have learned to hide their feelings of embarrassment or shame behind this mask of courtesy. Constant smiling is considered to be neither false nor deceiving, but an art that is admired and practiced with great skill. The Japanese put on a smile to avoid a sign of individual embarrassment and also loss of face. They will even smile at death or personal tragedy because they have been taught not to burden or disturb the peace of another person with their own troubles.

Jessica was a victim of this type of face during a business trip to Tokyo. When she decided to take in some local sightseeing, she took along a matchbook with the name and address of her hotel written in Japanese characters, but she lost it somewhere along the way and had no idea where her hotel was. Jessica hailed a cab and told the driver the name of the hotel. He smiled and pulled out a map, indicating for her to point to its location. When she told him she couldn't read the map, he continued to smile as he opened the door for her to get out. Jessica realized he had lost face because he couldn't help her. This happened to her twice in a row, and both cabdrivers never stopped smiling.

Understanding what face is, its nuances and intricacies, is only the groundwork for gaining face in the workplace. Next we will explore how to acquire face and how not to lose it.

How to Acquire Face

First let's take a look at the American workplace and how we do business. When you arrive at a client's office it is considered good manners to shake hands first, then place your business card on the desk. The client may not pick up the card immediately, but he or she will acknowledge it with a thank-you. Many people do not have business cards and it is not considered impolite to simply introduce yourself.

This would drive a Japanese businessman crazy. Even before you consider making a bow or shaking hands with a Japanese client, present your *meishi,* or business card. Your business card is your most important tool in making a first impression. Your company name, your name and title, and other particulars should be printed in English on one side, in Japanese on the other.

The company name comes first, frustrating many an American ego. An untitled Sony employee is more impressive to the recipient

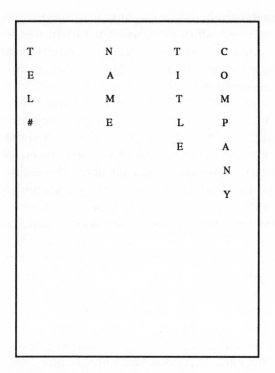

Figure 1. Business card layout for Japanese side.

of the card than the executive president of a small, obscure firm. Younger Japanese, however, are changing from the old way to the more western-looking horizontal style. The English side of your card is written in the normal horizontal manner.

Even if you have to postpone the meeting to have cards printed, it would be better than the serious loss of face you would experience by being without them. The Japanese believe that the business card represents your face and your reputation as a businessperson. (The latest fad is to have business cards made from one gram of pure gold flattened out to card size and encased in plastic—they can be printed or written on—and the cost is $45 per card.) The business card is an international icebreaker that transcends any language. You run the risk of being totally ignored or even forgotten if you don't have one. A business card can also help the Japanese businessman remember difficult American names. Have enough cards for everyone—fifty or more at a formal meeting is a safe quantity. If you give your card to someone and allow him to use it as an introduction, it's as good as lending him your good name. Some business cards now come with bar codes, including your telephone number and other private information (such as your resumé), that can only be retrieved through a scanning device. In a more personal introduction, the place where you were born as well as what college you went to may even be included on the card.

Business cards are presented with great ceremony and pride: hold the card with both hands (between your forefingers and your thumbs) and present it with the Japanese side toward the receiver. The Japanese businessman will do the same. Study the card carefully, noting the name of the firm and the title. This is how the Japanese determine rank and position—the most important things you must know to do business with them. Also, never address a Japanese businessman by his first name, and avoid direct eye contact (too much eye contact is considered disrespectful). Do not stuff the card into your pocket or scribble on it in his presence. The card represents your dedication to your company and also determines *keigo,* or rank, so that each of you will know how to bow to the other.

Bowing is a custom that not only frustrates most Westerners but also intimidates them. Bowing arose as a means of acknowledging a person's place and preserving harmony in a crowded society. It is not a submissive gesture, but a sign of respect. The lower the bow, the greater the respect. In general, the younger person bows to the older; the lower-ranking employee bows to the employer. Traditionally, women bow with their palms touching their sides. A ninety-degree bow is perfunctory when the big boss enters the room. And a Japanese boss with great face does not bow low. (The head of one major Japanese company has refined the corporate bow into a quick nod.) The person who bows last has the most face—and a slight edge in business negotiations. In the West, the Japanese businessman will usually extend his hand, since a handshake is acceptable and known internationally as a sign of friendliness and respect. It can be managed without anyone losing face.

When traveling abroad, many Americans are instructed by their companies *not* to bow, but not bowing can be interpreted as American arrogance in certain situations. With a slight bow you can signal to the Japanese businessman your respect for his customs. This goes a long way in building trust—something the Japanese value above all else. Trust is also the reason why the all-important introduction by a go-between (*komon*) or written instructions (*shokai-jo*) by a Japanese colleague are vital. (Banks in Japan even require a letter of introduction to open an account.)

An improper bow could be misconstrued as a sign of disrespect and loss of face. This can be the case when a Westerner attempts to bow without understanding the subtleties.

Scott, an experienced company man with a good record, found himself in an embarrassing situation when he made varying degrees of bowing every time his Japanese boss entered the room: sometimes he bowed low, sometimes he barely nodded. He obviously didn't know what he was doing, and, at times, didn't seem to care. His lack of self-discipline was obvious to his Japanese boss, but he said nothing. Scott, however, soon found himself transferred to another department at a lower-paying position. He was moved from the department because he didn't observe *amae*, that is, he didn't fit into the spirit and body of the group. It is part of everything the Japanese do and is more important to them than experience or work produced.

Amae is the practice of self-discipline by which the Japanese judge themselves and others. For example, there's the story of the Japanese Army officer who engaged his men in maneuvers for sixty hours with only ten-minute opportunities for sleep. "My men don't need training in how to sleep," he supposedly said, "but in how to stay awake." Self-discipline can take on another form as well. Policemen in Japan are taught how to pour tea and how to arrange flowers as part of their training.

Face to Face

The Japanese dislike doing business over the phone, especially if the caller never makes an effort to meet them in person and develop a relationship. This personal touch is necessary on a face-to-face level so that the Japanese feels he knows you and can trust you. This is also true within the company structure.

Whether it's a large plant or a small office, it's best to deliver your intentions or requests at a face-to-face meeting rather than through numerous inner-office phone calls or memos. Also, the Japanese prefer oral agreements over written ones, and tend to favor vague and flexible contracts, usually only a few pages long. The *keiyaku,* or contract, is considered to be the tangible binding of your relationship, based on harmony and conciliation. Intuition and face often play more of a part in reaching the contract stage than logic does.

Face on the Line: Losing Face

Losing face can be a trying and perplexing experience. Take Frank. He was new in the company and didn't understand the subtleties of working for the Japanese. When he was asked by a Japanese co-worker to do a job in the office he couldn't handle, he refused the job in a blunt manner, causing his colleague to lose face. Frank also asked numerous questions, and when he didn't get an answer from a Japanese colleague, he would raise his voice, nearly shouting at times. He also had a habit of criticizing the competition and usually arrived late for meetings. But the worst mistake he made was when he publicly embarrassed a Japanese co-worker who refused to change his mind about the outcome of a sales meeting, even after Frank had proven him wrong. Frank didn't understand that the Japanese will hold to their decisions even if they know they are wrong so they don't lose face. He also didn't realize that he had hurt the face of his entire section (*ka*) by his actions and that every member had taken it personally. What should Frank have done?

How to Do an About-Face: Saving Face

Saving face takes a few techniques that can be applied to any situation. For example, Samantha understood the importance of giving her Japanese co-workers leeway in overcoming a difficult situation. During her weekly staff meetings, she would routinely make suggestions to the group about how to change a procedure without actually telling them they must do it—she merely wondered out loud what would happen if things were done this way or that.

When she wanted to use the phone in another office or borrow some material, she implied her requests rather than asking a direct question. If she had to deny a request from a Japanese co-worker, she was always careful to make it as pleasant as possible, never raising her voice, and she avoided using the word *no.*

Being sensitive to their feelings is the most important factor in dealing with the Japanese on a day-to-day basis. When they ask you for criticism of their work, they are actually asking for reassurance, and expect it to be given in return. In addition, a long delay regarding a business decision could simply be a face-saving measure; do not be fooled into thinking that a compromise is in the offing. A compromise can be construed as a loss of face because it means something has been lost. Maintaining personal dignity as well as company face is the most important thing to your Japanese boss and co-workers.

But what is company face?

Types of Face

A Japanese businessman may sometimes indicate that he can't do something because he might mar his company's face. This is the company symbol handed down since the old days when the name or crest of a business owner was imprinted on the *noren* or split curtains hanging in front of a business. Over the years this has become the most important symbol of company pride and it is not uncommon for them to say they will not do something out of respect for their company's "face."

The Japanese language is also filled with colorful expressions that when translated can give you a deeper understanding of the meaning of *kao* or face. From keeping the potholes in the road in front of his house filled to being known at the highest levels of business, a person who has a broad face (*kao ga hiroi*) is said to have many business contacts. A businessman must continuously work hard to keep up these contacts and this is called *kao o tsunagu,* or tying up his face. If someone wants to talk to you, they will often say *kao o kashite,* or lend me your face.

And when his face is on the line, a Japanese businessman will say, *"Kao o tatette kudasai,"* please save my face.

4

Playing the Work Game by Japanese Rules

If we had recognized the Japanese as the threat
they were, we could have done things differently.
—Gordon E. Moore
Chairman, Intel Corporation

Making the Commitment to the Japanese Way

Haruki was worried. He had been sent by the Tokyo home office
to oversee the opening of the hyper-market in the suburban American city, but sales were going nowhere. The store included everything from restaurants to a cosmetics counter, even a fresh fish
market, but he couldn't find enough qualified workers to staff it.
The butchers didn't understand the Japanese way of cutting fish
filets to minimize waste, the cosmetics girls didn't know how to
hold the products and present them with grace, and no one
seemed to understand *sabisu* (service), a general willingness to
favor the customer in any way deemed important. The customer is
not just treated like a king, Haruki would tell his employees, he is
a god.

After weeks of disappointing results, Haruki decided to change his tactics. He held special classes to explain not only the rigors of the Japanese work ethic (long working hours, few promotions, and constant attention to details), but to explain the rewards as well. He taught his workers how to take pride in doing things the Japanese way: a work ethic that is skill-directed, service-oriented, and product-driven. He broke down the language barrier, explaining technical terms and product names. He even wrote a company song and played it each morning before the store opened. The workers responded enthusiastically once they understood they were working toward a common goal. It wasn't long before Haruki's store became a top-grossing company store—and it was all due to his multiethnic force of workers who had learned the Japanese way.

What Haruki taught his American workers isn't new. It wasn't so long ago that America embraced the same work ethic.

That's the Way It Was in the American Workplace

We've all seen groups of Japanese in shopping malls or at theme parks snapping up American culture with their cameras. Who are these hard-working, curious Japanese who study diligently and have even brought up the learning curve of our own students? (In fact, in order to compete with Japanese students entering U.S. colleges and universities, eighty-seven percent of college-bound American high school students now take extra classes to earn higher grades on the annual college entrance exams.) They are no different than we were back in the 1950s and 1960s, when regular rises in productivity and living standards were the norm in the United States. (We went from corporation management in the 1960s, to strategy management in the 1970s, and into the "me" generation of money management in the 1980s.) The Japanese have reminded us of this strong work ethic by copying our past and obtaining the same positive results.

Much of their success has been attributed to the formation, in the late 1940s, of *Keidanren,* the Federation of Economic Organizations, which helps direct business development and ensures support from the Japanese government by controlling business donations to political parties. *Keidanren* is credited with being the voice of Japanese companies, and it helped bring about much of the current prosperity and success Japan now enjoys. We know it better as Japan Inc.

Inside Japan Inc.

Many major global businesses started out as mom-and-pop operations, but unlike American corporations that become faceless enterprises, Japanese companies like to believe they retain that familial structure. They view their businesses as having the same internal, contained organization as a family, based on traditional Japanese attitudes and values. Employees are encouraged to regard their supervisors and management personnel as parents. In turn, these supervisors are expected to take a personal interest in the affairs of their employees and guide them through what can be lifetime employment. However, it has been argued that lifetime employment is actually offered to only about half of all Japanese workers and it isn't really part of a cultural root, but actually a product of the fast-moving 1960s progressive upswing in the Japanese economy, when companies tried to hoard the labor needed to continue their hectic pace. It has also been likened to a feudal hierarchy, where a worker has little personal freedom and where the company succeeds at the expense of the individual.

Whatever the basis, lifetime employment usually offers little opportunity for the worker as far as promotions and advancement, and salary is tied to a seniority system called *nenko joretsu-sei* (age-seniority system). This system determines pay on seniority defined primarily on the length of service with the company, rather than on the worker's personal achievement or individual ability. (A recent survey, however, has shown that some Japanese companies are beginning to advance American employees on merit.) Still, Japanese workers put their company first, themselves second, and their families last. In a society where titles and personal relationships are top priority, they have no choice: the sense of belonging in the Japanese culture centers on your job. Your company is the pivotal point in your life. For example, a Japanese salaryman would rarely contest a job transfer. As more than one Japanese worker has said when asked why they don't job-hop: "If you lose your job, you lose your friends." The reason for these feelings is because the company is often the center of the worker's life, providing him with status and a sense of belonging in a culture that values personal relationships and group dependency above individual wants.

On the other side, lifetime employment isn't always a plus for the company. New employees are normally recruited once a year directly from colleges or high schools and are more likely to be hired on their personality (the better to keep the *wa* within the organization) rather than on their skills and knowledge. This puts the company at a disadvantage in the long run since it can't always fill its competitive needs with entry-level workers. Employees are put through rigorous training, including lessons on everything about the company and more, even public speaking. As they progress through the company structure, they are trained and retrained as needed. When business is bad, few companies will dismiss workers, instead they will try to find some use for them within the company. Between the ages of fifty-five and sixty, most Japanese workers are given a lump-sum severance and a pension (female workers are usually not given retirement benefits). Those who keep working are given a desk by the window and called *mado no hito* (window people). They are paid at a much lower pay scale and given a less important job. However, they are still in service to the company, which is important to the Japanese psyche.

The inner workings of Japan Inc. are not perfect, but the Japanese have devised a method of production and management that has proven to be the driving force in their economic success during the second half of the twentieth century.

Let's take a look at production first.

Japan's Lean, Mean Production Machine

When Vince returned from a business trip to Japan, the first thing he put up in his office was a sign that read: "Inventory is the cholesterol of industry." The young manufacturing vice-president had been impressed with the Japanese approach to inventory control, but what he didn't know was that it had its origins in the way the

Japanese live their daily lives. Every morning in America we climb out of bed and head out to work, while in Japan, every morning before hopping on the train, the *futon,* or bedding, is carefully folded up and put away in a cupboard. No space is wasted. It's no wonder a Japanese engineer approached production in his factory in the same way.

Taiichi Ohno, production chief at Toyota, realized that the American system of keeping huge inventories was not only using up valuable space in the factory, but also tying up even more valuable capital. By eliminating excess inventories of backup parts, he devised a way to keep the parts on the assembly line moving at the same precision speed to coordinate with the main parts. He called this system "just-in-time" (*kanban*).

But speed is not the only advantage of this lean production. Instead of reworking errors in the completed vehicle, quality was improved by allowing assembly workers to stop the line to correct defects immediately. Ohno also organized the workers into teams and gave them the responsibility for quality checks, as well as for production improvements. This allows Japanese workers to assemble a car in sixteen hours, while in the United States it takes workers twenty-five hours.

Lean production started more than forty years ago and has helped advance the Japanese auto industry to its present dominant position. (So-called "fat" manufacturing has been blamed as part of the problem in Detroit's inability to win back its lost market share from the Japanese.) Just as Henry Ford revolutionized auto production at the turn of the century, the Japanese took it one step further by not only making cars more affordable, but also by ensuring employment for Japanese and American workers. Ford Motor Company is now using lean production, as is GM's new Saturn plant.

Let's see what it takes to work for a Japanese boss on the production line.

On the Production Line

Adam put down his pencil and handed the test to the Japanese supervisor. He heaved a sigh of relief. Thank goodness *that* was over. He had started the interview three hours ago and he prayed this was the last of the tests. This was his fourth and, hopefully, last interview since he had first applied for the production job at the Japanese automaker plant. So far, he had been through three personal interviews with various supervisors, he had been shown a video about what a day at the plant was like (including the morning exercises and the company uniform), and he had attended a class on team meetings and the importance of upholding the values of the company.

He knew they were looking for employees who were high-paced, conscious of quality, and who understood the group dynamics of working as a team. Adam soon found out that teamwork was the most important part. He was placed with a group of sixteen people and given an assignment in his field of expertise. No leader was appointed. As a trained observer watched them, Adam's team assembled the part. Then they were told to do it again, but to do it better and faster, to make cost-saving measures.

When the task was completed, not everyone on the team was hired. Adam made the cut not only because he showed skill in what he did, but because he was willing to work hard and able to fit into the team spirit of the group. He also demonstrated management capability when he was asked to simulate being a manager. His assignment was to talk to an employee who was always late and convince him to change his habits. When the time was right, Adam would be sent to management school in Japan.

When Troy applied for a job at an electronics plant, he had six interviews. Instead of the usual questions about job history, he was surprised when the Japanese managers probed him endlessly about his own ideas of product quality. Just as important to them was his knowledge of Japanese culture. Although Troy knew little, his work experience and his interest to learn about the Japanese earned him the position he wanted. Afterward, however, Troy realized that his performance was not judged on his individual initiative, but on his ability to work as part of a team. For example, if he had a problem, at least four other engineers had to sign off on the solution.

Other Americans working in production have reported comparable incidents in dealing with Japanese companies, but the biggest problem still hinges on one simple element: quality control.

QC: No Room for Second Best

Tony was sweating under the collar. The production meeting at the Japanese automaker had been part boot camp, part revival meeting, and it wasn't over yet. He had sat for the past two hours listening to testimonials from numerous auto-parts makers who hailed the Japanese method for quality control as not only being the path to salvation, but to profits as well. If his auto-parts supply company did not bring up its standards to match those of the Japanese, it would certainly be left far behind. Tony reviewed the statistics about the big gap in the quality of parts bought domestically and those imported: around one thousand defective parts out of every million shipped by non-Japanese suppliers were found. It was only a rate of one-tenth of one percent, but even this was not acceptable to the Japanese.

Defect rates were found to be a hundred times higher for components supplied by seventy-five American and European companies than for those supplied by nearly twice that number of Japanese companies. (Motorola, however, has implemented the Japanese management style and slashed its overall defect rate from nearly three thousand per million products in 1983 to under two hundred today.) Although on-time delivery also remains a concern to Japanese automakers, the number-one issue continues to be quality. The Japanese have implemented *kaizen* (continuous improvement) to promote awareness of quality among employees. The first step is not to look for a quick fix, but to search for the root of the problem. Is the working environment *kitanai* (dirty), *kitsui* (hard), or *kiken* (dangerous)? These are known as the "3 K's" and have to be resolved before activating the elementary points of *kaizen: seiri* (arrangement), *seiton* (order), *seiketsu* (cleanliness), and *seiso* (cleaning). With the help of the group leader, as well as a work evaluation system and a specially designed production procedure, *kaizen* can be implemented in the workplace.

So how can you implement *kaizen* and improve quality control in your workplace? Start at the top.

The Executive Suite: Japanese Style

The hum of machines mixed with the tapping footsteps of the company president as he walked through his plant. The employees noticed his presence but continued working at their jobs. They showed their company pride by their work rather than by anything they could say. Edward was proud of his company. Since they had adopted the Japanese system of total-quality management, they had turned the company around in less than two years. The plant had posted dramatic increases in on-time delivery and worker productivity, and morale was at an all-time high. So were profits.

Edward remembered the days when he had agonized over quarterly reports and fluctuating stock prices before the stockholders' meetings. With the Japanese, it wasn't unusual for stockholders to wait for four years before questioning the productivity of a company. Edward's company had cut that time in half.

How did Edward achieve such dramatic results? It starts with the men at the top. Instead of dealing with decision making as a one-man job with plenty of ego attached, the company president learns to share that process with his workers on the floor. (Honda realized the importance of this when it began its biggest reorganization ever by dispensing with middle management.)

Japanese executives have always believed that total quality management is economically driven. They make sure that everything in the company's portfolio, including employees, methods, and policies, is geared toward the continuous improvement of performance and products. This not only prevents defects but keeps costs down. In most American companies, defects are weeded out *after* production, again exemplifying the American need for the quick fix as opposed to the Japanese system of looking for the root of the problem. Some companies are taking this system one step further and applying it to the development of new products.

The Japanese have been successful by targeting their cost up front according to market conditions, then they direct their design teams to meet that price. Their goal is to get to the market quickly and gain a substantial share of that market for the company. Attending seminars and meetings is important to sustain the ongoing process of quality and cost-control management, but understanding the many layers of the Japanese meeting is still the quest of American businessmen.

Not *Another* Meeting?

According to most Westerners, Japanese meetings or *kaigi* are frequent, no one says much of anything, they seem to accomplish little, and the whole thing starts all over again the next day. However, there are calculated reasons behind the Japanese system of constant get-togethers. Let's go to a typical meeting at a Japanese company with an informed perspective and see what is really happening.

The meeting is set for ten o'clock, but even before the scheduled time you notice what appears to be a private meeting taking place among the Japanese supervisors. What's going on?

In every Japanese organization, meetings or informal conferences take place early in the negotiations or at the beginning of a new project. These prebriefings are held to secure a basic consensus before the main issues are formally introduced later at the meeting. It is important to remember that these types of informal meetings (the process is known as *nemawashi, or attending to roots*) will continue to take place at all stages of decision making and are important to make everyone feel involved. If the Japanese do not preconsult with each other, the entire project or proposal could be in jeopardy for that reason alone.

You arrive at the conference and the meeting starts on time. You're ready to talk business, but all the Japanese want to do is exchange gifts and talk about the unusual weather they're having today (even though the forecast hasn't changed in a week). What gives?

The Japanese are getting to know you. They know where *they* stand as a group (remember those prebriefings?), but you are still an outsider. It's important that you accept this at the first meeting and not try to push for more. The quickest way to offend the Japanese is to insist on reaching a conclusion at this time. The main purpose of this meeting is to build a strong, personal relationship. Many Westerners complain the Japanese talk only nonsense at the first meeting and they often end up agreeing to things they don't understand. The most important thing to agree on is to meet again.

At the second meeting, you may feel you're two steps behind. You're not. Present your ideas smoothly and with enthusiasm, but don't be dismayed by the silence. The Japanese are giving thought to what you've said. You can gain more favor for your proposal by practicing silent communication and not making concessions just because there is "empty space" between you. Never show any emotion, especially anger, at a meeting. This weakens your position.

Also, do not be fooled into thinking that the senior Japanese boss usually does not understand English. Many times he may speak English very well, but he knows that his best offense is his interpreter. By the time his interpreter has finished translating what you've said into Japanese, he's already formulated his answer and has had the opportunity to think it over before giving you his reply.

Many meetings have no tangible results other than to necessitate having another meeting. Sometimes this makes it difficult to separate what happened at what meeting, and where the project or proposal stands at a particular time. The Japanese have a solution for this as well: *ringi-sho* (circulating written proposals). These proposals are prepared at lower-level management and are circulated for approval up the ranks and may even be approved before your original meeting takes place.

This often leads many Westerners to believe that the outcome of the meeting has already been decided even before they walk through the door and that they are going around in the proverbial Japanese circle. There are times, however, when even the circle can be stretched a little if you know what to look for.

Michael was looking for a Japanese investor, but he knew the minute he sat down in the meeting room he was in trouble. The Japanese boss was seated behind the conference table away from the door, while Michael had been placed in a seat directly opposite him—with his back to the door.

What was going on? The Japanese boss was seated so he could see who was coming and going, as well as keep an eye on everything happening in the room. When he had directed that Michael be placed away from him with his back to the door, the American

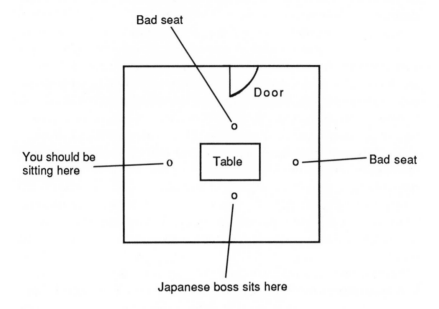

Figure 2. Seating for meetings.

knew the boss didn't want to talk to him. The Japanese had already made up their minds about his project, and it was up to him to change that decision. Michael presented his perspectus, but now he was more tuned in to the reactions from the Japanese. Wherever possible, he changed his tactics during the meeting and was able to secure a second meeting for the next day. He knew his strategy had worked when he was seated closer to the senior boss. He used this to his advantage and presented his material in such a way that he was able to change their minds and secure his desired outcome.

Japanese Traditions That Shape the Workplace

The Buddhist temple was filled with blue-suited salarymen, coming to pay their last respects. Heads down in silent prayer, they listened solemnly to the chanting of the priest as incense filled the air and the flames consumed the remains. The salarymen prayed for continued success in business as they added their own contributions to the fire: semiconductors, floppy disks, and computer pins. Floppy disks? That's right, floppy disks. This was a ceremony steeped in the Buddhist tradition that a day should be set aside to pay respects to things useful in everyday life that give of themselves. There's also a day for junk cars and broken needles.

Japanese businessmen believe they must pay tribute to things used in the past in order to have the proper attitude for things that have not yet been created. They believe such tributes help them keep their competitive edge. However, they lose sight of that edge when the tribute is steeped in strong tradition.

Tokyo's Narita Airport has only a single runway, and its expansion is nearly twenty years behind schedule, because farmers have owned the adjacent farmland (21.3 hectares) since World War II and refuse to abandon tradition. And Japanese society as a whole will not countenance their forcible removal. For these farmers represent the oldest form of the Japanese work ethic of *taue,* or rice transplanting. For centuries, the unremitting labor in the rice fields required a complex system of irrigation and the cooperation of everyone in the village. As the population grew, links to other villages created an even bigger network. This interlocking system of neighborhood responsibilities for channeling water is representative of modern Japanese big business.

It is a facet of Japanese society that still confuses Westerners, and it has caused an uproar because Japan protects its rice market. Some have charged Japan with forging an economic conspiracy against the rest of the world. The Japanese, in their view, are protecting a living tradition; however, they have finally conceded that they cannot expect to dominate the world economy while remaining a closed society and restricting imports. Talks on rice imports continue, but even with the sanction of Japan's most powerful business organization, *Keidanren,* as of this writing, Japan still has not agreed to the GATT (General Agreement on Tariffs and Trade) proposal that would open up its $23.5-billion rice market (13 million metric tons), even though imports would be limited to a maximum of 3 to 5 percent.

The potential opening of the rice market is simply the implementation of another Japanese work ethic foreign to the United States: *gaiatsu,* or foreign pressure. Like the ancient art of judo (waiting for someone else to make the first move), the Japanese will only succumb to foreign pressure when they think it is in their national interest, but without taking the responsibility if things should go wrong.

Although Japan's work ethic remains rooted in its feudal past, it has embraced some modern conventions that often leave American companies fighting not to win the game, but just to stay alive.

All's Fair in Big Business, or Is It?

Gary was very nervous as the white-gloved Japanese policeman politely escorted him into the Tokyo District Prosecutor's office. He was certain the doors to his American medical supply company would be locked after he handed over his financial records. He still couldn't believe that his company had been accused of giving bribe money to Japanese university professors to influence their procurement decisions. Although it is common for a Japanese company to offer large sums of money for such a purpose, he speculated that he had been singled out for such action because of his rising success in the Japanese market. He was surprised to find out that a Japanese company would never get caught because they either kept two sets of records or used a creative financing system with ambiguous payment terms. He was even more surprised at the outcome of his meeting: as long as he promised to keep his silence and not to do it again, he would be left alone.

Another practice that often frustrates American businessmen is *dango,* or bid rigging. Japanese construction executives meet in secret to determine which companies will submit the winning bids (they often signal bids to each other on the back of their business cards—everyone bidding higher than the predetermined winner), thereby guaranteeing their domestic firms the business. Some will also risk exposure and public scandal by illegally arranging stock-price manipulation.

Japanese businessmen are averse, though, to taking risks when it comes to research and development. The Japanese government provides the answer by supporting industry with bank loans, tax credits, and, sometimes, protection. This so-called guidance, or *gyōsei shidō,* is not founded in any written law, but is part of a tradition that has come to be expected by Japanese companies. This kind of gentle persuasion by government stands in place of any overt means of regulation, its subtle nuances again reflecting the Japanese style of indirect approach.

There are times when the government's protective attitude becomes too much for some Japanese businessmen, who then resort to unusual means to achieve their goals. When the Japanese decided to enter the art world, they did it in a big way: five of the ten highest-priced art objects, including Van Gogh's *Dr. Gachet* (the buyer, who paid $83 million wants to have the painting cremated with him when he dies), were purchased by Japanese businessmen and companies.

However, some of these purchases were not the result of a love of fine art (although many famous paintings now hang in public galleries around Japan or in private collections), but merely a clever method of concealing the transfer of millions of dollars and evading high Japanese taxes. (Large Japanese corporations are taxed at the rate of 37.5 percent and are hemmed in by countless regulations.) By brokering huge sums of money through French officials for paintings, one large Japanese corporation funneled $30 million out of its company profit coffers. But according to a recent investigation, the Frenchmen don't even exist. Also, the "Big Four" brokerage house scandal in 1991 brought to light news reports that the Japanese securities companies allegedly failed to report millions in taxable transactions. According to the National Tax Administration Agency, four out of five corporations investigated by officials from July 1990 to June 1991 had either partially concealed or failed to declare their total income.

Speaking of taxes, the Japanese figured that if it works in Japan, why not in the United States as well?

Why Don't U.S. Japanese-owned Companies Pay Taxes?

As twilight invaded his tiny office, Albert adjusted his glasses and checked over the income tax reports for the fifth time. He couldn't believe it, but it was true. The well-known and prosperous Japanese corporation listed on the tax return wasn't paying the U.S. government a dime in taxes. An experienced IRS agent, Albert pulled out another file listing a Japanese corporation as owner and discovered the same thing. He tried another and another all night until dawn, but each one was the same: Japanese firms have continuously claimed over the past few years that they have made a net profit of less than twelve cents per one hundred dollars, thereby avoiding paying millions of dollars in U.S. taxes. (The IRS estimates the United States is losing as much as $30 billion a year in tax revenues on foreign companies.) At the same time, American companies reported profits seventy times those of Japanese companies. Albert checked the returns for any wrongdoing on the part of the Japanese, but he found none. There was nothing he could do.

Japanese securities analysts and financial institutions don't focus on consolidated earnings to determine the strength of a company, but on the earnings of the parent company worldwide. Consequently, a Japanese corporation puts all of its corporate income into one basket: the parent company. By shifting profits to overseas parent firms, Japanese companies in the United States are able to report lower taxable profits and avoid paying higher U.S. taxes.

So what happens when a U.S. company decides to operate in Japan?

How U.S. Companies Can Succeed in Japan

Everyone told Greta that her family-owned retail clothing store would never make it in Japan. The Japanese distribution system was too tough to crack, they said, and there were endless restrictions to cut through, not to mention the lack of real estate available to build a store. But Greta was determined. She was certain that if she made a long-term commitment and created a high quality store that met the growing Japanese demand for designer clothing, she would make it.

Greta soon found out that small retailers in Japan are often required to wait as long as ten years for various approvals needed to open their doors and are required to go through wholesalers who control designer labels through licensing agreements. (According to a new Japan-U.S. agreement that went into effect in January 1992, a large-scale retail stores law will shorten the period for large stores to obtain permission to open an outlet to a one-year maximum.) Any unsold merchandise is returned to the wholesaler, making markdowns almost nonexistent (Greta couldn't imagine a department store without half-yearly sales). Every time she would check on the status of her proposal with various agencies, she was politely told: "We're studying it," or "We'll get back to you." Famous last words when dealing with the Japanese, according to more than one American businessperson. Greta could see her dream crumbling. What should she do next? Then along came her rescuer. His name was Motoki.

The Consulting Biz: Waving the Magic Wand

Motoki shuffled through his lists of thousands of properties before showing his client a suitable building just perfect for her store. Greta was impressed with her cross-cultural consultant. Ever since she had hired him, things had started to fall into place. After finding a building for her store, Motoki cleared the way for the approvals needed, and had the deal closed in a short time. Next, he set her up in a joint venture with a Japanese retailer with the similar background of running a family-owned business. The match proved to be beneficial for both, with Greta operating under a licensing arrangement and the Japanese retailer retaining full control of the franchise. Greta's store is now so successful she's thinking about expanding into other parts of Japan.

Motoki is a member of a new and upcoming breed of bicultural consultants who are more than matchmakers in Japanese and American joint ventures. Besides acting as an interpreter, a consultant can breach the gap between the two cultures and help the American businessperson understand the reasonings behind the actions of the Japanese. Westerners may not always like what's going on, but understanding it can often mean the difference between giving up the project or turning it into a success.

Take an American businessman who is preparing to meet his Japanese counterpart for the first time. While the American may worry about whether to bow or shake hands, the Japanese businessman is more concerned with overcoming other strong cultural differences, like a dissimilarity in approaching the marketplace. For example, to create a brand awareness and stimulate demand, Japanese consumer-products companies often advertise their merchandise on television years before the products are actually available on store shelves.

During the first meeting, the American may be more interested in determining how profitable the venture will be—and how soon he can reap those profits. The Japanese wants to know if he can trust the American. This is why many consultants enact "role-playing" with their clients even before a meeting is set up so the Americans can be prepared for confusing and tension-creating encounters with the Japanese *before* they happen.

Whether it's a joint project in the United States or in Japan, success often depends on whether you can recognize the many differences between how the Americans and the Japanese operate in the workplace.

Vive la Difference: Japanese and American Businessmen

Imagine playing a video game we'll call "Salaryman Commandos," starring an American businessman named Nick and a Japanese named Nobuo. Let's see how they score in the game of international big business.

Nobuo racks up points for his extreme politeness, while Nick loses some for being too brash. But give Nick bonus points for his generous nature. None for Nobuo—Japanese are perceived to be selfish in the world of big business. Nick loses points for his impatience, while Nobuo gains some for his perseverance. Americans are perceived by the world of big business to be better teachers— Nick gains points, but as business leaders the Japanese are more respected. Nobuo is ahead, but the game's not over yet.

Japanese businessmen are reputed to be stingy, keeping the best technology, vendor contracts, and profits for themselves. Americans, on the other hand, are more equitable toward their customers and judge on merit. Also, Americans tend to increase the quality of life in the areas where they invest. Nick goes to lunch with his workers, but Nobuo's hierarchical tradition excludes him from mingling. Nick's company has always given to charities and helps the community, while Nobuo's company is only beginning to give large donations and do community service work. Nobuo learns about the outside world through massive links of commercial information operations worldwide. Nick doesn't have those kinds of contacts within his company. Nobuo establishes business based on personal relationships. Nick prefers contracts, not contacts.

The final score is even. Nick and Nobuo come from different worlds, different systems, but in the final analysis, there are both positive and negative points about each method of doing business. The bottom line is: We *can* learn from each other and must continue doing so.

5

Sex and the Japanese Salaryman

Be prepared for the fact that in Japan there
is no sin, original or otherwise.
—Bernard Rudofsky
The Kimono Mind

Sex in the Japanese Workplace

A rainy mist fell on a narrow street in Tokyo as a car entered an
underground parking lot beneath a high-walled building. A metal
door quickly and efficiently slid shut behind the car; not even the
most keen-eyed observer had time to note the car's license plate or
recognize the man and woman inside. For visitors to Hotel Passion, secrecy was most important.

Inside the "love hotel" the man used a special credit card with
his own private number to check in. After choosing a room (without ever seeing another person—everything was done by computers and tape recorders), the couple retired for the next two hours

72

for an afternoon tryst—complete with food and drink, movies (pornographic, if desired), and, of course, a supply of condoms. They could even videotape their antics for future viewing.

Afterward, the man and woman left discreetly and returned to work in the same office. There was no softness in the eyes when they looked at each other, no casual brush of hands as they passed in the hallway. No one would ever guess they had just spent their lunch break in the grips of passion.

Not all Japanese businessmen spend their lunch hours in sushi bars. There are 20,000 love hotels available for the afternoon rendezvous (the fee is 20 percent higher for an all-night session) where Japanese businessmen often bring their secretaries for a little love—even getting some work done on occasion. If you want drive-up service, there are private drive-ins in Osaka where you can park your car inside a secluded cabin-like garage, choose a movie, and close the shutters.

Yet there's another side to the Japanese businessman that can burn you like hot *sake* if you don't know how to play the game.

The Flip Side: The American Point of View

Nancy was a bright young businesswoman working for a multinational soft drink company when she received an overseas assignment in Tokyo. Although she knew it was a good opportunity for advancement, she had heard numerous stories about the sexual appetites of Japanese businessmen. But much to Nancy's surprise, she was treated well by the men in the office. No one made a pass at her—except for an American colleague. He made no secret of his interest in her, openly flirting and asking her out to lunch. His antics, however, did not go unnoticed by Nancy's Japanese boss. The American man was quickly transferred to another branch of the company and no mention was made of him again.

Nancy believed that her Japanese boss was being considerate of her position in the workplace, but he was merely putting sex in its proper place. As long as Nancy was within his circle (in this case, business associates), she would be treated with respect.

This double standard may confuse Americans. The Japanese

man is permitted to indulge in sex on his lunch hour, yet the American employee strikes out in the office before he can even get to first base.

Sex in the workplace exists in both Japan and in the United States. However, because the rules are not always the same and are often confusing to American workers, let's take a look at some of the various Japanese approaches to sex in the workplace.

To understand sex in the Japanese workplace we must first understand exactly *how* the Japanese view sex.

Two Souls Are Better Than One

The Japanese believe we all have two coexisting souls. One is spiritual, timeless, and uplifting—this is the soul that works long, arduous hours and puts company and family obligations first. The other soul is earthbound and pleasure-seeking.

The Japanese do not believe the pleasures of the flesh are evil. On the contrary, Japanese men believe it is their *right* to enjoy sex.

Sixty percent of Japanese men surveyed said they would have an affair with a woman if given the opportunity (meaning to the Japanese way of thinking, when they could afford it), while 30 percent said they absolutely *had* to have an affair. The remaining men wouldn't discuss it.

As a rule, the Japanese businessman believes that his family and marital obligations are separate from other emotional attachments. Only his wife and family are within his primary circle of obligation. Mistresses and other women are strictly on the outside and, therefore, are not important. Extramarital sex is acceptable as long as it keeps a minor place in their lives.

The Floating World: The History of Sex in Japan

For centuries, Japanese men enjoyed a society where a world of geisha and prostitutes tended to their every need. It was called the *uki-yo*, or "floating world," referring to a fleeting sensation.

This was an era when the samurai ruled with their strict, unbreakable code of *Bushidō*, and sex was a game indulged in frequently, often lasting days or weeks with numerous ceremonies and frequent changing of partners. Every city had its own prostitution quarters, but Yoshiwara in Tokyo was the most famous.

Meaning "Plain of the Reeds," Yoshiwara was the favorite place of courtesans and common prostitutes alike. Finely dressed women in silk and brocade were lined up in cages for viewing and picking, while old, diseased prostitutes (their faces painted white and candle wax molded to replace their noses, ravaged by syphilis) wandered the streets, hugging ragged blankets at their sides, ready to drop them to the ground for services rendered on the spot.

So protected and beloved were the prostitutes of Yoshiwara that when thousands of them died while trying to escape their burning quarters after the earthquake of 1923, a monument surrounded by trees and flowers was erected in their memory. After the disaster the prostitution quarters were the first buildings rebuilt and open for business.

It finally took an edict from the United States Army to tear down Yoshiwara forever. In 1946, the Allied Command sent a memorandum to the Japanese government asking for its compliance in abolishing prostitution in Japan. The members of the Japanese government were distressed and confused—where would men go to satisfy their sexual needs? By 1952 the Japanese Ministry of Health and Welfare estimated there were around 70,000 prostitutes catering to the American forces—earning well over $200 million a year. No wonder it took the government until 1957 to officially close the doors of Yoshiwara.

But when one door closes, another one opens.

Sex in Japan Today

Jiro is a hard-working typical Japanese salaryman. It's not unusual to see him riding the train to work every morning or slurping a bowl of noodles at lunchtime while reading a comic book. His favorite comic tells the story of a man kidnapping a beautiful model, abusing her, then making love to her. Or Jiro imagines a galaxy far, far away where robots carry off blond, round-eyed girls and rape them to their heart's content, or a room where a beautiful, buxom brunette in a tiny bikini is chained to a post while a man repeatedly whips her with delight. These *manga*, or comics, present a modern version of the mythological Japanese *kappa,* a flat-headed, *sake*-loving creature who sometimes sexually assaults maidens and yearns to be human, like the overworked salaryman of today.

More than 124 million Japanese spent $39 million on comics in 1991—that's 36 percent of all books and magazines sold in Japan. Japanese *ero-manga,* erotic comics, reflect their national attitudes toward sex: it's natural and it's fun. And it often includes little girls—from the racks of soft-porn magazines in neighborhood markets filled with promiscuous characters who look like children to cute little girl singing "idol" stars on nightly television. The Japanese man's fascination with little girls, called *rori-kon* or Lolita complex, is so rampant that advice columns in newspapers often offer advice to parents on how to protect their little girls from *rori-kon* madness. According to the *Shukan Post,* seductive schoolgirls in sailor-suit uniforms (the all-time favorite fantasy of Japanese men) are especially appealing to the 300,000 latent Japanese *rori-kon* fans.

More than two hundred serialized comic magazines hit the newsstands every week. One-third of them have sexual titles like *Rapeman,* where a man targets a woman, hunts her down, and rapes her, but is never caught. Pornographic comics are even sold in vending machines. However, in 1990, 1,300 comics with titles like *Lemon Angel* and *The Season of Young Girls* were judged by the National Police Agency to be harmful to young people. Publishers report they will put a warning label on the comics, but there's no such warning in Tokyo's red light district, where the light never dims.

Just take the subway to the JR station in the Shinjuku district to the brightly lit entrance of the Kabuki-cho, sometimes called an amusement park for sex. Numerous sex-trade clubs, stores, and hangouts offer everything from massage parlors to peep shows. At last count there are twenty pornographic book stores, two hundred love hotels, ten peep shows, one hundred massage parlors, and nearly two thousand snack bars and cabarets. The cabaret shows feature everything from exotic dancing to S and M clubs.

Asian prostitutes, known as *Japayuki-san,* flock to the streets and clubs, plying their trade under the guise of doing a "soap dance" (*awa-odori*). Jeff didn't know what to expect when Kumao, his Japanese client, took him to a soapland establishment. He felt very uncomfortable. He had no idea that Kumao was trying to show him how exalted he was in his eyes. Taking Jeff to the soapland was an honor, not a mandatory request to become Japanese. Jeff mumbled something about having to get back to the hotel and asked Kumao to take him. The two men sat in silence during the ride back. It took many months before they were able to joke easily between the two of them again, and even longer before their deal was finalized.

Both Jeff and Kumao were acting according to their cultures, and neither understood the other's point of view. Kumao learned always to prescreen a Westerner, either back in the United States or before venturing out for a night on the town, to see if he was interested in that kind of activity. Jeff later found out that he should not have refused the invitation with a direct approach. Giving the appearance of being interested would have been enough. Both men also learned that understanding the other's culture stretched farther than the boardroom.

Dress and Undress in Japan

Carolyn was excited by the prospect of working for a large Japanese bank. She was a college graduate and had spent a few years working for a large American financial corporation. She prided herself on having good taste and always being professional in her appearance. She usually wore conservative designer clothes and soft makeup, but when she accepted the position with the Japanese she soon found out that she would be required to wear a uniform and was encouraged not to wear makeup or jewelry (some Japanese companies even forbid their office workers to wear makeup or jewelry). Carolyn realized that if she wanted to work for the Japanese, she would have to change her style. It was a difficult decision, but she decided that the opportunity to work for an international company and gain valuable experience was worth it. She went ahead and took the job and saved her designer look for her free time.

For centuries the Japanese have adhered to a strict pattern of behavior that dictates everything from manners to language, even to the way they dress.

There is a prescribed uniform for every stage of life in Japan: from the brass-buttoned uniform of the schoolboy (the design was taken from nineteenth-century German naval academies) to the blue suit of the salaryman. It is only during the teenage years that the Japanese veer away from this practice, spending their free time dressing up in outrageous clothing.

When a salaryman gets his first job, blue is the only color acceptable for him to wear (although younger men are more open now to wearing gray and other colors, the freedom to deviate too much from the norm is frowned upon by Japanese management). These attitudes are similar to those in the U.S. workplace, where the type of company often dictates the style of dress (more freedom is found in creative fields, such as film and the arts). Women, however, (usually secretaries) must wear a company uniform to the office. These uniforms for both men and women are supposed to keep their minds off sex in the workplace. That's usually not a problem for the Japanese. Ninety percent of Japanese salarymen have no contact with women at work. Women are not included in many work related activities and are not encouraged to attend the after hours social drinking. Many salarymen live in remote company dormitories with early curfews. No wonder the average Japanese businessman is sexually frustrated, but he has found interesting ways to relieve that frustration. Phone sex (also the latest fad among Japanese teenagers) is very popular because it allows the Japanese to continue his usual manner of not looking into someone's eyes when he speaks. Also available are pornographic videos, titillating television shows (one quiz show features young Office Ladies who strip off a piece of clothing every time they give a wrong answer), and *nudo gekijo*, striptease theaters, offering live sex shows with audience participation.

How Japanese Women Cope With Sex

A Japanese man often has a wife, a girlfriend, and a mistress, and each knows her place. Only the girlfriend can ever hope to enter the circle of being a wife, while a mistress (known as a *nigo-san,* or a Miss Number Two) is relegated to remain on the outside.

Some women prefer it that way. After all, it is the wife's obligation to pack a supply of condoms in her husband's suitcase when he leaves on a company-sponsored sex tour to Hong Kong or Thailand. The wife also dutifully pays the bill for any of his sexual excursions. However, as long as her husband fulfills his obligations and puts his family first, she will usually close her eyes to his indiscretions, although younger women are changing their attitude toward this practice and are not accepting such behavior from their husbands. If a married woman should stray, she upsets the social order.

Sometimes you can get into trouble through no fault of your own. Paula was a married woman working in a Japanese manufacturing company, making good money, and with a fair amount of responsibility. She was treated with respect by her Japanese boss and her colleagues. Then she was divorced, and more than her marriage fell apart. Paula noticed a subtle change in her Japanese boss: he began to watch her more carefully around the male workers and slowly began taking away her responsibilities. Paula discovered the changes were because she had gotten a divorce. In the eyes of her Japanese boss she couldn't be trusted now that she was a divorced woman. Paula tried to remedy the situation, but to no avail. In her frustration, Paula left the company.

The Japanese have a place for single or lonely women to vent their frustrations: escort bars. These so-called "host clubs" cater to women only and have such exotic names as Club Taboo, Blue Bird, and Club Love. The women come from every part of society: wives of businessmen, entertainers, even old ladies who've made a killing in the rich real-estate market. The clubs have their roots in the Edo Period (1603–1867) when wealthy ladies from the *shō-gun's* court would amuse themselves with the kabuki actors, often paying them for their services. Today these gigolos are called *tsu-bame,* or swallow. They cater to the needs of many neglected Japanese wives in their forties and fifties who are trapped in arranged marriages and prefer to enjoy themselves in an accepted manner rather than risk everything in an illicit affair. They are also popular with young women who prefer the controlled atmosphere of a host club over the uncertain outcome of a night at a disco. Like similar clubs in the United States that feature male dancers, Japanese host clubs employ fantasy characters (sumo wrestler, shy young salary-man, movie star), and for many Japanese women these clubs pro-vide the romance (and, at times, sex) lacking in their lives.

However, the rules of the Japanese vertical society (everything according to rank and position) apply here as well. On a lady's first visit she is permitted to sit with any man or men she chooses. On subsequent visits she must choose one specific host and see him only. Like everything else in Tokyo, love comes with a price—about sixty dollars for the company of the man of your choice for the evening (sex is not included and is arranged separately).

The hosts must also follow the rules. If several men are sitting with a lady, only the highest ranking man may light her cigarette. The men involved in this sort of prostitution are rewarded well for their loving glances and attentive gestures. The average Japanese gigolo makes around $8,000 a month—without tips and other ser-vices rendered. The most popular host at Tokyo's leading club has been known to receive around $40,000 in tips for a night's enter-tainment with several ladies.

Not every woman is lucky enough to afford the luxury of her own host. In fact, most Japanese women are romantically frus-trated as well. In a recent life insurance poll, 47 percent said they couldn't remember the last time their husbands said, "I love you." (In the Japanese dictionary, the official definition for love refers more to filial love than to romantic love. "I love you" between the sexes is usually said only in novels and films.)

However, it's the younger Japanese woman who is standing up for her rights: 90 percent of women in their twenties are urging their husbands to come home earlier at night for a romantic rendez-vous. However, when the men *do* come home, the Japanese woman has little choice regarding the contraceptives available to her.

Contraceptives: The Condom Versus the Pill

Condoms are nothing new in Japan. Hundreds of years ago a sheath for the penis was developed to prevent pregnancy as well as to increase enjoyment. A specially hardened rubber was used with rings of various sizes and widths. Raised corrugations and other protuberances, often comb-like and prickly, were added to the face of the sheath to make up for any shortcomings on the part of either partner. (Foreigners in Japan are often surprised to see an ad in an English language magazine offering *gaijin*-sized condoms for sale—a set of six imported from Europe for ¥1000, or $7.25.)

Condoms have gotten a lot of use through the centuries since they were not only the main source of contraception, but also a popular form of sexual enjoyment. Oral sex was rarely performed by either partner (even to this day most Japanese men have not experienced oral sex with their Japanese wives). The man did not engage in any kind of breast fondling, either orally or manually (Japanese men have since discovered big-breasted women— breasts implants are very popular among young Japanese women, about 20,000 silicone gel implants have been performed in Japan since 1979, according to the *Japan Times*). Women usually took the initiative in the sex act, although always making sure they did not appear to dominate the male. Even today, it is the duty of working women to supply condoms in a relationship.

As depicted in the works of the great pornographic artist, Utamaro (1754–1806), the sex act was strictly controlled: no sudden embraces or taking off the clothes of the intended female. Once again the woman had to adhere to strict protocol. Her most attractive asset was her hair (often trailing down to her knees or longer) and it never came in contact with the mat, floor, or her lover's hands; she always kept it floating. This kept the erotic activity going until the man entered her, and hopefully closed his eyes for a few minutes so she could relax. Not even when she reached orgasm could she forget about her hair.

A similar kind of sex act often goes on in the workplace. While some American men are fond of casually touching female employees on the shoulder or elbow and an occasional knee pat, Japanese bosses keep their distance. Or so Rita thought. Rita worked in a big city travel agency for a Japanese tour company. She would often ride home on the subway with a male Japanese boss. It didn't take her long to realize that the salaryman with the deadpan face who only came up to her shoulders enjoyed bumping into her on the sardine-packed transit system.

This is not an unusual phenomenon. Japan's crowded subways are filled with pinchers, grabbers, and mashers known as *chikan*. In a survey of 516 Office Ladies, or OLs, 96 percent of them said they had been the victims of these salacious salarymen. The Japanese OLs often use their bags as shields, but Rita was afraid her temper would get the better of her and she might hit him on the head with her bag. She didn't want to risk offending her Japanese boss so she began taking taxicabs home. The extra money it cost her was worth it: she allowed her Japanese boss to save face and she kept her job. She's now leading tours to Japan, where the pill is still not available.

In 1965 the Health and Welfare Ministry planned to allow the use of the birth control pill in Japan but dropped the idea because too many people believed it would promote sexual promiscuity. In 1986 they decided to re-evaluate its use and were expected to legalize the pill by 1992. In mid-March 1992, they put off that decision again, fearing the spread of AIDS if the pill replaced the condom (according to a Mainichi newspaper, in 1990 condoms were used 74 out of 100 times to prevent pregnancy).

The pill has never been given the opportunity to challenge the condom and considering the current concern about the spread of AIDS, it may never get that chance. The Japan Medical Association (dominated by men) has been the major force in keeping any kind of pharmaceutical device off the market. Even though the Japanese Diet passed a law in 1948 providing for the dissemination of information about contraceptives, there remains only one alternative to the condom for Japanese women who want to avoid unwanted pregnancy: abortion.

Abortion in Japan

Abortion is a common practice among married women in their thirties and young Japanese women as a method of birth control. Even if the pill were available, it's difficult to know how many women would use it. Many Japanese women still have an hysterical fear about the side-effects of the pill, created by exaggerated claims made by the Health and Welfare Ministry, as well as doctors and women's groups (they associate the proposed introduction of the pill in Japan with the chemical poisoning scandals of the 1960s). Consequently, many Japanese women believe that abortion is a better alternative than the pill.

According to Japanese Law, abortion is permitted when the woman's health "may be affected seriously by continuation of pregnancy or by delivery, from the physical or economic point of view." There are various statistics available on the number of abortions, but the most reliable sources estimate that at least one million abortions are performed in Japan every year. Some experts tally the figure as high as two million (this in a country whose population is 124.04 million as of October 1, 1991).

Abortion has had a great effect on the birthrate in Japan. According to the Department of Health and Ministry, the number of babies born in Japan in 1989 fell to a record low of 1,246,802— this is a decrease of 67,204 from the previous low of 1,314,006 in 1988. In 1991 the birthrate for Japanese women hit a new low of 1.53 children per woman. There are now commercials on Japanese television urging women to have babies. The government is offering ¥5,000 (or $38) a month for the first child (more for the second and third).

The spirits of these aborted, unborn children are not forgotten. Temples and cemeteries have been built around the country, complete with numerous rows of stone dolls about three feet high, each holding a colorful pinwheel in their hand to honor these unborn children. Small offerings (or prayers written on note paper) are often left at the feet of these dolls by the "parents" as a soft breeze blows the pinwheel around in a continuous circle of spiritual unity.

AIDS

In a recent Japanese newspaper a woman wrote to an advice column asking if she could get AIDS by holding onto a handstrap in the train that had been touched by a foreigner, meaning, very probably an American. The Japanese consider AIDS to be the American Disease and a significant contribution to what they believe will be our ultimate decline. (This isn't the first time they've blamed the West for disease: in the 1930s, the Japanese founder of the Society for Dermatology and Urology wrote that syphilis originated in America.)

Although there are 1,955 known cases of AIDS in Japan, many Japanese do not know how the AIDS virus is transmitted. (About 10 percent of Japan's population is homosexual or has such tendencies, according to a sociology professor at Tokyo's prestigious Gakushuin University.) Some Japanese businessmen even believe they can catch AIDS by drinking our water or breathing our air. Adding to the confusion is a new board game introduced by the Yonezawa Corporation called Bacteria Panic; the loser is left holding a card marked "AIDS" at the end of the game.

In the past the Japanese have approached sexually transmitted diseases with their usual duplicity. In the 1950s brothel owners formed the All-Japan Association for the Prevention of Venereal Disease. The main purpose of this group, however, was really to prevent the passage of the antiprostitution law. The law was passed anyway, and the association quickly disbanded.

Japanese businessmen today are pretty much on their own, although many prostitutes eagerly flash their AIDS-free certificates as an incentive to would-be buyers. As a second precaution many businessmen also invest in pharmaceutical companies on the Tokyo stock market, hoping they find a cure for the disease.

AIDS, however, hasn't stopped the increase of whirlwind sex tours for businessmen to other parts of Asia, especially Thailand, making it probable that the number of infections will increase. According to the Thai Red Cross, about one out of every eight prostitutes in Thailand is believed to carry the AIDS virus. The World Health Organization's latest estimate of HIV-infected Asians is now more than one million. WHO predicts that with two-thirds of the world's population in Asia, 40 million people worldwide will be infected with the AIDS virus in nine years. The global AIDS Policy Coalition, however, predicts that there could be 110 million adults infected with the HIV virus by the year 2000.

Making a Pass: Flirting the Japanese Way

George was a likable young guy with a Japanese auto manufacturing company. Every time an attractive secretary would walk through the plant, he made remarks about her obvious physical attributes. His Japanese boss said nothing, but George soon found himself transferred to the night shift.

What George didn't know is that such comments are taboo in the workplace. Japanese bosses use more subtle ways of making contact with the opposite sex—any kind of blatant and direct propositioning will land you in trouble.

While the office is now the primary meeting place for 30 percent of single workers in the United States, in Japan this is only a recent phenomenon that began with the passing of an equal employment opportunity act in the 1980s and also when companies cut back on executives' expense accounts at hostess bars. The recent hiring of young female employees, or Office Ladies, has made Japanese men more aggressive in the workplace, but their approach is still indirect, as Monica found out when she took a job in a Japanese trading company.

Monica was assigned as a personal assistant to a senior Japanese boss in the company and was required to spend a lot of time with him away from the office, attending meetings and working on team projects. Her Japanese boss began giving her gifts: expensive perfume, designer scarves, fine chocolates. Then he began to target her Japanese girlfriends with his charm, dropping hints that Monica would get a better job, more gifts, etc., if they encouraged her to have an affair with him. To Monica's surprise, not only did they encourage her, but they warned her that if she didn't, she might be replaced. Monica realized that the Japanese girls enjoyed the idea of her having an affair with the boss and would keep it secret. Both Monica's girlfriends and her boss were experiencing the purest form of the Japanese delight in sexual sensation without emotional involvement. Monica, however, decided against getting involved with her Japanese boss. She firmly but politely refused his advances and went to great lengths to prove her professionalism in the office. Her boss began to back off, and soon directed his attention to another woman in the company. Monica sensed a new respect in his eyes and became a role model for the other women in her office.

When Shannon went to work in management in a Japanese company she also found herself deluged with gifts; not just from one man in her department, but from several—and they were all married. These Japanese businessmen were involved in a political courtship of Shannon, not because they wanted to have an affair with her, but because of her position in the company. Shannon said nothing and the situation only got worse, with each man trying to outdo the other with more and more expensive gifts (even though the gifts were given privately).

Shannon met with each colleague privately and let him know she wasn't interested. That took the pressure off of her and her Japanese co-workers. The gifts and the courtships stopped.

Fraternizing in the Workplace: The Difference Between the United States and Japan

Carl hadn't worked for a Japanese company for very long when he met Mariko in the accounting department. She was one of the first Japanese women to be assigned to a U.S. transplant, and he was surprised when she agreed to go out with him. They began a serious relationship, and when Carl asked her to marry him, she agreed. Carl assumed she would quit her job, as was the Japanese custom, but Mariko told him that times were changing—she intended to stay and work right alongside her new husband.

According to a survey by Japan's Health and Welfare Ministry, 50 percent of all nonarranged marriages are now between employees of the same company. Some Japanese companies are even actively getting involved in the dating process: Toyo Sash Company provides a matchmaking service in its company newsletter, and Tokyo Electric Power Company has set up a marriage-counseling corner for its employees. Another company even has a go-between service called *Maidenmate.* In contrast, in many U.S. companies, married co-workers are frequently encouraged to transfer to a different department within the company; fraternization between unmarried workers is usually discouraged.

Some American companies have recently become interested in promoting non-fraternization policies that prohibit managers from dating their staff members. This is particularly true in industries with large numbers of female employees (for example, hotels and restaurants). In a recent poll, most of the office romances in

U.S. companies surveyed did not result from close contact on the job: 12 percent worked together, while 46 percent worked in other departments of the company.

According to a 1990 national survey conducted by Loyola University in New Orleans, American men get involved in office relationships for their egos 56 percent of the time, while American women become involved for love 61 percent of the time. Japanese men never get involved for love—it is strictly ego. They believe it is their right to be promiscuous in the workplace—and the number of women conquered is limited only to what they can afford. When former Prime Minister Sosuke Ono was forced to step down because of his affair with a geisha, popular opinion said it was not because he had a mistress, but rather because of his failure to bestow expensive gifts upon her.

Of course, it is still up to the employee to make the final decision whether or not to date or become involved within the company. Although there are differences between American and Japanese companies regarding fraternization, one rule remains constant: discretion means the same in both languages.

6

Through a Glass Darkly: How Japan and America View Each Other

Of all the gifts that God could give us,
to see ourselves as others see us.
—Robert Burns

How the Japanese See Us and How We See Them

It is well known that smiling Japanese often stare openly at foreigners. What are they thinking about? Dan, a reporter on assignment in Japan, was determined to find out.

However, he discovered it was not an easy task to get anyone to talk to him. He was the only one on the morning train not reading a newspaper, book, or comic book. It was hot and humid in the commuter train, but Dan was the only one sweating. As he loosened his tie he watched the cool Japanese with envy. He didn't know that many Westerners have come to the conclusion that the

Japanese must have a slightly lower body temperature than we do to allow them to survive in a climate habitually thick with humidity.

He would have also been shocked to find out that Japanese perceive all Westerners as having a strong body odor—luckily Dan had used deodorant that morning. He finally struck up a conversation with a young Japanese man and was surprised to find out that the "kid" he was talking to was in his middle thirties. He was just as shocked when the Japanese figured him to be about ten years older than his real age. (In Japan all foreign men are perceived of as enormous in stature and as having big noses, while all foreign women are considered to have big breasts.)

Throughout his stay in Japan Dan continued to try to find out what the Japanese thought of foreigners, but with no success. He did note that his foreign appearance always evoked courtesy and a willingness to help. Giggling students would try to practice their English on him and shy housewives would turn around for a quick look at him. He was asked out to dinner several times by Japanese business associates, even invited to be a guest at the wedding of someone he hardly knew. His most baffling experience came when he stopped at a small *minshuku* (country inn) outside Tokyo and was turned away by the owners, even though they had several guest rooms available. He learned later from an American expatriate that they had done this because they were afraid the *gaijin* didn't know the rules and they wouldn't be able to please him. He also learned that no matter how long you are in Japan, whether it's twenty minutes or twenty years, you will always be a *gaijin*.

Gaijin the Barbarian

In the middle of the seventeenth century Japan had just been through a long, bloody civil war when a shipload of red-haired barbarians from Portugal insisted on them opening their doors to trade with the West. Most of the *gaijin* were sent back from where they came—minus their heads. The Japanese weren't taking any chances on being contaminated by the smelly, bearded Europeans with their loaded guns and bad manners. The Tokugawas (the shōgun Ieyasu Tokugawa and his succeeding government during the

Edo Period, 1603–1867) had just consolidated their power and didn't want any political intrusion taking over what they had won. Under penalty of death, they forbade travel by any Japanese citizen outside of Japan, and even refused to allow shipwrecked Japanese fishermen who had been rescued by foreign ships back into the country. They outlawed trade with any country, except China and Holland, even refusing permission for any foreigners to bury their dead on Japan's sacred soil. They were completely and contentedly isolated from the rest of the world and gave no thought whatsoever to foreigners.

Their seclusion lasted for two hundred years until 1853 when Commodore Perry sailed his seven black ships into Japan with a letter from President Fillmore, demanding that Japan open her borders and trade with the rest of the world. By 1868, Japan had accepted her place in the modern world (although there were several subversive groups against this, one with the slogan *sonnojoi*— revere the Emperor and expel the barbarians). The Japanese began to adopt Western ways (even corsets and bustles were in fashion for a brief time), but they continued to believe they were a superior people, culturally, racially, and spiritually. The Japanese consider themselves to be homogeneous (less than 0.8 percent of Japan's population are non-Japanese), while they like to refer to the United States as a genetic brawl. Over the next seventy-three years, the Japanese learned from the West; but with the invasion of China in the 1894–95 Sino-Japanese War and their entrance in 1904–5 into the Russo-Japanese War, the real brawl hadn't even begun yet.

World War II: Lost and Nearly Forgotten

When Edith accepted a new teaching job at a junior high school in the southern town, she had no idea that several of the students in her history class would be the children of Japanese bosses from the new plant. She was soon impressed by how well the young Japanese spoke English, but she could see they were having a difficult time studying World War II. One young girl went home crying and refused to return to school. Edith reasoned it was probably hard for her to understand Japan's involvement in the war, but when she talked to the girl's father, she discovered the young Japanese girl didn't even know Japan and America had fought against each other in a war. All mention of the conflict had been taken out of her history books back home.

In 1986 Masayuki Fujio, the Japanese Education Minister, ordered that all Japanese textbooks be revised to read that Japan was not the aggressor in World War II, and that the atrocities in Asia, such as the Rape of Nanking in 1937, were exaggerated. The attack on Nanking is now recorded only as an advance by the Imperial Army in Japanese textbooks. (This has been challenged by an historian named Ienaga, who took his case to the Japanese Supreme Court. The court's decision allowed most of the Education Ministry's expurgations to stand, but they did award Ienaga ¥100,000 ($710) in damages for his inquiry.) Even on film, they've changed the record. In the 1988 movie *The Last Emperor,* Japanese censors edited and removed the narration from the newsreel footage showing the assault on Nanking so as not to offend anyone.

This way of thinking stems from the new revisionist historians who believe that Japan should not have to accept the guilt for what is now considered to be ancient history by Japan's younger generation. When these historians tried to justify Japan's invasive march into China, they met with no resistance from the prime minister or the general public. On the contrary, numerous letters poured into newspapers supporting their ideas. At the same time, the Japanese believe that Americans have a guilt complex about the atomic bombings of Hiroshima and Nagasaki. True, some Americans *do* have a guilt complex about the bombings, but for a humanitarian reason. We did not initiate the conflict. Many Japanese agree. When two officials of the Japanese Ministry of Education argued that the Japanese people were not the aggressors in World War II but that the Americans were, they were both forced to resign.

Oscar-winning director Akira Kurosawa presented his viewpoint of World War II in his 1991 film, *Rhapsody in August,* the story of the bombing of Nagasaki in 1945. At the Cannes Film Festival in 1991 he told the press he had made a film about the children and their perspective of the bombing. Yet he was still taunted by Western reporters who accused him of not dealing with Japan's accountability for her part in the war. The eighty-two-year-old director countered by saying the Japanese people were a victim of Japan's military leaders and should not be held accountable for their mistakes. He believes that war itself is to blame.

It is true that no stories of Japan's heavy military losses were made known to the Japanese people until after the war. Many Japanese didn't even know the war was over until they heard the Emperor speak on radio for the first time. Yet if they continue to claim they were merely victims of Japan's militaristic leaders, how can we explain that the Japanese government still keeps its military hardware out of sight of Western reporters, but conducts tours of battleships for Japanese tourists? What *is* visible to Western eyes is a heroic statue of a World War II kamikaze pilot returning from a successful mission. After the war American soldiers ordered the statue destroyed—but the villagers buried it, then dug it up after the Americans left.

Some Japanese seem to have no guilt at all about the war and are glad they lost to the Americans, especially the young Japanese who are not anxious to atone for their parents' mistakes. Do Americans also want to forget the part of the Japanese in World War II?

Japan Bashing: An Old Story

Everyone in the house was stunned when they heard the news broadcast on the morning of December 7, 1941, but no one seemed more upset than fourteen-year-old Margie. She had just gotten her first pair of high heels and had also made the school debating team, but now it all seemed to be coming to an end. Margie was *Nisei*, first generation Japanese-American.

Margie and her family joined thousands of other Japanese-Americans in various internment camps until the end of the war. Emotions ran high among Americans after the bombing of Pearl Harbor, and the camps provided both a safe haven for Japanese-Americans and a way for the American government to keep an eye on them. After all, the Japanese in this country retained dual citizenship, unlike the Italians or Germans. There were about 30,000 Japanese-Americans in Japan at the beginning of the war; 20,000 of them were inducted into the Japanese Army. The induction was made compulsory—the Japanese government completely ignored their American citizenship.

The Japanese who were interned in the United States, however, probably fared much better. The camps had schools, beauty parlors, Saturday night dances, newspapers, even golf courses. They also had the highest birthrate in the country at the time. But even though they tried to make the best of it, life in the camps was not easy for these Japanese-Americans. They were forced to live in cramped barracks under constant guard, often without the proper food (many planted their own gardens on the near-barren land), alongside total strangers. And many returned home after the war to discover that their homes and farms had been sold, their personal belongings vandalized, and their businesses ruined.

Yet it wasn't until the late 1980s that the U.S. government recognized that the nearly 120,000 Japanese interned during World War II were entitled to any kind of reparation—they received $20,000 each. So why is it only recently that we hear so much about the Japanese: what they think, what we think? Why not directly after World War II? True, Japan was devastated and totally dependent on the United States to get through that first winter after the war without complete starvation, but part of the reason for the lack of communication is simply that the Japanese were forbidden to travel outside of their country until 1964. During their second period of self-imposed isolation, Americans conjured up their own version of the Japanese; for example, two political cartoons of the day show them as apes or as little men in little cars. Many Americans viewed the Japanese as an amusing, munchkin-like people who somehow learned how to function in the modern world with our help. We watched the industrial power of Japan grow rapidly in the 1970s, yet ignored them in world politics when President Nixon opened up negotiations with China without any prior warning to Japan.

But we weren't alone in our prejudice. Two other images we've seen are a French president who once called the Japanese prime minister a transistor salesman—and a past French prime minister who has likened the Japanese to ants, seeking to swallow the world economy.

Today's American press has gone to the opposite extreme,

sometimes picturing Japan as a sumo wrestler with a frail Uncle Sam. Another image of Japan seen in the media is that of Mercury, the god of trade—small, deceptive, tricky, and surrounded by a pack of hard-working dwarfs. A 1991 CIA-commissioned report (entitled *Japan: 2000*) prepared at the Rochester Institute of Technology stated that Japan is an amoral nation that seeks "worldwide dominance" through financial and industrial power. Many Americans believe that's a valid description, especially after one of Japan's most controversial politicians decided to get on a soapbox.

The Japan That *Did* Say No

The phone on Ed's desk wouldn't stop ringing. Everyone wanted to get a peek at his copy of the bootlegged edition of Shintaro Ishihara's polemic book, *The Japan That Can Say No*. Ed was one of several editors debating over whether or not to go after the book for the American rights. The savvy editor, however, was still reeling over the allegations made by the Japanese novelist/politician. Unlike others who had read the photocopied version, Ed wasn't fooling himself into thinking he was getting a sneak look into a dangerous and hidden side of the Japanese mind. His interest had been purely business when he started reading it. Now he wasn't so sure. His blood pressure continued rising when he read Ishihara's contention that Japan could cause havoc with America's security by redirecting their semiconductors to the Soviet Union and altering the global balance of power. (Japanese semiconductors make far more accurate nuclear missiles.) But Ed couldn't help but laugh out loud when he read Ishihara's assertion that there were nothing but buffalo in America during Japan's glorious Edo period (1603–1867).

Ed had been told that the bootlegged version was riddled with misreadings of the original manuscript. Then why would Akio Morita, Chairman of Sony and the book's coauthor, take his name off the title page? he wondered. Not unless there was a lot of truth in what he was reading.

Ishihara also portrayed the United States as a meddlesome, declining power that Japan should say no to more often. He didn't mince words when he accused the United States of using the atomic bomb out of racist attitudes and that racism is the root of much of America's Japan bashing and trade friction. America can't compete because of the decaying of our system, he charged, and we blame Japan for our problems instead of looking for solutions. He even claimed that in Pentagon planning documents, Japan is listed as enemy number three, after the Soviet Union and China respectively.

According to Ishihara, the American political and management systems are the real reasons for our decline. Yet he is the only Japanese politician who will admit that his country's economic system is often rigged against American imports (in a speech in Detroit he specifically cited the case of Motorola when Japanese bureaucrats kept out the U.S.-made high-quality cellular telephone in favor of a substandard domestic product). But Motorola persevered and has started marketing the Micro TAC in Japan—a pocket-size gadget that has captured about one-third of the world's $1.2-billion cellular phone market.

Although the Japanese have an economic dependency on America and want to keep our goodwill, the publication of Ishihara's book was seen as a display of Japanese pride and nationalism. It also hit the bull's-eye in pinpointing Japan's residual inferiority complex; yet we often perceive the Japanese of having a sense of superiority.

Life on a Seesaw: The Inferiority/Superiority Complex of the Japanese

Anson couldn't take it anymore. He was going to make a complaint about their new Japanese section chief. Yoshio, who had just arrived from Japan, spent more time hanging around the water cooler than in his office. Also, he wandered around the floor constantly, poking his nose into everybody else's work and asking them what they were doing. Anson wasn't the only one who felt that way. Other employees in the company had also noticed Yoshio's behavior and had formed the same opinion: the Japanese boss thought he was better than everyone else.

The Japanese do believe that the world should look up to Japan as a model for hard work and quality, and that their methods are superior. They also believe they are morally and intellectually superior to everyone else (except the Germans). This superior attitude is actually a defensive play against having a history of being dumped on and bashed by other nations throughout history. Every Japanese child in school is taught that being constantly aware of what is going on around them is the only way to maintain self-preservation. Also, Japan is a country with no natural resources and must import everything from oil to iron to meet its industrial needs. Consequently the Japanese continuously vacillate between an inferiority and a superiority complex and can change views overnight.

One view that seems to be more and more prevalent these days is the Japanese myth that the reason the West is having so many problems with Japan is that we just don't understand them. Even a panel of experts set up in September 1991 and led by former President Jimmy Carter and ex-Japanese Prime Minister Yasuhiro Nakasone agrees: they said that "if the economic frictions, compounded by the cultural differences [between America and Japan] are allowed to continue they could lead to misunderstanding and chaos." This problem has been enhanced by a Japanese businessman named Ochiai Nobuhiko who maintains that the stock scandal of 1991 was actually a secret strategy of the United States to "rob Japan of strength and power." Arrogance such as this has caused many Americans to perceive the Japanese in a bad light, even when a cultural difference is the reason behind the problem, as in the case of Yoshio.

Yoshio was experiencing a kind of culture shock when he came to work in an American-style office. Although he would never mention it, he wasn't used to having his own office. In Japan office space is so expensive there isn't enough room for individual offices. Instead, Yoshio had worked in a large, open room with desks arranged in a particular order, according to rank. The atmosphere was often chaotic with telephones ringing, computer keyboards tapping, people talking. The big room had been filled with computer terminals, file cabinets, and more desks than an office-furniture showroom. Yoshio felt isolated and lonely in his private office, and was merely following the Japanese custom of gathering around the water cooler, chatting, and drinking tea. This is the way they work, often holding minimeetings in such a manner. They don't have the same pressures as in an American company, although when they come to America they feel the pressure to try to fit in. If you find yourself in this situation with a Japanese boss or co-worker, by understanding their different system you can help them not only fit in, but smooth over differences with your American colleagues as well.

You Can't Win With a Japan Basher

Jack figured he should have seen it coming, but he didn't. Every night for six years he had been stopping off at Bonnie Sue's Bar and Café after work. He'd have a beer, some of their famous biscuits and gravy, and talk shop with the other guys from the plant. But things had begun to change over the past few months. After several guys had been laid off from their jobs, Jack had decided to go to work for the Japanese at the auto transplant. He liked his new job. He thought the Japanese were down-to-earth people and that their production ideas made sense.

Others, like Sam, had nothing good to say about the Japanese. Sam was a union man and couldn't even get his foot into the door of the new plant. But that didn't stop him from spouting off at the mouth every night at the bar—especially when he saw Jack. He called him derogatory names and made cutting remarks about the Japanese. Jack finally lost his cool one night and socked Sam in the jaw. Later he realized that although he felt better, it hadn't resolved the situation. This is typical of one problem you may come up against while working for a Japanese company: the Japan basher who won't go away.

T. Boone Pickens, the Texas businessman, had more than his share of problems when he tried to obtain a seat on the board of a Japanese company. He spoke for a segment of Americans when he stated his personal viewpoint and said that a lot of people in the United States "don't like the Japanese . . . I think you're going to find that the Japanese will be a major issue in the 1994 political campaign." If you run up against people with the same viewpoint as Pickens, it can be difficult if not impossible to change their minds. If they are young, there's a chance they may change their way of thinking if they are exposed to a positive relationship with the Japanese. Older workers tend to be set in their ways and very difficult to deal with, especially if they remember World War II (that was one of the reasons that the Japanese hired only young workers in Harrodsburg, Kentucky, a town that lost several native sons in the Bataan death march).

Whatever their ages, sometimes all you can do is just cope with Japan bashers by dealing with them politely. Try to avoid falling into the pattern of using their negative terms, and if they don't find an audience for their remarks, they may at least keep their thoughts to themselves.

The Ugly American-*San*

Sumi and her friends were still laughing over the antics of the popular Japanese comic Tokoro Joji as they stopped for a snack at their local Makudonurarudo—McDonald's (there are 809 McDonald's restaurants in Japan). Sumi especially liked his joke about Japanese-American relations: "Japan lends money to America," the comedian said in his act, "so people can maintain living standards three times higher than ours."

As Sumi paid for the expensive Western-style snack, chosen from a menu which included the usual McDonald's fare plus the addition of soup, soy-chicken sandwiches, and other dishes to appeal to the Japanese taste, she was certain it was true. She often heard her father say that Japan was rich, but the Japanese were poor. He isn't alone in this view. Many Japanese agree.

America bashing can be nearly as prevalent in Japan as Japan bashing is in America. Some Japanese housewives are dismayed by the pushy, arrogant attitude of the Americans they see on television, and more than one salaryman believes that Americans do not appreciate the hardworking attitude of the Japanese people. In a poll conducted by a Tokyo research organization, 71 percent of the Japanese said they consider Japanese products to be superior to American products, and 86 percent said they would not buy an American car. (Let's not forget that Japanese automakers hold 30.5 percent of the American car market and 10 percent of the

European car market.) Only 26 percent of the Japanese in the study said they consider Japan to be a *political* superpower, while 65 percent of those polled consider Japan to be an *economic* superpower. Yet 76 percent of the Japanese polled admitted they cannot buy a house with their present income.

They blame this problem on America. The popular sentiment is that when the U.S. economy goes down, up goes the Japan bashing. Many Japanese like to say that America's deteriorating economy is our own fault because of our poor quality, outdated factories, and inefficient, lazy work force. (This comment was echoed by the speaker of Japan's lower house who called American workers "lazy" and also by Prime Minister Kiichi Miyazawa, who in February 1992 told lawmakers in the Diet, Japan's parliament, that "I suspect that American workers have come to lack a work ethic.") Our consumer products suffer not only from a poor image of inferior quality in Japan, but also from inefficient after-sales service. The Japanese aren't the only ones who think so. A survey by the Brookings Institute in Washington found that a decade of poor products and poor service is to blame for Detroit's losing its share of the auto market to Japan.

A recent consumer report showed that 52 percent of Japanese customers who bought a foreign-made product needed after-sales service—and that 62.3 percent of them were dissatisfied with that service.

General Electric hopes to solve such problems by forming a joint alliance with Toshiba to sell American-made refrigerators in Japan. Large-capacity refrigerators are a hot item in Japan (the Japanese are used to a smaller product that must fit into the tiny space of a typical Japanese home or apartment). GE will manufacture them and Toshiba will service them in Japan.

But not even double-door, ice-making refrigerators can cool off some Japanese. Many will not even travel to the United States because of our high crime rate. (Experts believe this is part of the reason that Japanese overseas tour bookings fell 9.3 percent in June 1991 from a year earlier.) Statistics show that in Tokyo, a city of 8.3 million, there were 121 homicides in 1989, while in Los Angeles, a city of 3.5 million, there were 877 homicides during the

crime

same period. The number of robberies also substantiates America's image of being unsafe: 1,993 in Tokyo compared to 30,705 in Los Angeles.

Even Japanese comic books took a stab at America bashing in 1990 when *Silent Service* hit the newsstands. This adult comic explored the saga of a Japanese submarine crew that obtains nuclear missiles, provokes a confrontation with the United States, and declares a war for Japan's independence. The popular pulp provided an outlet for the Japanese people's frustration about America's Japan bashing. Although no one took it seriously, it does speak of a growing mood of Japan's nationalism that worries officials on both sides of the Pacific. According to the book *The Coming War with Japan* by George Friedman and Meredith LeBard, they may have something to worry about.

The amount of bashing back and forth across the Pacific continues to be a sparring match with no end in sight.

Opinion Polls: Barbs Across the Pacific

When the Mansfield Center for Pacific Affairs and the Dentsu Institute for Human Studies analyzed a number of stories regarding Americans and the Japanese, they had no idea their results would show that one in ten articles published in each country included negative portraits of the other side. Americans were pictured as an "arrogant, emotional, extravagant people in economic decline," while the Japanese were "insular, opportunistic, and a treacherous people." During the one-year period studied (beginning in late 1989), America had 70 newspaper reporters in Japan, while Japan had sent 237 correspondents to the United States.

Another poll by the East-West Center in Honolulu supports these findings: both American and Japanese reporters stationed across the Pacific think the bashing will get worse before it gets better. However, both sides said that much of the problem lies with their editors back home who overdramatize what is going on. Language difficulties continue to be a major problem for both countries in covering local stories. U.S. reporters claimed they had to spend too much time reporting on business trends, while the Japanese said that Americans k   story or way of life.

For years Japan and Am   r's poli- cies; now we are beginning to criticize each other's lifestyles. What these polls reveal about our knowledge of each other shows that we have much to learn about our respective cultures. One thing we do have in common is the aging of our population. America's baby boomers (those born between 1946 and 1964) are getting older, and Japan's labor force is aging faster than any other nation's. By the year 2020, one-fourth of Japan's population, or 30 million people, will be senior citizens.

Japan's Elderly: The Silver Society

The silver-haired *obāsan*, grandmother, swept the porch of her veranda every morning and every afternoon with her aged broom, just as she had done for the past forty-seven years since she had been brought to the house on her wedding day. She was proud of that broom. It had been given to her by an American GI who had seen her crying on the steps of her house not too long after the end of the war. She had been weeping because her husband was coming home and she had no broom to clean the veranda. Every- thing must be clean to heal his wounds, she had told the American soldier, both in his mind and his body.

She never forgot that GI and still remembered many other Americans who had been kind to them during those hard years. When her grandchildren complained about their cramped style of living and said that Americans have bigger houses and swimming pools, she would mutter, *"Shikata ga nai."* It can't be helped.

This attitude permeates the Silver Society in Japan. Most older Japanese were grateful for America's help after the war. If they had had any idea of changing things when they were young, once they assimilated into the corporate hierarchy they followed the paths of those who had gone before them. Some Japanese from World War II, however, still harbor resentment because the con- quering Americans did not come from a noble warrior class. They hold to the idea that America doesn't understand Japan at all. They believe that today's political structure in Japan mirrors the oligarchical system of the 1920s that led Japan into a world war with devastating results. Some of the younger generation agree.

Japan's Teens: The Pepsi Generation Wannabes

Midori and Goro were among the crowd of teenagers hustling through the lunch line at the American high-school cafeteria. They both picked up cans of Pepsi as they loaded up their trays with tacos and hot dogs and headed for the cash register. The Japanese teens were eager to try the cola drink on their first day in the new school. They were the children of Japanese managers who had been transferred from Japan to the auto transplant in the southern town. They had been drinking Coke for years, but in 1990 Pepsi had only 2 percent of the Japanese market—and the youngsters were anxious to try everything American.

Six months later they weren't so sure. The brother and sister now ate lunch only with the other teenagers of Japanese managers from the transplant, and none of them had made many American friends. They usually talked to each other in their native language, and consequently their English had not improved. Goro especially found it difficult not to react to quips in the hallways made by the American kids about Japanese imperialism. By her sixteenth birthday, Midori had had only one date because her parents pressured her not to date Americans. They were afraid of all the stories they had heard about wild sex parties.

When the situation didn't get better, Midori, Goro, and the other Japanese teens were asked by the school to join a "prejudice reduction committee" to help ease rising tensions between Japanese and American students. The American students were unhappy because the Japanese ruined the grading curve with their excellent marks and study habits. The Japanese students countered by saying the Americans should give up their football practice and drama club and study more. The Americans accused the Japanese of not participating in class discussions. The Japanese explained that in Japan the teacher gives the students the material and they were responsible only for memorizing it. They hadn't been taught to express themselves or defend their opinions in front of anyone. The Americans thought the Japanese were always talking about them because they never spoke English anywhere except in class. The Japanese criticized the Americans for not learning more about Japanese culture and customs.

With more than 200,000 Japanese bosses and their families settled in America as neighbors, classmates, and employers, the friction is not likely to decrease soon. In fact, a *Wall Street Journal* poll found that Japanese teens listed the United States as the country they were most likely to go to war with in the future. The young Japanese aren't like their parents and grandparents—they don't always approve of the bullying ways of the United States. Their open nationalistic attitude stems from the fact that many of them believe that Japan has already surpassed the United States as a world economic power. They don't bear the scars of World War II and they believe that Japan should be more arrogant in taking its place in the global power structure. More and more you hear the word *kojinshugi,* individualism, in connection with young Japanese citizens as we move toward what some experts are calling the Pacific Century.

Japan Bashing: Is There a Solution to the Problem?

The Japanese believe *they've* found an answer to Japan bashing—it's a computer game introduced in 1992 in which the player proceeds to bash with statements like: "Japanese should make wheat their staple food." The ultimate outcome for the player is a complete Japanese buyout of the United States. The game (which retails for $66) has an unusual twist: it's sold only in Japan.

With *kenbei* (hatred of the United States) the latest buzzword among the Japanese, it's more important than ever that the United States and Japan adjust their way of thinking toward each other.

Japanese businessmen have repeatedly advised Americans working with the Japanese to work hard and be patient. But this familiar advice has another side to it: the Japanese know they are different and sincerely believe they are doing *their* part by acting differently to sell overseas. They also believe that first-hand experience in America is the key to their success. Of course, it's not logistically possible for every American worker to spend several years in

Japan, but it is possible to learn more about Japanese language, customs, and culture and to observe some simple rules of international etiquette to help eradicate bad feelings between the two countries. For example, Japan's advice to America regarding how to reduce the U.S. trade deficit meets with little approval over here. They say we should limit the number of credit cards an individual can have, end income tax reduction on home mortgages, and pay more taxes and save more—Americans' personal savings rate is a meager 3.6 percent (an average $4,201 in savings accounts) compared to a new Japanese low of 7.2 percent (an average of $45,118 in savings accounts) in fiscal year 1990.

However, the Japanese are trying to improve their own self-image. In August 1991, the Economical Planning Agency (EPA) advised the Japanese government that it is "important that our country [Japan] develop better international relations with other countries and make our policies clear." A new consensus by the Japanese government calls for Japan to send civilian volunteers to foreign disasters and for refugee assistance. Also, Japanese companies have increased their charitable contributions from $30 million in 1986 to $500 million in 1991 to help bring a halt to Japan bashing in America.

Many Japanese are also changing their attitudes toward the United States. In a survey taken by the Japanese government in 1991, 78 percent of the Japanese questioned said they felt close to the United States, up from 74 percent in a similar survey a year earlier. What also makes this significant is that this percentage was higher than any other country listed in the survey.

Multiculturism is the key to providing a better workplace for both Japanese and Americans in the future. Americans can help further good relations with the Japanese by not participating in Japan bashing in the workplace. We can no longer expect the Japanese to abandon their ethnic roots and become Americanized. We are mutually dependent economies and experts predict this will continue well into the twenty-first century.

7

The Japanese Pride and Prejudice

> People create prejudice, so we can change it if
> we want to. My dream is equality for all the
> people of the earth.
>
> —Sue Sumii
> Japanese novelist

The Homogeneous Society Versus the Outside World

Sheryl watched her fifth-grade class with pride as they sat quietly in their seats and listened to the Japanese visitor explain that he had come to honor them and to promote friendship and love to American children. Her inner-city students were mostly black and Hispanic children from lower-income families and had no idea what had prompted the vice-president of the Japanese company to visit their school. As Sheryl watched, the smiling businessman give out novelty items such as elephant coin holders and gorilla pens to the wide-eyed kids. It was hard to believe that he was the head of a company that practiced racial prejudice against African-Ameri-

105

cans. She bit her lower lip in frustration. Hopefully, her students wouldn't have to face a world filled with such injustices when they grew up. Who would have thought the Japanese would be prejudiced?

She remembered how shocked she had been when she was called into the principal's office to see the Little Black Sambo toys with very black faces, large white eyes, thick lips, and other exaggerated features. It shocked her even more when she discovered that these offensive toys and beachwear were being sold and distributed at three thousand Sanrio boutiques in Japan. (The Little Black Sambo character was created in 1898 by British author Helen Bannerman.) These toys had been brought to the attention of the principal by a concerned parent who had brought them back from Japan. Now, with Sanrio shops opening in shopping malls in their city, the parents, school principal, and teachers were worried about what kinds of toys they would be carrying in their U.S. stores. They were not the only ones to protest the racially insulting items. Hundreds of black Americans also made their views known, and even though the Japanese insisted they viewed the hot-selling toys as "cute" and not offensive, they agreed to remove them from the shelves.

Takara, the Japanese company that makes Transformer robots and the dancing "Flower Rock" toys, stopped selling a black inflatable plastic doll with big round eyes wearing a grass skirt. Another Japanese company recently agreed to drop a racially offensive trademark: since 1923 the label on Calpis bottled yogurt had shown a dapper black minstrel sipping a tall, cool Calpis. It took ten years for the company to change their logo, but not all Japanese feel the pressure to change. There is a pub in Tokyo called Little Black Sambo with a log-cabin decor and featuring specialties such as "little black fried chicken" and "little black potatoes." It has been open since the early 1980s and has no intention of changing its name or its menu.

Most Americans don't perceive the Japanese as being racists—they're a homogeneous society, right? Their doors to the outside world have been closed more than they've been open, but their attitudes about racism have recently come under fire.

The Japanese Parliament: Their View From the Top

On the CBS Evening News in September 1990, the justice minister of Prime Minister Kaifu's cabinet said during an interview that Japanese prostitutes were just like blacks in America because they were ruining neighborhoods. Many black Americans shook their heads in disbelief. But it wasn't the first time in recent memory a member of the Japanese government had uttered a racial slur. In 1986 former Prime Minister Nakasone said that "the level of knowledge in the United States is lower than in Japan due to the considerable number of blacks, Puerto Ricans, and Mexicans." Two years later, the policy chief for Japan's ruling Liberal Democratic Party, Michio Watanabe, said that American blacks have no qualms about defaulting on their debts.

Apologies followed, but Americans were beginning to question the sincerity of the Japanese, especially in the case of Seiroku Kajiyama, the justice minister. He apologized for his remark only after Prime Minister Kaifu rebuked him during a cabinet meeting. Then both he and Kaifu rejected repeated calls for his resignation until Kaifu was urged by his supporters to reshuffle his cabinet, although doing little to change the balance of power. What prompted this sudden switch in policy? Was it the two month long "informational picket line" in front of the Japanese Embassy in Washington? The meeting of the NAACP director with Japanese business representatives? Or was it due more to the buying power of black Americans—an estimated $230 billion annually?

Whatever the answer, the Japanese view of black Americans remains a problem, and in the words of the U.S. ambassador to Japan, Michael H. Armacost, Kajiyama's remark "struck a sensitive cord with all Americans, not just black Americans." There is also the unanswered question of how the average Japanese views black Americans. Not all agree with Kajiyama or Nakasone, of course, but in a survey conducted at Ibaraki University, only ten percent of the students interviewed in the English department knew anything about the late Reverend Martin Luther King, Jr. Such ignorance is further complicated by the Japanese penchant for caricatures in their daily newspapers, such as black American baseball players with exaggerated "Negro" lips or a Hawaiian sumo wrestler with "bulbous, mindless eyes," in the words of a reporter for a Japanese magazine. The Japanese don't think of these cartoons as racist, some say, but as part of their fun-loving nature, in which they poke fun at everyone from movie stars to old ladies.

Even in private the Japanese have difficulty explaining black Americans to their children. They don't mean to be offensive; it's just that they've never before had to deal with anything of a similar nature in their culture. For example, when a black woman sat down next to a Japanese man and his young daughter on a Tokyo train, the child pointed to the woman and innocently asked, "*Kore wa nan desu ka?*" "What's that?" The father answered by telling his daughter an old Chinese fable popular among Japanese children in which the hero is named "Songoku." Songoku is a monkey.

Black leaders in America perceive the situation to be even worse in American companies where Japanese bosses tend to bring their prejudice with them. This often shows up in employment discrimination. In the words of one black entrepreneur, "We may be replacing white American overseers with Japanese overseers." Some black Americans blame these prejudiced attitudes on a Japanese culture that promotes racial homogeneity, while others accuse white Americans of introducing bigotry against blacks to Japan, especially the U.S. troops who have been stationed there since the end of World War II. Still, black leaders agree that reversing these attitudes won't be easy.

Several Japanese companies, however, are now directing their advertising toward blacks. Toyota contributes to the United Negro College Fund, Hitachi has designated about $4 million for minority projects in the past five years, and Mitsui grants $10,000 annually to the National Minority Business Council. In addition, Sony has instituted an award for black creative artists, and Nissan is now advertising in black magazines.

We can hope that Japanese government officials have learned their lesson. After all, Kajiyama did lose his job as justice minister and was reassigned to a different party job as chairman of the Liberal Democratic Party's Legislative Affairs Committee.

Opposites Attract: Interracial Relationships in Japan

The table setting looks perfect, Lydia thought, admiring the floral display. She was so proud of her *ikebana,* flower arrangement. When she had signed up for the class in the ancient Japanese art she hadn't been sure of herself, but her *sensei,* teacher, Etsuko, told her she was a true artist. Lydia had insisted that the Japanese-born woman come to her home for dinner and bring her husband. She was very nervous. Lydia had heard how fastidious Japanese men were—she wondered if the fun-loving, smiling Etsuko she knew was a different woman around her stern Japanese husband.

When the doorbell rang, Lydia answered it, but she wasn't prepared as Etsuko introduced her husband: a tall black American.

A new phenomenon has taken over a segment of Japanese women, who traditionally have been given little choice about the direction of their lives: marriage to black Americans. American and European men have long enjoyed the company of Japanese women—but relationships between Japanese women and black Americans began only after World War II when U.S. troops were first stationed in Japan. The U.S. government went to great lengths to protect the interracial families when they came to the United States by stationing them in Mid- and Southwest locations, according to Japanese-American playwright, Velina Hasu Houston, herself the daughter of a Japanese woman and a black American. She has written a play called *Tea,* the story of Japanese war brides, as well as a screenplay based on Sawako Ariyoshi's novel, *Not Color,* also the story of a relationship between a Japanese woman and an African-American. Another female Japanese writer, Amy Yamada, is the author of *Bedtime Eyes,* a controversial and sexually explicit bestselling novel about a Japanese woman and a black American soldier, that was made into a feature film in Japan.

Black culture continues to permeate the Japanese landscape. Motown and rap music have invaded the clubs in Tokyo's fashionable Roppongi district where young Japanese dress in black fashions, wear dreadlocks, and bronze their skin. Their adoption of black culture also extends to a few rare cases where young Japanese women hire black American marines to engage in sex parties at bridal showers. But these are the exceptions rather than the rule in a country that has never easily accepted the existence of minorities.

Racism Wasn't Born in a Day

In his book, *The Japan That Can Say No,* politician Shintaro Ishihara stated that race is "the most important factor moving history." It is perhaps never more true than in Japan. The we-Japanese-versus-the-rest-of-the-world syndrome has endured throughout history. One of the most interesting cases occurred in 1791 when an American ship loaded with animal skins landed at Kushimoto-Oshima, southeast of Osaka. The American captain had hoped to sell the skins to the Japanese, but they considered anyone who worked with animal skins an outcast and ordered the Americans out of the country. When a volcano on Shimbara Peninsula erupted, destroying twenty-seven villages and killing thousands, the Japanese blamed it on the intrusion of foreigners into Japan.

Disaster became associated with the intrusion of foreigners into Japan. The Japanese believed that the gods were angry with them for allowing foreign ideas into their country. After the Great Kanto Earthquake of 1923, a similar viewpoint caused the deaths of thousands of Koreans living in Tokyo. They were hunted down and killed by Japanese who blamed their intrusion into the "land of the gods" for the natural disaster. These ideas are not necessarily representative of Japan today, but they do offer insight into the history of modern Japanese thinking.

Racism was not confined to the shores of the Japanese islands. During World War II, over 20 million Chinese were killed by Japanese soldiers. More evidence of Japanese prejudice toward other races was revealed by the discovery of the remains of thirty-five bodies, unearthed in July 1989 at a government construction site in Tokyo where the Japanese Army Medical School stood until 1945. Historians believe the bones are the remains of biological experiments carried out by a notorious secret division known only by its unit number, 731. The 20,000-member unit was organized in strictest secrecy in the 1930s to conduct experiments in biological warfare and operated in occupied China and Manchuria. According to Japanese Army documents that weren't released until the early 1980s, about three thousand human guinea pigs were transported to laboratories in Harbin in northeast China, where they were either killed by exposure to germs and extreme cold, or by other inhumane treatment. The bodies were dismembered in laboratories in China and sent back to Japan for forensic research. Most of the prisoners were either Chinese, Koreans, or Russians—although some members of 731 have testified that during World War II American and British POWs were also interned there.

We may never know for certain if any Americans or British fell victim to these atrocities. The Japanese Health Ministry has refused to put pressure on the local government to identify the bones. The police will not open the case as homicide because the bones have been buried for more than twenty years, and, according to Japanese law, the statute of limitations for murder is fifteen years. The historians argue that the bones can't be Japanese because they would have been properly cremated, and if they were Japanese victims of Allied air raids, other parts of the bodies would have been recovered.

Yet the Health Ministry continues to wear a face of unaccountibility. They claim they have no obligation to identify the bones— not just because a criminal case can't be proven, but because no one has come forward to claim them. Japanese historians, however, continue to press for justice for these victims. More and more modern Japanese are coming to terms with the recent history of Japan's racial injustices and are trying to do something about it. For example, in the 1980s Japanese author Seiichi Morimura wrote a bestselling book on the subject, *The Devil's Gluttony*, to bring it to the attention of the Japanese people, and a Japanese filmmaker made a film called *731*.

But these dead soldiers are not the only victims of racial pride and prejudice. Some Japanese have lived with it since the day they were born.

The *Burakumin:* Japan's Untouchables

Gordon was still reeling from his strange conversation with his Japanese boss regarding the young man he had interviewed for an opening in their Tokyo office. Although Gordon spoke fluent Japanese, he had only been in Japan for a short time and he hadn't been prepared for the startling information he had unearthed that morning. He had recommended a young Japanese named Hiroshi for the job, but after an investigation by his company, Gordon's Japanese boss suggested that he keep looking. Gordon couldn't understand why his opinion was being challenged, so he read the investigative report. Everything checked out fine except for one thing: Hiroshi's family was linked to the *burakumin,* Japan's untouchables.

The Japanese have discriminated against their own kind for centuries. The *burakumin* (literal translation: "hamlet people") were once called *eta,* or "much filth." This meaning stemmed from the fact that they were the butchers, tanners, sandal makers, midwives, and undertakers.

Most Japanese don't even know the origin of this prejudice, although even today the sight of an old woman in a patched, dark kimono will evoke whispers among Japanese schoolgirls who refuse to get off the bus in front of a *buraku* district. It is most likely that the prejudice against these people originated in the obsession with cleanliness and purity stemming from the Shinto religion, as well as from the introduction of Buddhism in the sixth century, with its restrictions against the slaughter and cleaning of animals. Death and disease became associated with these *burakumin* who lived primarily in the south and west (the locations of their villages were deliberately omitted from maps).

Even though the *burakumin* spoke the same language and looked the same as other Japanese, strange superstitions began to surround them. They were thought to stink and were labeled habitual troublemakers, liars, and thieves. It was only the indispensable nature of their jobs that saved them from extinction within their own country. They produced magnificent leather saddles and fine bowstrings for the samurai to use as they rode into battle in a period of long civil wars. But with the Tokugawa Shōgunate (beginning in 1603) came peace—and no further need for the military goods produced by the *burakumin.*

Restrictions regarding their dress, abode, even their lifestyle, were formalized in the Edo Period (1603–1867) when hereditary social classes were given a permanent station in life. They were forbidden to smoke or eat with "commoners," as Japanese people called themselves, and marriage with a Japanese was unthinkable. In 1859, a judge declared that if a Japanese killed a *burakumin*, he could not get the death penalty because the life of the untouchable was worth only one-seventh of that of a regular Japanese citizen.

Although the *burakumin* were legally emancipated in 1871, even today schools in Japan hold separate athletic games so that regular Japanese students don't have to hold hands with *burakumin* children. Some *burakumin* parents become so distraught at the birth of a child, there have been isolated cases where they tried to murder their own offspring to spare them a "living hell" on earth. Among the estimated one to three million *burakumin* now living in Japan, many end up as day laborers or join criminal gangs (*yakuza*). They disappear like fine threads into the tapestry that makes up modern Japan, never acknowledged, yet still part of the same cloth.

The *burakumin* may be the untouchable Japanese, but they are not the only ones shown discrimination.

Yearly Fingerprinting of Japanese-Koreans

When Steve stopped by the pachinko parlor to see his friend Taizo, he was surprised when the cleaning lady handed him a note. Steve didn't understand his friend's message. Taizo had gone with his family to be fingerprinted for his yearly alien registration card.

Even since the American student had wandered into the noisy, smoke-filled pinball-machine parlor one day after class, he had become friendly with the son of the owner, a young student like himself. It hadn't occurred to Steve that his friend was different from any other Japanese. Taizo was born in Tokyo, spoke fluent Japanese, and had never mentioned that his ancestry was Korean. What Steven discovered about the nearly 700,000 Japanese-Koreans living in Japan was something he would never learn in a Japanese university.

From 1910–1945, Japan's military leaders directed their sights to colonizing Korea and forcibly brought Koreans to Japan to work as slave labor in Japanese factories. Until May 1992, when the proposal to end the fingerprinting of Korean, Taiwanese, and other permanent foreign residents was approved by Japan's Parliament, all Koreans (even those born in Japan, who know no other country and speak only Japanese) had to submit to yearly *shimon,* or fingerprinting, as aliens and carry a registration card on their person at all times. Unlike the United States, where citizenship is determined by place of birth, in Japan and other countries, citizenship is a matter of blood, not birth. Even if a Korean decides to renounce his heritage in the naturalization process, his offspring will still carry the "stigma" of Korean ancestry on all official documents throughout the next four generations.

During the political scandal of the late 1980s (where questionable political donations were reputed to be laundered through Korean-owned pachinko parlors), Japanese-Koreans experienced a surge of violence ranging from verbal abuse to bodily harm. The North Korean residents' association wrote to Prime Minster Kaifu to put an end to this treatment, but received only a curt reply instead. "I didn't bully anyone myself . . . ," Kaifu replied to their letter, "and I'm not in a position to go and look for the bullies, either." Since then Japanese-Koreans have stepped up pressure on the government to eliminate the national identity-card system.

They did gain a slight victory when Emperor Akihito made a speech to South Korean President Roh Tae Woo in August 1990 acknowledging Japan's militaristic aggressions in the past. However, even then the Japanese government went to great lengths to assure Korean officials that the Emperor's "August words" or *okotoba* were not an apology (which could render former Emperor Hirohito's words to Korea in 1965 to be insincere), but a statement of regret. Even more confusing to Koreans was Japan's apology to North Korea in September 1990 for its past aggressions when concessions were also made by Japanese political leaders for economic compensation—then a few months later, Japan formally rescinded such compensations. (Japan did agree to pay South Korea $500 million in restitution but continues to shun any responsibility for the years after Korea was divided.)

Even in the face of disaster, Japan still turns its back on Koreans. None of the 30,000 Japanese-Korean *hibakusha,* or victims of the atomic bombing of Hiroshima, have been entitled to compensation. In addition, so strong is the prejudice against Japanese-Koreans that the memory of those who died at Hiroshima was not allowed to be honored alongside the Japanese who perished that day. Instead, a small memorial to Japanese-Korean victims was erected in 1970 outside the boundaries of the Hiroshima Peace Park by the Japanese-Koreans to honor their dead.

Many Japanese-Koreans, however, will go to great lengths to avoid the stigma of their ancestry.

A Different Kind of Japanese Prejudice

The early morning mist only added to the fairy-tale effect of the wedding, Boyd's wife assured him as they watched the Japanese bride and groom exchange vows before the Shinto priest. Boyd did admit his Japanese business partner's bride looked beautiful in her white silk wedding kimono overcoat (*uchikake*). Boyd remarked to his wife how very Japanese she looked.

The American businessman and his wife enjoyed the wedding more than anything else they had seen since they had come to Japan—and they remarked to their host that they had never met so many wonderful Japanese people all in one day, especially the bride's family. They were so open and friendly, the couple said, unlike some of their other experiences in Japan where they were treated like strange *gaijin*.

Boyd and his wife didn't find out until years later that his Japanese partner's new bride was Korean—and that her "wonderful Japanese" family were actors paid to pose as her relatives. (The actors who played her mother and father received double the fee for their roles.) It was important to the young couple that everything be perfect in the public eye: the cost of the wedding of an average Japanese couple exceeds ¥7.55 million ($55,000). On the rare occasion when a Japanese family will consent to their son marrying a Korean girl, it would be unthinkable for her Korean family to mingle with their Japanese relatives. Since tradition dictates that the bride's family must be in attendance, hiring actors was the simplest solution so no one would lose face.

But what about another side of Japanese prejudice—which no amount of playacting can change.

The Handicapped: Japan's Invisible People

The Shibuya train station in Tokyo was filled with commuters as Karen tried to find the right train. As she looked for a way to get to the platform she was conscious of the curious stares from the Japanese travelers who brushed by her quickly. One nearly knocked her over, but she steadied herself just in time. In frustration she asked a train attendant in Japanese if there was an elevator that would take her down to the platform. He simply ignored her, trying with difficulty not to stare. Karen was a rare sight in a Tokyo train station: she was in a wheelchair.

Even if Karen could get down to the platform, she would be unable to board the train: in Japan there is a gap between the height of the platform and that of the train door. And there are not elevators at every subway station, as in some U.S. cities. In fact, there are *no* facilities for the handicapped in Japan.

This is not unusual in the eyes of the Japanese because in their daily lives, most Japanese never see a disabled or handicapped person. The Japanese attitude is that they should be cared for out of sight of the normal population. This is not to say that the handicapped are forbidden to move outside their homes or special schools; in the Japanese way of using indirect means to accomplish their needs, the handicapped are merely discouraged from doing so by the total lack of accommodations for them.

Since World War II, under the auspices of the Japanese government, the handicapped have been placed in special homes or schools where they spend their time in training and/or therapy. It wasn't until 1979 that Japan decreed that every disabled child was deserving of an education—albeit in a special school, away from normal Japanese schoolchildren.

Although the Japanese attitude toward the handicapped seems unjust and unfeeling, it is necessary to explain the root of such action. Japanese society is built around the principle that no one should look or act differently from the majority. This principle of sameness has moved the machinery of Japanese life for centuries, where only hard work and conformity were respected. Japan is a skill- and achievement-oriented community where the importance of the individual is relative only to his or her ability to contribute to the welfare of the group as a whole.

When Karen visited a school for the deaf, she discovered you can make a difference. With Karen's help, the Japanese children eagerly began learning to speak English by imitating how she moved her mouth when she spoke. Karen was impressed with the children, but worried about their future. These young people would always be treated as outsiders, even in their own country.

And they're not alone.

Discrimination Comes in All Colors

The sumo match was already underway when Walt arrived with his Japanese co-workers. He had been assigned to study the company's operations in Japan for a year and this was his first opportunity to see a sumo match. As they took their seats, he heard someone yell, "*Taichiai!*" The charge. Before Walt knew what had happened, the nearly five-hundred-pound wrestler named Konishiki had squarely defeated his opponent. While Walt was still trying to figure out what had happened, the Japanese sitting next to him uttered an expletive, showing his disappointment at the outcome of the match. When Walt asked why, he said that Konishiki wasn't even a Japanese, but a Samoan-American from Hawaii who was often booed more than he was cheered. Some sumo fans had mounted a "stop Konishiki" campaign and one disgruntled fan had nailed a voodoo doll bearing his likeness to a tree at a Shinto shrine. This was an example of nationalism in Japan that Walt never knew existed.

Walt remembered the incident later in the week when he was touring the company's facilities in Osaka. He decided to take a detour and ended up in Nishinari Ward—home to Kamagasaki, Japan's largest labor market, or *yoseba*. It was like something out of a bad movie—the streets were filled with dirty-looking men who smelled of urine and cheap wine sleeping on the ground. This slum area was run by local gangsters, or *yakuza*, who eagerly handed out construction jobs to men without an identity (illegal workers or Japanese without a home or family) then cheated the men out of their pay with rigged gambling.

These unfortunates, as well as the gaijin sumō wrestler, are only two examples of the discrimination faced by anyone in Japan who does not fit the mold. Their presence is tolerated because they provide services—services Japan will continue to need more than ever as the next century begins to dawn.

In 1988 there were 100,000 illegal workers in Japan—the numbers have swelled in 1992 to 200,000, with no signs of slowing down, according to the Justice Ministry's Immigration Bureau. (The present Japanese immigration law passed in 1951 forbids entry to unskilled workers.) These illegal workers perform many of the "dirty" (*kitanai*) jobs that Japanese are no longer willing to do. (Many fast-food restaurants have been forced to close or curtail their hours because of a lack of workers to fill the jobs. To attract workers, for example, McDonald's offers nearly twice the salary in Tokyo that it does in the United States.) Also, the sweatshops, or *takobeya* (literally, octopus rooms), are filled with illegal workers who grind out scraps of metallic debris accumulated from auto graveyards to sustain Japan's booming scrap-metal industry.

In a poll by the Justice Ministry, 47 percent of the Japanese said they supported the use of foreign workers if Japanese could not be found to fill undesirable jobs. Yet, these workers (Pakistanis, Bangladeshis, Filipinos, Thais, etc.) are forced to live in slums with no rights to better living conditions. It doesn't appear that things will improve. A report issued by the National Police Agency stated that Pakistanis are "smelly people with skin diseases who speak poor English, get mad when they are fed pork without being told, and tend to lie in the name of Allah during interrogation."

The bottom line is this: The work gets done, the wages for these workers stay low, and as long as they stay out of sight in their ghettos (they're not even considered *gaijin*, but lower than that on the vertical ladder of Japanese society), Japanese leaders will continue to ignore the problem. After all, they argue, Japan is *tanitsu kokka, tanitsu minzoku*, one nation, one race, and they intend to keep it that way.

What the Japanese have not recognized is they must not only provide jobs for these people in the future, but a decent living standard as well as assimilation into their society. Most of the foreign workers live in apartments isolated from their Japanese neighbors, including the 150,000 Japanese-Brazilians who came to work in Japan as "trainees" when a revised Immigration Control Law went into effect in June 1990. There are also many native Japanese who are still discriminated against—like the 20,000 Ainu who live in northern Japan, as well as the descendants of sailors from an American whaling ship who settled in the Bonin Islands south of Tokyo in 1830. And many Japanese continue to promote an attitude of superiority toward Japanese-Americans. When *Nisei* (first generation Japanese-American born in the United States) speak Japanese clearly and precisely, the Japanese will often just stare at them or walk away.

Many experts say that the Japanese attitude toward ethnic minorities originated back in the late nineteenth century during the Meiji Period when homogeneity was used to control the society, its attitudes, its work ethic, its future. Control over minorities is something that the Japanese *don't* have in the American workplace, and it's a situation that may get worse before it gets better.

Japanese Prejudice in the United States: It Doesn't Play in Peoria

They were never going to make their deadline, Ronald thought as he waited impatiently for the temp to finish preparing the computer printouts. Luckily his Japanese boss had consented to hiring the extra help, but they were still behind schedule. "Here are the printouts, corrected and up-to-date," the temp announced proudly. Ronald looked over the work. He was impressed. The young woman was not only accurate, but fast, just the kind of employee his company needed. He hired her on the spot, and expected her to move up quickly in the company, but after several months nothing happened. Every time he brought up her name for a promotion his Japanese boss gave him another excuse. Soon Ronald began to get the picture: the young woman would never get anywhere in the company because she was a woman. Ronald also began to realize why *his* career was stalled: he was black.

Ronald's experience is not unusual. The hiring and promoting practices of Japanese companies in the United States have come under scrutiny by the Equal Employment Opportunity Commission. The Japanese have been criticized for not promoting American workers, even if they are not minorities. According to a survey of 585 Japanese companies by the Japan Society, 30 percent of

DISCRIMINATION '

them have been involved in discrimination complaints for failing to promote minorities, women, and older people. For example, Toyota is being sued by a white American male mid-level manager who alleges that he has been denied promotions to upper management during the ten years he has worked for the company because he is not Japanese. He contends that American managers have no real power.

It can be difficult to deal with Japanese companies that cling to some very old Japanese customs as a means of doing business. For example, the founder of Toyota was named "Toyoda," but the number of strokes needed to write his name was ten, an unlucky number. The company was named Toyota: the number of strokes needed to write it is eight—a lucky number. Even today Toyota continues to consult a Shinto priest to decide which direction a new building should face. And companies such as Mazda and Sumitomo Bank also use the services of a Shinto priest to perform a *jichinsai,* or ground-blessing ritual, to bring about a certain trust basis with the earth before they start building on a site.

American managers can learn to deal with such cultural differences, but not with cultural injustices. Once the Japanese come to terms with the fact they are doing business in a multicultural arena they will be able to avoid expending large amounts of capital on lawsuits: Honda agreed to pay $6 million to 377 female and black employees as a result of past discrimination in hiring and promotion, and Sumitomo Corporation of America agreed to pay $2.6 million in settling a federal lawsuit that asserted Japanese and American males were favored over women (the case took twelve years to resolve and generated a Supreme Court ruling that civil rights laws apply to the U.S. subsidiaries of foreign companies). Also, Matsushita's Quasar was found guilty of discrimination when manager layoffs in 1986 affected only its American staff. (However, in December 1991 a federal appellate panel overturned a $2.5 million damage award won by three former managers of Quasar Company, stating that according to a treaty between the United States and Japan that entitles companies of each nation to employ executives of their choosing in foreign subsidiaries, it *is* legal for Japanese-owned companies to show hiring preference to Japanese citizens.) Japanese companies have even been accused of discrimination in hiring practices. For example, a Los Angeles-based Japanese employment agency devised a code to screen applicants on the basis of race and age. "I want to speak to Adam in suite 2035" meant that the employer wanted to interview a white man between the ages of twenty and thirty-five, and "Don't speak to Maria" meant that a Hispanic would not be considered for the job.

Another factor to be considered regarding minority hiring is understanding the Japanese corporate way of thinking. If they can avoid a problem altogether they will. Consequently, many Japanese manufacturing plants are located in the rural areas of the Midwest where white workers predominate. Although it has not been proven this is the reason that the Japanese set up many of their transplants there, many Americans speculate this may be true. When confronted with this fact, the Japanese insist that their decisions are based solely on geography and cost (real estate is cheaper there and many state governments offer tax breaks for companies who locate there) and that they do hire minorities: in American border towns.

Head for the Border: The Mexico Connection

During the free-spending years of the 1980s, many Japanese companies traded yen for pesos—and lost a lot of money in the process. They weren't used to the surplus of flexibility in Mexican law that allowed the government to change laws six times in six years. The Japanese prefer a stable environment where the laws are in force on a long-term basis: twenty, thirty, forty years. In the eyes of Japanese investors, Mexico began to suffer from a "high-risk" stigma. Then devaluation of the Mexican peso sent many Japanese executives heading back for the border. A new word became popular in the boardrooms of Japanese companies: *maquiladora* (a foreign-owned manufacturing or assembly plant set up in the border region to produce goods for export). The Rio Grande Valley in Texas is very popular with Japanese investors, and Japanese consumer-electronics giants like Pioneer and Matsushita presently lead the Asian manufacturing boom in Tijuana, providing jobs for workers. Sony has just expanded its Tijuana plant from 280,000 square feet to 500,000 square feet and increased its work force from 800 to 1,500 workers.

This sounds like a good beginning, but the Japanese have little choice. The makeup of the American workplace is changing rapidly. By the turn of the century, it won't be the same.

America 2001

Masahiro couldn't find the words he was looking for in his Japanese-English dictionary: diversity, pluralism, and niche businesses. Of course, he had been carrying around the compact dictionary for a long time, many years before he began hearing those words in the American workplace. These new buzzwords, as his American colleague called them, had a strange ring to them, but he was beginning to understand what they meant. He had even put them to work when he hired the new woman engineer last month, as well as the two African-American managers during the past year. These people had been well-qualified for the jobs, and Masahiro had eagerly explained to them that the Japanese consensus-style of management equalized the decision-making process, tearing down many of the barriers that had previously existed. Other Japanese companies were following their lead: Mitsubishi Bank of California, for example, had made a real effort to include women and minorities in its senior upper-level management.

Masahiro looked at his watch. He was scheduled to have lunch with Daniel, his new executive vice-president, and the man who had shown him the way. He would ask him about "segmentation, targeting, and multicultural." Daniel is *ichi ban*, number one, Masahiro thought, smiling as he closed his dictionary. Even for a *hakujin*, a white man.

As the twenty-first century begins to emerge from the shadow of speculation, new statistics have begun to appear. The national unemployment rate in the United States is expected to decline from the 1991 figure of 6.6 percent to 4.6 by the year 2003. Working women will represent the most dramatic change according to the U.S. Bureau of Labor Statistics: in 1990, 38 percent of women were in the workplace (74 percent were between the ages of twenty-four and fifty-four), and by the year 2000, they will make up 47 percent of the work force.

Immigration is expected to increase from 685,000 in 1991 to 800,000 in 1993. The Hispanic population should be the fastest-growing segment of the work force, making up 9.2 percent of the total number of workers by the year 2000. The labor force, however, will face its biggest change over the next twenty years: the percentage of white workers will decrease from 75 percent to 64 percent; black workers will increase from 12 percent to 14 percent, Asians from 4 percent to 7 percent, and Hispanics from 9 percent to 15 percent.

Japanese companies know that they are facing a great challenge in the future with a changing work force. Hopefully, they will learn from the earlier mistakes and realize that doing business with minorities is good business. Americans can do their part by working together to build a bridge between all races and all cultures.

8

The Story of an American Working for the Japanese

> "As you are a trainee–"
> "I suppose I am, at Sony . . . but I do have two master's degrees and considerable computer experience."
> "I see. . . . Since you are a trainee at Sony . . ."
> —Gary Katzenstein
> *An Outsider's Year in Japan*

Mr. Jones Learns the Japanese Formula for Success

Mr. Jones had only a few hours left to spend his bonus allotment before losing it, and his feet were killing him. He had walked around the sprawling shopping center all day with his special Japanese corporate credit card in hand and his company pin shining brightly in his lapel. He didn't have much time left.

As Mr. Jones browsed through the men's department in the upscale store, he wouldn't have believed that working for the Japanese could be *this* much fun. Skiing equipment, a new CD player, Nike Air Pumps, a new set of golf clubs, and he still had money left over, he calculated. But then again he had earned it—many hours of overtime, attention to details, team effort. Mr. Jones had learned a lot since going to work for the Japanese boss, but it hadn't been easy. His early days on the job had been a combination of communication problems, confusion, and downright frustration. At the beginning, the hardest thing he had to learn was patience—now it was how to spend the bonus money his company had given him and two hundred other company dealers before the weekend was over.

Mr. Jones's company offered the incentive program to their hottest dealers every year. Each dealer was given an average of $10,000 (some as much as $50,000) to spend during a $2-million weekend spending spree in such shopping meccas as Trump Tower in New York and the Neiman-Marcus flagship store in Dallas.

Incentive and performance rewards are one way the Japanese are trying to Americanize their U.S. operations. What makes this so unusual is that by nature Japanese companies adhere to a culture that doesn't accept the concept that money is the bottom line for many workers. In a survey done by the certified public accounting firm of KPMG Peat Marwick of eighty-six Japanese-owned companies, only 38 percent of them said they used performance incentive programs for their U.S. employees. Companies with long-term programs numbered even less: only 7 percent of them implemented a multiyear incentive plan for their workers in U.S.-based companies, compared to 90 percent of U.S. companies. But as more and more Japanese companies admit they must change their strategy to succeed in the American workplace, these types of incentives are becoming more commonplace and are a top priority in their long-range plans.

Mr. Jones had to admit that the Japanese did things right—from choosing the upscale mall for their bonus sweepstakes to the reception afterward, right down to the free foot massages. Yes, he thought, closing his eyes as the masseuse worked on his tired feet, going to work for the Japanese was the best thing he had ever done.

But it hadn't started out that way.

Don't Call Us, We'll Call You. . . . Maybe

The employment agency told Mr. Jones that the Japanese company where he wanted to work was very explicit about their job qualifications. Although Mr. Jones knew his education and experience were top-notch, he wasn't sure if that was enough. He had heard how rigorous the interview process was, and knew that some Japanese companies even made employees write a paper on loyalty as part of their interview.

Mr. Jones believed that working for the Japanese offered him a good opportunity to be on the inside track for the future of global business. Although his verbal communications were good (he made an excellent presentation explaining why he should be part of their team), he soon realized that the American way of converting an interview into an offer right then and there wasn't going to work with the Japanese. He told them he had a keen interest in the Japanese culture, but when he admitted he didn't speak Japanese he was afraid he was out of the running. He went home and waited.

Several weeks went by, and Mr. Jones was considering another job that he had been offered with an American firm, although he felt there wasn't the same potential there as with the Japanese company. The American workplace has changed drastically—ten years ago there were ten potential candidates for every middle-management opening. Now there are three hundred. Three million jobs have vanished from the Fortune 500 companies, with mid-level management positions the first to go.

Then the phone call came. The Japanese company wanted Mr. Jones to start immediately. What would be his job title? he asked. He was told only that he had been accepted and that they looked forward to having him with the company. Mr. Jones was puzzled, but excited. He was working for the Japanese—but what was his job? What Mr. Jones didn't realize was that it is typically Japanese for workers to have an unstructured job description. They are given time to learn every facet of their area of expertise to broaden their knowledge, which in turn makes them more valuable to the company.

Mr. Jones decided not to worry about it. Working for the Japanese couldn't be *that* different.

Getting to Know You

During his first day on the job Mr. Jones noticed that his new company's organizational chart was put together in the Japanese style and showed only collective units, not individual names, their positions, or titles. He was confused. How would he remember everyone's name? Of course, he wasn't the only American on the team, but he was determined to show his Japanese boss that he could adapt to their ways, especially in being on time for work in the morning. (Japanese employers expect their workers to arrive at least five minutes early so they can be hard at work by starting time. According to the study prepared by the accounting firm KPMG Peat Marwick, 81 percent of Japanese companies study company records for employee tardiness, with 30 percent of them considering one minute as being late.) However, Mr. Jones did like the idea of spending the first half-hour reading the newspaper. Keeping up with the world and local news was considered part of his job. But the rest of the day wasn't so easy.

After Mr. Jones called his boss by his first name a couple of times and he acted like he didn't hear him, Jones asked a co-worker for help. He found out that in speaking as well as in writing Japanese, the family name is mentioned before the given name (Japanese do not have middle names), and first names are never used except among close friends. He also noticed that the Japanese in the company usually used the term *-san* after someone's last name, but that the most senior officer in the company was addressed as *"sensei,"* a term of respect also reserved for teachers, medical doctors, and politicians. Mr. Jones was amused to discover that the term *"-chan"* was used only among children or young lovers, and that male employees often addressed a junior or younger male colleague with *"-kun."*

Jonzu-*san* (as he was now called) became friendly with a young Japanese who helped him over the hurdles of the first day—from explaining that everyone worked in an open desk area that usually held eight desks (the number eight is considered to be lucky) situated according to the hierarchy to bowing every time he passed a fellow employee in the hall. Employees worked their way up the section of the basic work group (the *kachō,* or section chief, is set off from the rest). His co-workers showed Jonzu-*san* where the company library was and helped him order his own *hanko,* or personal seal, that he would use to give his consensus on company documents.

But Jonzu-*san* was confused when his boss gave him a vague outline of his job responsibilities. It was up to Jonzu-*san* to analyze the job and interpret it. (The Japanese believe that their employees will do more on their own initiative than what they are told to do.)

After a few days, Jonzu-*san* was feeling like an old pro and ready to take over some responsibility. But he still had a long way to go. As his young Japanese colleague told him, working for a Japanese company was a lot like studying judo: "When you get your black belt, you become a beginner."

Boot Camp: Japanese Style

Observers have often said that Japanese bosses can be as exacting as boot-camp drill instructors, and in many ways working for a Japanese company can be compared to serving in the armed forces. Every company provides its own distinct kind of training, which is one way that Japanese companies make certain their employees don't switch jobs. Companies rarely value each other's training programs, making it nearly impossible for an employee to make a step up if he does change jobs. Usually, changing companies means a step down with less job security, pay, and benefits; however, in today's changing Japan, more and more salarymen are taking that chance. According to a government survey, 2,570,000 Japanese changed jobs in 1990, a 23 percent increase over the year before, and the biggest increase since the agency began keeping track of job-hopping in 1984.

Jonzu-*san* had no idea what to expect when he began his training. Some companies, like Matsushita, provide two different kinds of training: one covers the basic skills needed for the job, while the other teaches the fundamentals of the company's values. Employees are required to extol the company's values as well as its relationship to society. It is becoming more and more important for workers to verbalize their views as Japanese companies struggle to implement "Americanization" into their corporations.

Jonzu-*san* was surprised to discover that *all* employees were required to give a short talk on the company values on a frequent basis. This self-indoctrination to persuade others can be traced back to the teachings of the founder of Matsushita, Konosuke Matsushita, who advocated that the most effective teacher was actually on-the-job experience. Matsushita was the first corporation to have a company song and to institute the organization experience for its workers. Some Japanese companies, however, like Komatsu Forklift USA, offer two- or three-week training sessions in their Japanese home offices or plants. Yaohan Inc., a supermarket chain with stores in the United States, gives its employees a booklet advising them on "how to live" and sends them for "heart education" to the Seicho No Ie (House of Growth sect, founded in 1930) training center for five nights and six days.

Although these sessions can be as difficult to graduate from as a Marine boot camp, Japanese companies are proud of their track record. Their success in the global marketplace indicates their training does instill a sense of pride into their employees. That sense of pride translates into products that sell, and into job security for their workers.

Even after the initial training sessions are over, management training continues at every level. However, as Jonzu-*san* discovered, the most important facet of that training is nurturing the relationship between the Japanese boss (*senpai*) and the junior worker (*kohai*).

The Boss Is Not the Enemy

Jonzu-*san* discovered one of the most surprising aspects of working for a Japanese boss when his *senpai* stopped to ask a line worker what ideas he had for improving the quality of their product. The smiling young man eagerly outlined a couple of ideas that made sense. Later, Jonzu-*san* asked the worker if he wasn't afraid that he might be suggesting himself out of a job. The man quickly answered that not only was his job secure when he proposed new ideas to the Japanese company, but unlike what happens in some American companies, he had the power to put them to work.

In a Gallup poll taken for the American Society for Quality Control, half of 1,237 employees surveyed said that their companies stated that quality is a top priority, but only one in three believed their companies followed through with effective programs. And only 14 percent of those surveyed felt that they had the opportunity to participate in such programs.

However, Jonzu-*san* didn't understand why his new boss seemed to spend more time on furthering their personal relationship rather than on asking him for *his* ideas. He knew he wouldn't have been hired if his technical expertise hadn't met their requirements, but what he didn't realize was that his show of promise of being a loyal, committed employee was what had landed him a spot in the company in the first place. Also, he didn't understand that the Japanese way of training on the job is to focus on the relationship between the boss and the junior executive as two workers linked together for mutual benefit and striving to meet a common goal within the company. During this "training relationship" period he learned not only his own strengths and weaknesses, but his boss's as well. He learned to work with his boss as a unit where they would utilize each other in a way in which they both benefited.

Next, Jonzu-*san* learned the importance of the group.

Fitting In: Teamwork on the Job

As Jonzu-*san* walked over to his group members, his hands were sweating. Even though he was nervous, he was determined to go ahead with his plan. He had been practicing for a week and now was the time to try it.

"*Kyō wa watashi ga gochisō shimashō ka,*" he asked, hoping his pronunciation wasn't too bad. ("Would you like to go to lunch today?") To his surprise, they looked at one another and answered, "*Tabun. Ikitai to omoimasu.*" Quickly he looked up the words in his phrase book. "Maybe, I think I want to go," they had said. He also discovered that the word for "probably" was exactly the same as the word for "maybe." Jonzu-*san* didn't know what to do, so he did nothing and ate lunch by himself.

Poor Jonzu-*san*. This is an example of why it is so important to not only understand the Japanese language, but the cultural nuances as well. The group members' response to Jonzu-*san*'s invitation to lunch showed the reluctance of the Japanese to answer in a way that could be deemed as being self-centered and direct. This often makes it extremely difficult for Americans to participate in employee activities on the job.

Be aware that language and cultural differences still account for much of the friction between American and Japanese staffs. Although there was a time when Japanese companies believed they could prepare American workers if they needed to go overseas, that point of view is slowly changing. Learning the language and culture is at the top of the list of requirements, and an MBA graduate who has spent time in Japan and speaks Japanese can practically write his own ticket.

After a few more weeks on the job, Jonzu-*san* tried his "lunch" speech again, this time allowing for the indirect response of his co-workers. He asked them to go to lunch exactly the same way, they gave the same answer, but this time Jonzu-*san* told them he had reserved a table for noon. They acknowledged his request with "*Hai*, we understand," and they all enjoyed a pleasant lunch together. As they toasted him, Jonzu-*san* knew he had achieved the prime qualification of working for a Japanese company: acceptance by the group.

American companies have often failed in using the team approach to business because they don't realize that these teams require quite a bit of nurturing to sustain themselves. Extra time must be set aside for the additional meetings required to discuss the issues at stake. Japanese companies stress that managers be available to employees who need to talk and be unbiased listeners. This is part of building relationships, or *ningen kankei*, that goes along with group maintenance. The Japanese also rotate employees through different jobs to make them more adept at teamwork. Remember, it is proper to request things from your employees, but not to demand them. This works very well in Japanese companies, since the Japanese are much more accustomed to behaving in this manner in their own culture. An indirect request is the most desirable, but make certain there is no language disparity among your Japanese boss, co-workers, and yourself. Finally, avoid using the words *me* and *my* when discussing the company; instead, use *we* and *our*. This change of pronoun goes a long way in verbally communicating your commitment to the team effort.

Your Secretary Is Not Your Slave

Jonzu-*san* was not only surprised by the lack of private offices in his Japanese company, but also by the lack of private secretaries. In fact, the boss-secretary relationship as it exists in American companies is rarely seen in Japan. Even though secretaries are just as essential to business on both sides of the Pacific, in Japanese offices their alliance with the boss is not based on a "wife away from home" relationship where they share company duties as well as a part of each other's lives. This type of bonding is reserved for the *senpai-kohai* relationship. Japanese companies usually have a clerical pool that more than meets the needs of the staff. The cultural difference here is that, as a rule, secretaries are not being groomed for management, therefore, the Japanese do not believing in burdening them with duties that go beyond clerical tasks. This often confuses Americans working for the Japanese and they feel slighted if they don't have their own personal secretary. But that's not the only problem.

What If You Just *Can't* Get Along?

Jonzu-*san* was worried about his American co-worker, Smith-*san*. He wasn't fitting in with the team. He had been very upset when his entire department had been rewarded with a bonus for their performance. Smith-*san* knew that it was his initial plan of action that had earned them that recognition, and he was used to being praised for his individual efforts. He didn't understand that in order to maintain harmony Japanese companies don't reward individuals. For weeks he refused to attend meetings and started coming in late to work.

Jonzu-*san* tried to explain to his American co-worker that the Japanese were attempting to "glocalize" (a recently coined word referring to the attempt by Japanese companies to blend both cultures together by implementing local ideas and methods into their U.S. operations), but Smith-*san* reminded him that not much had changed. The Americans didn't have their own offices yet and the Japanese were still only "talking about" changing the pension plan. He accused the Japanese of being ignorant of American management practices, making him feel "used" for his talents and experience without being given anything in return. Also, the Japanese set impossible target goals, never considering the possibility of a mistake and never admitting when they were wrong (they wouldn't want to lose face).

Jonzu-*san* had to admit that Smith-*san* was right. On the other hand, the *kachō,* or section chief, mentioned to Jonzu-*san* that his co-worker seemed to lack commitment and loyalty to the company. His "I'll try" attitude when asked to do a job represented defeat before he got started in the eyes of his Japanese boss.

Jonzu-*san* noticed this was only a part of the hostility and suspicion between the Americans and the Japanese, especially among the internal Japanese groups where no one knew who did what. Friction was created by numerous Japanese managers coming and going within the company. Some came from the home office in Japan and stayed three to five years, and some were hired locally. At times no one knew who was in charge, no matter what their title. But there were also problems between the Americans who spoke Japanese and those who didn't, as well as between the employees who put in their time and went home, and those who were committed to the company for the long run.

At times, even Jonzu-*san* became frustrated. He now could see that it took an average of ten to fifteen years for a *gaijin* to get his foot into top management. Even though he was learning Japanese, he often felt excluded from the flow of critical information. The Japanese did encourage him to continue his efforts, but when junior Japanese executives often got more information than he did, he began to wonder if they were sincere. Jonzu-*san* also realized that factors like age, loyalty, and educational background were more important to the Japanese than personal achievement and competence.

Jonzu-*san* knew he was in line to be sent for special training in the Tokyo home office. Maybe that would boost his career. He hinted to his boss that he would like to see the cherry blossoms in the spring. His boss got the message.

Jonzu-*san* received his plane ticket for Tokyo a few weeks later and he was off to Japan for several months of training. It was a trip he would never forget.

Destination Tokyo: Working Abroad

The crow of the neighbor's rooster awakened Jonzu-*san* every morning at 6:20 A.M. in the tiny community outside of Tokyo. As he put away his futon he yawned sleepily. At least that was *one* Japanese neighbor he had no trouble understanding. Ever since he had arrived in Japan all he did was look up words in his dictionary, especially at work. His *kachō,* or section chief, had said little to him since he arrived. That was also part of his frustration— he was left on his own to figure out what to do. He read reports and attended meetings but he rarely understood what was going on.

His *kachō* suggested that he could get a better understanding of the language and culture if he moved into the company housing (*shataku*) outside of Tokyo. (Ninety-six percent of Japanese companies offer such housing, where single workers pay approximately $930 a *year* in rent, or 4 percent of their annual salary.) Jonzu-*san* enjoyed practicing his Japanese with his neighbors when he saw them, which wasn't very often. He spent most of the day either at the office or commuting to and from there by train. However, he knew he was lucky to have an apartment to himself. The other bachelors in the office lived in company dorms, or *ryō,* that usually consisted of a room about eight by twelve feet with old, worn-out carpeting, no air conditioning, and just one small sliding-glass window. No one stayed there indefinitely. There is an unwritten rule that Japanese workers (single or married with families) must save the bulk of their salary and move out of company housing in their early forties to buy homes of their own. However, this is becoming less and less of a reality with the average cost of a home in Tokyo reaching the half-million-dollar mark for only 675 square feet. It's no wonder the Japanese call their homes and apartments *usagi goya* (rabbit hutches).

Jonzu-*san* sat down and poured some *coco-paya* (coconut papaya) flakes into his cereal bowl. He couldn't get used to the usual Japanese breakfast of seaweed, raw eggs, rice, fish, soup, and vegetables. (He still wondered how Japanese babies ate rice with sardines in the morning.) He looked at the clock. 7:00 A.M. Time to hit the train.

Riding the Rails to Work

Jonzu-*san* grabbed his briefcase and headed for the train station. He grabbed a copy of *Wedge* (a bimonthly Japanese news magazine that claims it can be read during a three-hour commute) from the train kiosk and he was off on his nearly two-hour, three-train, mostly standing-room-only, journey to his office in Tokyo, less than twenty miles away. *Tsukin jigoku,* commuting hell, the Japanese called it. Jonzu-*san* put on his Walkman, grabbed an overhead strap, and began reading his paper. He had gotten used to the idea that no one talked during the ride, but he still couldn't accept the fact that no one apologized during the human crush that inevitably developed every time the train stopped at a station and more commuters crowded inside the car. (Japanese commuter train cars are designed to hold 120 people, but during the morning, when nearly a million Japanese straphangers endure the agony of the rush hour, they are usually filled to 250 percent of capacity.)

By the time Jonzu-*san* arrived at his office he was hot, perspiring, had lipstick smears on his sleeve from bumping into a couple of Office Ladies, and he had left his briefcase on the train.

Before he could panic, a fellow worker called the lost and found department at the train station and reported the missing briefcase. (Inside the case was a video depicting company life, that Jonzu-*san* hadn't seen.) Jonzu-*san* didn't have much hope in getting it back, but he couldn't worry about it. He had a meeting with his *kachō* this morning.

The *Hai*s and Lows of a Day at the Office

Jonzu-*san* discovered that a day at the office in Tokyo was pretty much the same as back in the United States. The Japanese weren't so different from American workers. They worked hard at their jobs, and many considered themselves to be *shinjinrui,* Japan's new breed, who were trying to change the corporate workplace by proposing more leisure time and personal fulfillment. (Some older Japanese, however, disapprove of this group and the way they often mock tradition and Japanese values.) Still, many Japanese give up their weekends in the name of the company and often work until midnight during the week. The Japanese often work as many as eighty hours a month overtime, although some companies allow their employees to report and get paid for only thirty hours. There is a joke going around Japanese offices regarding the work week: "*Getsu, Getsu, Ka, Sui, Moku, Kin, Kin,*" (Monday, Monday, Tuesday, Wednesday, Thursday, Friday, Friday). This is because Japanese employees are obligated to make up any additional time off by putting in extra hours Monday through Friday.

In a 1990 Japanese government survey, 57 percent of those polled said they wanted more leisure time instead of a pay raise. In 1991 Japanese workers took an average of only 7.9 days of paid vacation a year. (The average U.S. vacation time was 9.2 days. The Japanese vacation days, however, also include their end-of-the-year holiday time, as well as other nationally observed holidays during the year.) There is no doubt that Japanese workers need more vacation days and time to spend with their families (some men say their wives ignore them even when they *are* home—which can average as little as five waking hours during the work week). In 1990 the average employee arrived home at 10:00 P.M.

Jonzu-*san* could understand their plight: he was living the life of a salaryman twenty-four hours a day and felt stressed out from the seemingly endless work load. He still had trouble with the language and some of the cultural differences in management style. He had even tried Regain, the pick-you-up drink that contains caffeine, a nicotine derivative, and vitamins C and B1. (The commercial for this drink asks Japanese businessmen, "Can you fight twenty-four hours a day?" The market for this and similar drinks is a $700 million-a-year business.) However, he preferred *Black Black,* a caffeine chewing gum.

Yet he realized that these stresses occurred in any global company, not just in a Japanese one. He did notice that the Japanese scheduled their time off when they did have it, and rarely wasted it. However, he had recently gone to the beach on a Sunday with some friends from Tokyo and had spent six hours on the expressway coming home—for a sixty-mile trip. (Japan has only 2200 miles of national expressways.)

As he finished up the morning meeting with his group, Jonzu-*san* was surprised when he received a phone call: his briefcase had been found. Would he please come down and identify it?

Japanese Company Life: The Movie

It was nearly midnight when Jonzu-*san* loaded the videotape into the VCR in his office and turned it on. He had already missed the last train home, so he decided to take a look at the training film in his briefcase. He still couldn't believe that his briefcase had been returned to him intact, down to the loose change he always threw into the bottom pouch. When he had shown up at the lost and found department at the train station, all he had to do was identify the contents and with a quick bow and a *dōmo arigatō* (thank you), he was gone.

The story of Japanese company life unfolded on the TV screen. Good grooming, work habits, the proper way of bowing (fifteen degrees for regular greetings, thirty degrees for customers, and forty-five degrees for managing directors) were all shown in story form. The main point of the tape was that individual employees should not in any way stick out. They were advised to get to work fifteen minutes early, after having read the newspaper and eaten a three-minute breakfast.

Women in Japanese companies seemed to receive the most training (although they had the least amount of responsibility, Jonzu-*san* had observed). They were taught proper telephone etiquette, like answering on the third ring (American companies are expected to answer on the first ring—another example of Japanese hesitancy). They also practiced their grammar and voice intonation with imaginary telephones and were taught to "smile with their eyes as well as their mouths."

Japanese workers were also taught proper *karaoke* (sing-along tape machines) etiquette when going out with a group from the office: do not hog the microphone and do not sing the boss's favorite song. The correct wearing of the *seifuku*, or uniform, also received attention in the video: female employees all wear the same colored skirts, white blouses, scarves, and jackets; salarymen are instructed to wear a dark suit, white shirt and tie, and gold company pin in their lapel. While some Japanese companies in America have made uniforms voluntary in some positions, in Japan all workers take pride in being a member of the team. (In some Japanese-owned companies in the United States everyone wears the same kind of smock on the factory floor, including the president.

Their different colors indicate job functions, not titles.) The uniform is seen as a reassuring symbol of group identity. Jonzu-*san* could understand that: he still had his high-school letterman's jacket.

At the end of the film, Jonzu-*san* was asked to take a quiz. Some of the questions weren't too hard: How do you present a document to a customer or a co-worker? Answer: Maintain eye contact with the person receiving the document while keeping it at chest level, and make certain it's facing the correct way so that the person can read it easily. (This is probably the only time you will maintain eye contact with the Japanese. In this case you are providing a service and you communicate that service in a nonverbal manner.) How do you open a door? Answer: If the door opens toward you, hold it open until the customer or boss goes through; if door opens away from you, go through the door first and hold it open until the others go through. But his favorite question was: What do you say before answering the phone to bring a smile to your face so that the caller hears a happy voice? The answer: Whiskey.

Junior Salarymen

Jonzu-*san* was still thinking about the training video when he started out for work a few days later (remembering the video's advice, he was leaving for the office earlier now). According to the film, the company created the lifestyle and it was up to the individual to fit in. Why did the Japanese worker accept this corporate structure so easily? he wondered. It must have its roots somewhere.

As the bong from the town's Shinto shrine gong echoed through the village, Jonzu-*san* noticed something he had never given much thought to before: a group of schoolchildren were going from house to house on their way to school to pick up their classmates. The group of eight students was totally organized, even carrying a flag, and already working like a team. That's where it begins, thought Jonzu-*san*, watching these junior salarymen.

Training in the group work ethic and self-discipline begins at an early age in Japan. Some experts attribute Japan's economic success to the weekly morning assemblies held in Japanese schools where the students must stand at attention for thirty minutes, often in freezing weather. Another *Bushidō*, or samurai credo, drawing criticism is the practice of seasoning six-year-olds (both boys and girls) to endure the cold during playtime in winter—by sending them outside without any shirts.

Every child *must* walk to school with his preassigned group, learning how to socialize and work toward a specific purpose. Students attend school six days a week (half a day on Saturday and occasional school activities on Sunday although the Education Ministry planned to introduce a five-day week once a month in Japanese public schools in fall 1992), and often visit the local factories to see cars or other products assembled. The Japanese believe it is important that their children are not only aware of the economic life of the community where they live, but also learn to share in the pride of its achievements.

In the classroom, the students are split into squads, or *han*, where every child is responsible for the behavior of the group. At the beginning of each period the group leader of the class announces what they are going to study next; at the end of the class, the group leader thanks the teacher for the lesson and leads the class in a deep bow. This group vigilance and attending to social responsibility carries over into adult life where their accountability lies more with each other than with the boss. Whether it's called the very basic of Confucian teachings or peer pressure, it works for the Japanese.

What doesn't work is that even with these skilled, dedicated workers, Japan is facing a growing labor shortage. So the Japanese have formed a new breed.

Robotics: Steel-Collar Workers

Just when Jonzu-*san* thought he was beginning to understand his Japanese co-workers both in the office and in the factories, he was transferred to another part of the company: automation. He had seen how robots had been implemented into the workplace in Japanese companies back in the United States: robotic welders, hydraulic lifts, and sophisticated lug-tightening machines.

Although robotics got its start in the United States in the early 1960s, Japan currently has two-thirds of the world's working robots—176,000 industrial robots to the U.S.'s 37,000. Now these steel-collar workers are taking on a whole new meaning: the

Japanese are investing heavily in automation to free up desperately-needed labor to run not just their factories but their service companies as well. Jonzu-*san* was most impressed by a robot developed by Sanyo Electric for the corner convenience market. He watched with amazement as the robot took a sandwich out of the refrigerator, put it into the microwave, and placed it on the counter for him when it was ready. (The robotic service industry promises to be a booming business: according to the Japan Industrial-Use Robot Association, it will grow to a nearly $1-billion-a-year business by 1995 and to more than $2 billion by the year 2000. For example, near Ueno Park zoo in Tokyo, there are sidewalk vendors with robots that make panda cupcakes, and Toshiba is working on a language computer speech system that can take orders from customers at a simulated hamburger shop.)

Jonzu-*san* took a bite out of his sandwich. "*Oishii desu,*" he said. "Delicious." He almost wished he had a robot to take his place in the United States so he could stay in Japan. He had learned so much from the Japanese, but he knew it was time for him to go back to the United States and put his knowledge to use.

Japanese Management: American Style

Jonzu-*san* arrived home on Thursday, just in time for the Fourth of July. He was surprised to discover that his Japanese company had decided to give its workers the Friday after the holiday off as well, making it a four-day weekend. This was another example of how Japanese companies were implementing Americanization into their management styles.

When Jonzu-*san* reported for work the following Monday, he personally called on his co-workers, giving each one a small gift in private. He understood now how important this was to the Japanese, who found themselves in a country where the telephone call had replaced the social call. He was excited about the business changes he had seen in Japan and was eager to share his experiences with his co-workers.

Toyota and Mitsubishi Motors are now experimenting with three shifts instead of two in their plants, and Kawasaki Steel has budgeted $385 million over the next five years for new company dorms and housing. Also, Toyota is promising that working in its new factory in Japan in 1993 will be like working in an office—the production line will be quiet enough to enjoy piped-in music. Mazda Motors has put a bar, Jacuzzi, swimming pool, gym, and audiovisual entertainment in the dorms for its unmarried workers.

Jonzu-*san* explained to his co-workers that all of these innovations were in response to the growing problems faced by *buchō,* or general managers, on both sides of the Pacific. Many executives in senior management are aware that an increasing number of younger workers are putting more value on their private lives than on their work. This is due in part to the internationalization of Japanese business and the surging emergence of women within the corporate structure.

All of these concerns come at a time when Japanese companies are struggling to cope with the hottest trend in marketing: *aidentiti,* identity. Identity is to management today what quality control was in the 1960s and 1970s. The word did not even exist in the Japanese *katakana,* syllabary (used only for foreign words and official documents), until a few years ago. Other new words like *puraibashii* (privacy) and *insaida* (insider) are also making their way, not only into the Japanese language and culture, but into Japanese management style as well. The first thing Jonzu-*san* noticed in his company was that control of daily management had been shifted to the Americans. And he had been promoted to be part of that management team.

Jonzu-*san* believed he could blend both cultures by teaching his workers the best of Japanese management concepts (for example: from Matsushita—that knowledge and intellect as well as intuition and willpower enable an employee to acquire the knack of good management; from Shiseido cosmetics—that ease of mind and physical well-being affect each other for optimum performance) and, most important of all, by teaching them to approach any problem in the workplace by first understanding the Japanese context of the situation.

And finally, as Japanese businessmen say to one another, *ganbare,* hang in there! With time and knowledge, plus application and perseverance, as well as understanding, it *is* possible for a *gaijin* to succeed in a Japanese company.

9

Union Blues Japanese Style

The right of workers to organize and to bargain
and to act collectively is guaranteed.
—Article 28 of the Japanese
Constitution, 1947

Japanese Union Busting

Jim wasn't the only worker who had decided to listen to the union organizer give his spiel out on the lawn that afternoon. Many of the workers in the Japanese transplant had taken their lunch outside to see what was going on. The warm summer sun cast a soft glow on the Kentucky bluegrass as Jim and the others listened to the union man talk about getting them better wages and more benefits if they voted in the union. He went on to say that it was un-American for them not to be in a union, even if they were working for the Japanese. After all, he argued, look what the unions had done for their fathers and grandfathers.

Jim sat down under a shady tree and thought over what the man had said. His words brought back memories. Jim's father was retired now, but back in 1963, when Jim was nine years old, he had gone to work for IBM in nearby Lexington. Jim could still remember his father leaving for work every day, wearing a clean white shirt with at least three mechanical pencils clipped in his shirt pocket. Jim Sr. had enjoyed being an IBM-er. He knew he had lifetime employment if he wanted it, along with solid benefits and a good salary. His immediate bosses, as well as the head man himself, constantly reminded the workers they were all family. Jim remembered watching his father play third base on the department baseball team, and every summer the entire family enjoyed an IBM picnic at a local amusement park.

The management stressed that loyalty was a two-way street, as did the Japanese company where Jim now worked. He also had a good salary and benefits, just like his father. And as at IBM, there were no unions.

In many ways IBM was the first Japanese plant in the United States, Jim thought. Was working for IBM un-American? No way, he decided. If it was good enough for his father, it was good enough for him.

Working for the Japanese was as American as working for Big Blue.

Jim's sentiments aren't that different from those of many other Americans who work for Japanese companies. As union membership continues to drop nationally (only 12 percent of the American work force now belongs to unions), organizers have begun to target white collar and service workers, as well as the numerous Japanese transplants on U.S. soil. As of this writing, only one Japanese transplant has been unionized: Mazda. Efforts to do so at others have failed.

As more and more Americans find themselves working for the Japanese and as union membership continues to decline, the question of unionizing these plants will continue to be a major concern for the American work force. However, in order to understand the pros and cons, we must first take a look at the union question on both sides of the Pacific.

The Life of Riley: A Union Dream or Nightmare?

He was the hero of every working man during the 1940s and 1950s, this mug-faced aircraft worker with the lunch pail under his arm and the perfect wife waiting for him at home. Chester Riley, the popular 1950s TV character, personified what every union man wanted: a good, stable job and a loving family. More than 71,000 American unions grew out of this dream that began long before Riley uttered: "What a revoltin' development *this* is!" Today he would probably be speaking about the situation of the unions in the United States, but it wasn't always that way.

The first modern labor union, the American Federation of Labor, or AFL, was formed in 1886 and helped turn the United States into an economic power at the beginning of the twentieth century. The International Brotherhood of Teamsters, Chauffeurs, Warehousemen, and Helpers of America was founded in 1903 and has since become the largest union in the United States with 1.7 million members in 1988. However, during the last set of negotiations for a three-year contract in 1990, that figure had shrunk to 450,000 members. Why? Because the unions haven't penetrated the growth industries, and the areas where they were the strongest have all declined, according to the Regional Federal Commissioner of Labor Statistics. And it's hard to say if they can reverse that trend in the future.

Union or No Union: That Is the Question

It was a dirty job and somebody had to do it, but why did that somebody have to be me? thought Manny as he continued making notes on his fact sheet. It was a problem he had seen coming for a long time and he had tried to avoid it, but he couldn't any longer. Half of the guys in his department wanted to form a union and the other half didn't. As supervising manager, it was up to him to present an unbiased view of the pros and cons of unionizing.

His biggest headache was still to come: rumor had it that the Japanese were going to buy a percentage of the company and were coming in to run things. Some of the guys figured that if they were already unionized, the Japanese couldn't take it away from them, while the other half wanted nothing to do with a union. So Manny had been chosen to present both sides of the argument, but he had never dreamed it would be *this* complicated.

Things didn't look good for their chance of unionizing once the Japanese took over: only about one-fourth of Japanese-owned manufacturing companies in the United States had unions, and most of these were seafood-processing plants. Also, the Japanese did not tolerate problems between management and workers: Japanese workers lost less than one-third the number of days in labor disputes that Americans did, and the time lost due to strikes was even less. According to the Ministry of Labor, the number of disputes per one thousand workers in Japan was 0.04 percent in 1989.

Manny looked over some of the antiunion comments from his employees: "I don't want to risk losing that promotion due me." "Who needs a union? I just put in my time and go home." "I'm afraid a union will attract the wrong kind of people." Some had justifiable fears, others were just plain ignorant of how a union worked. Yet no one could deny that unions had lost a lot of ground in the workplace over the past fifty years. Organized labor is not the power it used to be on the American scene. Two recent events attest to that fact: the rail strike in 1991 went virtually unnoticed (the rail strike in 1992 was ended quickly by Congress), and the unions were left holding an empty bag when the *New York Daily News* refused to bow to their demands. Some experts even blame Detroit's declining percentage in the automobile market on union work rules.

On the other hand, in 1992 several Japanese-owned companies in New Jersey were accused of union busting by the Teamsters: for example, Sanyo employees were put on notice that their jobs would end if President Bush pushed tariffs, and Otagiri employees went on strike to prevent cancellation of retiree health benefits.

For many, even the word "union" conjures up scenes of fat, union bosses out for themselves, making deals with mobsters. The working American often feels he or she has little in common with these union leaders. Consequently, union membership continues to drop. For example, who ever thought they'd see the day when the steelworkers' union would try to recruit office workers to expand its membership, which has fallen to half its numbers in just the past decade.

Yet no one can deny that in the past the unions *have* achieved better wages and benefits, as well as working conditions for the American worker. So what about Japanese workers?

Japan's Labor Pains After World War II

In the early 1950s several men huddled inside a closed-up car manufacturing plant. Outside, the workers picketed and threw rocks,
yelling and trying to break down the doors. The strike had been
going on for forty-four days and no negotiations had been started.
It's bad luck, more than one manager muttered under his breath,
meaning the combination of the number "four," which, pronounced *shi*, also means "death" in Japanese.

For more than six weeks, the managers of the company had
stayed in the plant and slept on their desks. To the strikers it looked
like they were crazy, but these men had a plan. They knew that if
Japan was going to survive the postwar trauma of not enough food
and low wages, there must be strong management *and* dedicated
workers.

The next day they opened up negotiations with the striking
workers, and a couple of weeks later everyone was back at work—
with a new company union in place.

It hadn't been easy. So many different unions had sprung up
after World War II that relations between management and labor
reached dangerous levels. These new unions were often headed by
left-wing communists allegedly released from jail by the U.S occupation forces. At that time, the United States was determined to
impose labor laws and unions on the Japanese "for their own
good." (Inadvertently, it was these same groups of communists
who ended up heading the labor unions—for *their* own good.) U.S.
politicians had no idea they would change their ideas during the
1950s. They originally believed that Japan would be economically
weak (kept in line by strong unions) and dependent on the United
States; at the same time they envisioned that Japan would
strengthen its military power and play a major role in the defense
of Asia. By 1957, even the Eisenhower Administration approved
of Japan's tough stand against labor. Secretary of State John Fos-
ter Dulles told the Japanese foreign minister and his aides that he
was "very happy that the Japanese government intended to deal
vigorously with the labor problem in Japan."

When the National Car Workers staged their fourteen-week
strike in 1953, it was management who finally won, when they

organized a company union that gave them not only cooperation from the workers, but also greater freedom to change unproductive working practices. Another strike at that time, by what is today the All Japan Textile Workers, lasted 160 days and, when it was over, three workers had committed suicide.

Labor organizing and strikes were still relatively new to the Japanese. They hadn't had much practice. The first labor union in Japan was called the *Yuaikai,* or Friendly Love Society, and was founded around the turn of the twentieth century. It was soon disbanded by the Peace Preservation Law of 1900. This law denied the workers the right to organize—a right that wasn't reinstated until after World War II, by the United States.

Since that time, the Japanese have added their own flair to the art of labor unions. There was a union for prostitutes (prostitutes were known as *kiken na dokubana,* or Dangerous Poison Flowers), the National Federation of Special Restaurant Workers, and a union for the 35,000 owners of Japanese brothels, the National Venereal Diseases Prevention Autonomy Council.

Today's labor unions may not have such an interesting diversity of members, but they are an important part of understanding the Japanese system.

Wearing the Union Label in Japan

In late 1989 three of Japan's weakest unions united under one banner: *Rengo* now represents eight million workers, or two-thirds of Japan's organized work force. They had little choice. In the past the unions were steadily losing members—from 28.9 percent of the work force in 1985 to a low of 25.9 percent before the merger into *Rengo,* according to the Ministry of Labor. Their workers' real-cash earnings index wasn't keeping up with their productivity: from 1985 to 1989 the workers' labor-producing index increased nearly thirty points, while their wages increased only ten points on the same scale, according to the Japan Productivity Center.

Rengo is intended to be the AFL-CIO of Japan and its goal is to strive for better wages and benefits for its workers. This represents quite a turnaround for modern Japanese labor, which has managed to keep its workers happy and its labor problems to a minimum since the organization of what are known as "enterprise unions."

After many major strikes and walkouts in postwar Japan in the 1950s, these enterprise unions now provide individual company unions for corporations, each offering lifetime employment and good working conditions to its employees. Workers feel secure in their jobs and, in return, complain very little about small grievances. The Japanese way of training employees to learn all phases of the job also solves what many American companies call "feather bedding" (stocking the company with workers who are not needed), as well as having to wait for a "union" man to make needed repairs.

This also illustrates a major difference in union organization in Japan: most unions have their roots in a particular industry and are *not* organized by job or occupation. (In NKK's U.S. subsidiary, National Steel, the number of job classifications was cut from eighty-six to sixteen.) This also brings managers into the unions along with their employees, guaranteeing that they are on the *same* side in any negotiations. However, Japanese workers are not always agreeable.

A demonstration of 50,000 members of the rice farmers' union, known as *Zenchu*, staged a protest in the summer of 1991 that was the largest of its kind since World War II. Japan's five million farmers believe that pressure from the United States urging Japan to open up its rice market will result in a loss of 64 percent of that market and ruin nearly a million farmers. As the possibility of an open Japanese rice market continues to grow, Australian rice has also been a target. A study by a group calling itself the Japan Posterity Foundation purportedly found Australian rice to be contaminated with "nerve poison" and unfit for Japanese consumption.

These accusations against foreign markets may sound like an old story, but with the strong traditional and cultural ties that rice holds for the Japanese, this is one area that offers no easy solution for the United States in the foreseeable future. The Japanese government has been negotiating with the United States about opening up its rice market, but their staunchest supporters, the farmers, are determined to keep it closed. Their protest caused a delay in the opening of the rice market and is a good example of how strong Japanese unions can be.

The major Japanese unions, however, are more concerned with providing their workers with enough money to purchase their own homes, as well as with reducing the number of working hours. Every year they launch their annual labor campaign to do just that.

It Happens Every Spring: Union Negotiations

Shouts of "*Washo! Washo!*" ("Go! Go!") can be heard in the streets in April as workers break their work patterns to join in the traditional "spring offensive," or *Shunto,* for better wages and working conditions. These twice-yearly meetings (also held in the fall) are not discouraged by management; on the contrary, the welfare of the workers is considered to be linked directly to the health of the company itself. These showdowns are seen as a constructive way for both labor and management to determine what changes are needed in the workplace so that little time is lost in production.

Wages are always on the agenda (an average increase of 5.65 percent was agreed upon in fiscal 1991 but for fiscal 1992 labor and management agreed to wage increases between 4 and 5 percent), but during the past few years talks have centered around such topics as more time off for employees around public holidays, the retirement issue, and lowering the annual working hours per year. The issue that raised the most concern recently was when executives and union leaders of several industries agreed to cut their annual working hours to between 1,800 and 1,900 from the present average of over 2,000. The Labor Ministry is planning to revise the Labor Standards to reflect this new change by fiscal 1992, and the largest union, *Rengo,* has targeted fiscal 1993 for compliance with the new 1,800-hour yearly average. A research study by the Labor Ministry showed that in 1990, 66.9 percent of the five thousand companies surveyed had introduced a five-day workweek. There is one industry, however, that is having difficulty with this ruling.

The Confederation of Automobile Workers said it was impossible for them to comply with the 1,800-hour-maximum ruling because they worked an average of 2,300 hours in 1990 (more than any other union). However, they assured *Rengo* they would do their best to cut their working hours to the desired number by fiscal 1995.

If the Japanese allow car unions to operate in Japan, why not in their U.S. transplants?

The Japanese Company in the United States: No Union Is a Good Union

The middle-aged man looked out over the Ohio River Valley and wondered what it must have looked like a hundred and fifty years ago. He could imagine trappers making their way down river with their furs; farmers and their families settling down and growing their crops; and curious Native Americans, still wary of the white man trespassing on their land.

The dark-haired man smiled. He wondered what the Native Americans would have thought of *him*. Eiichi was one of the Japanese managers assigned to the transplant in the valley. His company had chosen the area because of the tax breaks and the nonunion labor, which make transplants a common sight in Ohio, Tennessee, and Kentucky. It's not only auto plants taking advantage of the lower costs: aerospace manufacturer Rohr Industries of Chula Vista, California, recently built a plant in Arkansas in seven months and paid $750 in building fees. If they had built the same plant in California, construction would have taken at least three years, and fees would have amounted to $750,000.

As Eiichi drove back to the plant, he passed by an abandoned American auto factory. Rumor had it that it wasn't the arrival of the Japanese that had closed the plant, but the American unions with their skyrocketing wage settlements and difficult-to-follow work rules. Also, the unions seemed to have forgotten that they were among the leading proponents of bringing Japanese car production to the United States. What they hadn't counted on was their inability to lure the Japanese into their web of rules and regulations.

The Japanese avoided the unions by opening up plants in largely nonunionized areas instead of where the auto industry held a major foothold in the community. (Also, their factories are usually close to Japanese assembly plants.) The Japanese knew that by introducing the employees to *their* management style up front, they would be less likely to organize unions in the future. The Japanese know that if they *do* allow their auto plants to unionize, they must follow somebody else's rules, not their own.

Mazda Sets an Example

The auto transplant has a Japanese name and Japanese management, but the employees of Mazda America are members of the United Auto Workers. Ford owns 25 percent of Mazda, perhaps explaining why it is the only Japanese-owned unionized auto plant in the United States. Mazda is obligated to follow the dictates of the union regarding increases in production workers' wages and cost-of-living payments. When they agreed to accept the UAW's increase from $13.50 an hour to $16 an hour, observers predicted that other Japanese transplants would have to follow suit with matching increases—if they wanted to stay nonunion. Although the Mazda example seems to be working, other Japanese transplants are in no hurry to unionize and American workers in those plants are not organizing union movements. Why should they if they can secure the same wage benefits *without* paying union dues? But the Japanese are not resting on their past success. They've also introduced profit sharing for their workers that actually translates into a check, not just a promise.

Honda, for example, bases its profit-sharing formula on its worldwide net income, the number of total employees, and the number of workers at Honda of America. Payouts by the Big Three (GM, Ford, and Chrysler) are figured out using a complicated formula devised by the union that is based on U.S. automotive profits *alone*. Considering their recent dramatic losses in the automobile market, including a $2.1 billion loss for the third quarter of 1990, it is likely there will be no profit sharing for unionized workers for awhile. The unions, however, say they aren't worried. They have renegotiated a new formula to increase potential profit-sharing bonuses.

The UAW hopes to change the makeup of their workforce by

making their pension plan more desirable. By luring older workers into retirement, the UAW hopes to assemble a younger work force willing to dedicate itself to shrinking the competitive edge between American and Japanese automakers. However, not even the union could have dreamed up what happened when a Chrysler employee won a Honda on an Ohio lottery television show and she refused to accept it. "I'm union," she told the TV audience—except they never heard it. The producer bleeped her out, and caused an uproar the likes of which haven't been seen since the historic auto-workers' sitdown strike in Flint, Michigan, in 1937, when the UAW finally won recognition by the automobile industry. The woman gave more than a hundred interviews to the media and received numerous cars from American automakers before the furor died down.

When Worlds Collide: The Japanese Versus the American Unions

The two men squared off, fists raised menacingly, as they faced each other under the hot noonday sun. The striking engineers at the asphalt and concrete plant had been friends for years, but since the Japanese had bought a 50 percent share in the company and broken off contract talks during negotiations on wages and bene-fits, they were on opposite sides. Brent was a union man and believed that the Japanese were trying to break the union; Jerry felt the union had done what it could and just wanted his job back. Behind the men was a sign bearing the Japanese flag with a slash through it.

Brent continued to hold his strike sign high as Jerry crossed over the picket line and picked up a rock. He accused the strikers of wrecking a Japanese car as a publicity stunt, then hurled the rock at the sign, causing a gaping hole. Brent took a swing at his former co-worker and the two men scuffled in the dirt. When the strike was finally over a year later, Brent and Jerry never worked together again.

Their story is just one of many illustrating how the Japanese avoidance of unions in their U.S. subsidiaries has caused friction and bad feelings. Some American union workers believe that the

Japanese will often structure their investment in a company in such a way that the American owner is beset with union labor problems and forced to acquire loans from their Japanese owners to keep the company afloat. When the union workers strike for better wages and working conditions, the American owner is faced with the problem of defaulting on those loans from the Japanese and ends up forfeiting the company to the Japanese owner in what has been called a "secret takeover."

Union workers have also accused the Japanese of controlling their industry by fixing prices. Alaskan fishermen went on strike in protest against Japanese processors cutting their salmon prices from one dollar a pound in 1990 to less than forty-seven cents a pound in 1991. The fishermen accused the Japanese of keeping prices down to keep their profits up. When the strikers threatened violence against the fishermen willing to accept the lower price, the governor of Alaska issued an emergency executive order and closed the fishery.

The Japanese also created havoc in the sky when the 1,370-member Japan Air Lines Cockpit Crew Union went on a twenty-four-hour strike against the hiring of foreign pilots and flight engineers. The union contended that airline safety would be affected by the new hirings if the Japanese and foreigners could not understand each other.

The question of safety in the workplace has come under scrutiny in both American and Japanese plants.

Workplace Safety: Don't Be Half Safe

When 3,200 autoworkers walked off the job in 1991 at the General Motors plant in Baltimore, it wasn't because of a dispute in wages. The company had recently been the victim of significant layoffs, causing unsafe working conditions for the employees still left at the minivan plant. The UAW called a strike, citing that the layoffs of four hundred workers a few months earlier had left the plant with "dangerous working conditions." Their decision was not a hasty one; the last time the union had struck the plant was in 1970.

Unsafe working conditions were also at the bottom of an attempt of the UAW to get a foothold in the Nissan plant in

Smyrna, Tennessee. According to reports, the backbreaking work speed on the plant assembly line was causing injuries to workers, and reducing quality as well. Complaints were made that the Japanese cared more about their machines then about the workers. Although the union failed to unionize the Nissan plant, the effort did force Japanese management to take another look at working conditions. However, even the UAW acknowledged that the safety issue was only an excuse to attempt to secure a foothold in the Japanese plant.

Although the unions have been behind much of the past success of the U.S. economy, their attempts to unionize the Japanese plants have failed for one major reason: their inability to adopt a noncombative, pliable attitude toward management that goes beyond wages and benefits. Enterprise unions, which permit management and employees to work together as a team striving toward a common purpose, works in Japan, and they can work here, too. More and more American companies are adopting the Japanese management system of quality control that stresses teamwork among the work force and statistical process control to find and eliminate defects. But for this system to function employees must first be given a voice in the decision-making process.

The Japanese Enterprise "Union": Make It Work for You

It was 7:30 A.M. on a Monday morning as the department store employees parked their cars in the mall lot and went into the building. They were the only employees there at this early hour but no one seemed to mind. They didn't want to be late for their weekly team meetings.

As Georgia, the store manager, sat down with her team representatives from the different departments, she wondered why more American companies didn't adopt weekly meetings to iron out their differences and share their triumphs: Jennifer was eager to discuss her ideas for an upcoming sales promotion; Al had received the results of the customer-service survey and they were good; and Betty was still beaming about the promotion she had just received. They all relied on one another not only for moral support, but also because they believed in each other and in their store. They had learned from the Japanese who were now some of their best customers. They started a mailing list of Japanese companies and were sending them a brochure in Japanese advertising a "Welcome Sale" and highlighting items in the store that would appeal to the Japanese buyer (designer fashions at affordable U.S. prices, for example).

Georgia and the others belong to a new kind of system—whether it's American or Japanese—where workers bond together in a "union" atmosphere because they are committed to their company.

Here are a few suggestions to help you start your own enterprise union in your company. (1) Eliminate excess layers of management between you and your workers. The quicker workers have the opportunity to talk over their problems, the quicker problems will be solved. (2) Divide your employees into teams. Each team should have complete autonomy and allow the employees to learn all phases of your operation. (3) Delete any insignificant social barriers that may cause petty misunderstandings or feelings of inferiority. Everyone should eat in the same cafeteria, have equal parking privileges, and carry a key to the washroom. (4) Make *every* employee feel important: business cards for everyone in the company is becoming a standard practice. (5) Don't forget that service is a two-way street: treat your employees the way you treat your customers. Help them develop and grow, and they will stay with you for life.

Whether you work for a Japanese-owned company or a unionized American company dealing with the Japanese, your workers are your most important tool. Use them wisely and fairly, and your product quality and company morale will be higher than ever.

10

Why Women Are Over the Hill and Out the Door at Thirty

Women do two-thirds of the world's work, yet
they earn only one-tenth of the world's income.
—Barber B. Conable
President, World Bank

Special Problems Women Face in Japanese Companies

Susan could hardly wait to get back to the office after her vacation.
Even though she worked twelve to fourteen hours a day and nearly
every weekend at the Japanese trading company, she loved her job.
She was certain she was in line for a promotion. She had only taken
her vacation to attend her brother's wedding in another state. Now
she was ready to go back to work. But Susan's vacation lasted
longer than she expected. She was told she was being laid off for
economic reasons, but Susan knew that wasn't true. She had seen
it happen to other women managers, and now it was her turn. The
reason was simple: the Japanese were getting rid of her before they
would be forced to promote her to management level.

156

Susan was not alone in her predicament. Her counterpart, Ayaka, was hired by a company in Tokyo after graduation from college. Her bosses assured her she would rise in management quickly. Instead they assigned her to a desk. After two years at the same desk she still copies her own documents and often serves tea to clients, but she doesn't complain. Ayaka believes that if she performs to the best of her ability and shows patience, she will be promoted to management someday.

Both Susan and Ayaka are victims of Japanese bosses who don't want to recognize the fact that women are no longer willing to act as tea servers and office flowers. They are willing to work hard to be salarywomen, but the Japanese aren't giving them a chance, neither in their U.S. subsidiaries nor at home in Japan. For example, although women make up 40 percent of the Japanese work force (27.23 million as of June 1991), according to the *Japan Times* only 0.3 percent of managerial positions in Japan are staffed by women. Women working for Japanese-owned companies in the United States fare somewhat the same: according to a survey by the Council on Economic Priorities on five diverse Japanese companies, no women were found among their 1,493 managers. According to a Columbia University study, by the end of the 1980s only 2 percent of management positions in Japanese-owned firms were held by women. In contrast, the same study found that 37 percent of managers in American-owned companies in the United States were women.

Although Japanese companies are being prodded by their government to correct their hiring and promotion practices because of the labor shortage, the idea of being a "salarywoman" is still more myth than reality. So what *are* the duties of women hired to work for Japanese companies?

Women's Duties on the Job: Coffee, Tea, or Else

Luann never dreamed that a teakettle could weigh so much. Her arms were already aching, and this was only her second day in her new job in Japan. It hadn't been so bad the first time she lugged the large teapot down to the hot-water heater, filled it up, and carried it back to the office—but her Japanese manager told her she would have to repeat the whole process in the afternoon as well. Once she steeped the tea, she had to serve it to the twenty-seven men in her department, then hand-wash and dry the cups and spoons. At the end of the workday, her job still wasn't over—she swept and mopped the floor, even though a cleaning crew would come in late at night after everyone else had gone home.

Luann figured out that with all of her domestic office duties, she spent only an average of two to three hours a day actually working as a copywriter—the job she was hired to do. She complained to her Japanese boss that she had been hired to bring new ideas into the company—why not let the men get their own tea? she suggested. Then she would have more time for her work. That was a new idea. The company director thought about it, then took it to the next director, who thought about it, and so on until they made a decision: yes, Luann was right. If she didn't have to serve tea, there would be more time for work, they explained, but because she was a woman, that was part of her job.

Nothing changed, so, in frustration, Luann quit. But her Japanese bosses did change one thing: they hired an American man in her place—and because he was a man, he didn't have to serve tea and could spend more time on the job—as Luann had suggested.

Luann was up against a caste system that is used to separate men from women in the workplace. When you are hired to work for a Japanese company, your job *description* is vague; but your job *category* has definite boundaries. This is why women usually run on an outside track in career planning: they enter the company under the umbrella of *ippan shoku* (general office), which means less pay, regular hours (8:00 A.M. to 5:00 P.M.), and short-term expectations on the part of both the employer and the employee. It is something like the American version of the typing pool, but with a difference: more than one American executive has risen from the clerical pool or mail room to the boardroom, but the Japanese adhere religiously to their hierarchy. If you enter a company at the general office level, you stay at this level.

Yet Japanese bosses do not believe they are keeping women from entering higher management. After all, women have an unwritten agreement with their companies that after a maximum of five years they will leave to get married (their bosses often participate in the search for a husband). Many companies even have a rule that no one on the permanent staff can be a married woman, and most companies will not even hire a woman for full-time work after the age of thirty.

If women do return to work after marriage and children it is in a part-time clerical capacity that pays on the average of $3,700 a year (one-fourth of all female employees in Japan are part-timers). Even if a woman continues working and doesn't marry, some companies require knowledge of English for a promotion (but not for the men), or that they pass a special exam, requiring knowledge from training classes that women never have time to attend because they're involved in their "domestic" office duties. Yet, when they're asked why women aren't promoted, most Japanese bosses scratch their heads in bewilderment. Women have the same opportunities for advancement as men, they argue, they just don't take advantage of them. What these Japanese bosses don't want to admit is that with their unfair company policies, they make certain that women are prevented from advancing in the workplace.

In a recent survey by Philip Morris, K.K., the Japanese subsidiary of U.S.-based Philip Morris companies, 55 percent of three thousand Japanese women polled said they weren't being treated equally with men at work. Yet many still regard having a job as something to do between the time they leave school and get married. The majority of Japanese women aspire to marriage first, then a career, even if they have graduated from a top university. Considering the fact that Japanese women make on the average 51 percent of what men do (American women make 70 percent of what men make), many believe that being a housewife offers them a better life.

Japanese Housewives: From Electric Rice Cookers to Microwaves

Yuki looked at the clock on her kitchen wall as she put away the vacuum cleaner. It was nearly two o'clock. She had an hour to sit down with a cup of tea and watch her favorite soap opera before her son came home and she took him to "cram school" (the *juku*, or extra classes after regular school hours where students prepare for the final exams that will determine which university they will attend). Unlike her mother, she didn't need all day to do her household chores; she had plenty of time to go shopping and to have her hair and nails done at least once a week.

As she flipped on the TV, she remembered an old Japanese saying that her *obāsan* (grandmother) had been fond of repeating: A woman's role in marriage is like a job that includes three meals a day and time for a nap.

As Yuki became engrossed in the problems and passions of the female TV character trying to compete in the business world, she couldn't understand why any woman would want to have a full-time career outside the home. Yuki had everything she wanted: status, independence, and financial security. She smiled knowingly. But then, of course, what you saw on TV wasn't real life anyway.

Yuki is not alone in feeling comfortable in her role as a woman at home. In a 1987 government survey, more than one-third of the women and half of the men surveyed believed that a woman should stay home. Many Japanese women continue to agree, and see their roles as homemakers as a source of power and independence. Even though the husband is the sole breadwinner, he turns his paycheck over to his wife who gives him a weekly allowance for cigarettes, snacks, comic books, magazines, etc. In the old days, the husband was paid in cash and at least had a chance to gaze longingly at his hard-earned money; but today, most salaries are automatically deposited into banks and the wife depends on electronic banking to pay bills. Even when the wife gives her husband his allowance (which increased by 6.9 percent in 1990, according to a survey of Tokyo salarymen by JETRO), he may not see any cash: prepaid cards valid everywhere from department stores to gasoline stations are the latest craze to eliminate the need to carry cash.

Paying bills is not the only responsibility of the Japanese wife: she also makes the investments, decides which schools the children will attend, even what tie or suit her husband will wear to the office. She is in complete control of the house, choosing their home or apartment, and, if they live in company housing, she and the other wives control the on-site management duties. Even when couples go shopping together for a major purchase, it is the wife who decides what they will buy.

It is no wonder that many Japanese women want no part of the business world which would require them to work as hard as their husbands while still performing the same duties at home. Like some American women they are more than happy to continue their lives as *okusan* (wives), which means "inside the house." After all, they have been trained for this since childhood. Men prefer to keep them out of the mainstream and childlike—at least half of all Japanese female names end in -*ko*, which means child. Not surprisingly, in a survey conducted by Nippon Life Insurance Company in 1992, 1,557 Japanese salarymen said they like their women "cute, cheerful, and humble." In most Japanese schools, boys and girls are separated by gender in subtle ways—for example, roll call lists are divided into male and female, with the males being called first. As Japanese women progress into girlhood, they are trained in everything from flower arranging to tea ceremony to develop their sensitivity and feminine traits. When it's time to look for a husband, a Japanese woman first looks for kindness, then financial security, and, finally, attractiveness. The first problem, however, is often just getting the men to introduce themselves. Many Japanese men have difficulty communicating with young Japanese women (considering the fact that 28 million business cards are exchanged in Japan on a daily basis and take the place of verbalizing an introduction, it's easy to see why they don't have much practice). But the Japanese have found an answer: charm schools for bachelors to help them make that long trip down the aisle. But not every marriage lasts forever.

Divorce: Japanese Style

Saori ran her hands slowly up and down the worn paper doors separating her room from the rest of the house. The paper had yellowed on the *shōji* doors since she had first come to the house as a bride, nearly twenty years ago. So much had happened since then—the birth of her children, the long, lingering illness of her mother-in-law, not to mention her own lonely nights when her husband didn't come home. Now she was leaving her home to stay with her widowed sister and she would never again return. She couldn't take it anymore. She had made her decision. Saori was getting a divorce.

Divorce was traditionally considered a disgrace for Japanese

women and it has only been since World War II that women have
been given the privilege of seeking a permanent separation from
their husbands. Since the beginning of the 1980s nearly 70 percent of the 155,000 divorces filed annually in Japan have been ini-
tiated by women. The divorce rate continues to remain low compared to Western countries: only a little more than one in a
thousand marriages ends in divorce. Before the second half of this
century, only Japanese men could seek a divorce. It was as simple
as writing his wife a short letter of intent three-and-a-half lines
long, *mikudari-han*, citing one of the seven acceptable reasons
needed to grant his divorce. Among the reasons were talkativeness
and having a communicable disease. This kind of attitude perpet-
uates the view of Japanese men toward wives, as evidenced by an
old saying, "A *tatami* mat, like a wife, is best when new." But Japanese women haven't always been at the mercy of men.

When Japanese Women Were in Charge: Japan's Early History

The tall beauty on horseback rode at the head of her army as she
led her conquering soldiers into Korea on a bright, victorious day
in the year 200 A.D. The Empress Jingo was not only a great leader
but a strong woman who led the Japanese people in their first con-
quest of a foreign land—an accomplishment that would not be
repeated by a Japanese man until the twentieth century.

Yet she was not the only woman taking her place in Japanese history. The names of Koken, Komyo, Suiko, and Himeko are all
those of women who reigned as Empresses of Japan during the
early history of the Land of the Rising Sun. Even the premiere goddess and highest deity in Shinto mythology is a woman: Amaterasu-
Omikami, the Sun Goddess. By the eighth century, however, the
place of Japanese women in society had changed drastically: they
blackened their teeth to subdue their smiles, tottered about on
high platform *geta*, or wooden shoes, and wore their hair so long
(about fifteen feet in length) that it was too cumbersome to move
about freely. What happened?

Around the time of the sixth century, customs and ideas from
other Asian countries began to govern the attitudes of Japanese
men toward women. They began to question the intelligence of

women and ignore their talents in the everyday scheme of life, believing instead that women were fundamentally weak creatures and therefore more likely than men to fall prey to sinful activities. Women were taught that their only hope for salvation lay in their complete subservience to men. By the thirteenth century Japanese women were relegated to a form of mental slavery that continued throughout Japan's centuries of isolation.

When the island nation was opened to the West at the end of the nineteenth century, everything changed but the role of women. Even when Japan was on the industrial warpath during the 1920s and 1930s, women's jobs were always structured in such a way as to keep them from being exposed to the Western ways of social equality. However, in October, 1945, Japanese women were granted the right to vote and to hold political office. These rights were guaranteed to all Japanese women when the constitution went into effect on May 3, 1947.

But it's only recently that the role of Japanese women has really begun to change.

From Office Flower to Steel Butterfly: Japanese Women *Are* Changing

The young stewardess smiled brightly as she greeted the passengers boarding the Japan Air Lines flight to Los Angeles. No one would guess this was Kaori's first trip as a flight attendant. She looked so poised and confident, as if she'd done this a thousand times. She had worked long and hard to earn her wings. Kaori is one of six thousand young Japanese women who annually choose the airlines as their after-college job. Instead of looking for husbands or boring jobs as office flowers, they want to see the world and travel. According to a recent survey by Recruit Company (a major publisher of job-information magazines) more and more Japanese women are placing emphasis on their leisure time, with 69 percent responding that the purpose of work is to make money to pursue their hobbies, including travel.

In 1987 more than 13 percent of Japanese Office Ladies made trips abroad to such romantic cities as Rome, Paris, and Vienna. Unlike overworked salarymen who are not encouraged to take more than four days of summer vacation (if any at all), women office workers usually take anywhere from a week to a month for a holiday. Critics say that women need these tangible badges of achievement to overcome their lack of advancement in the workplace and to gain confidence about themselves. According to a survey, however, less than 47 percent of Japanese women are willing to work as long as possible. They usually have no choice and are forced out at thirty and into retirement.

For the remaining women who *do* want to work, however, the roads to advancement have been few.

The Women's Movement in Japan: Fact or Fiction?

When Teruko Kanehira was appointed to the post of vice governor of Tokyo in May 1991, she became the first woman to hold such a position in Japan. But along with Diet member Takoko Doi, she remains in the small minority of Japanese women who are in decision-making positions in government and large corporations. When Doi scored a major success in the summer elections of 1989, the media was quick to call the approaching decade of the 1990s *Onna no Jidai*, the Era of Women. Even though the passage of the Equal Opportunity Employment Law (EOEL) in 1986 assured women of the chance to take their rightful place in the job market, most Japanese women continue to ignore the challenge of feminists. Many find fulfillment in becoming involved with community service activities, which gives them a sense of accomplishment without having to tread on the toes of their salarymen husbands.

Another reason the women's movement in Japan barely crawls along is traceable to the fact that Japan has no recognized racial minority and concomitant civil rights movement that might arise from it. (Although Japan has Japanese-Koreans, *burakumin*, and now an influx of illegal workers, these groups have not organized to demand equal rights.) Many Japanese women don't believe they are oppressed, and many more don't want to join the Japanese work force, which subjects their men to sixty-hour workweeks with no time for family and hobbies. The government, however, has been successful in getting businesses to agree to cut down the hours in the workplace to a more respectable forty hours per week.

This could attract more women to pursue full-time careers in the business world and fuel the fires of the women's movement in the near future.

Sexual Discrimination in the Japanese Workplace

As she hung up the phone, Rachel was mystified. That was the third secretary she had sent over to Mr. Takahara's office this week for the job. None of them had worked out. All of the women from her personnel agency had more than met the job qualifications; one of the applicants had even studied in Japan. She couldn't understand what the problem was, but Rachel was determined not to lose the account.

She spent the next few days personally interviewing Mr. Takahara's staff and learning more about the Japanese businessman so she could fill his work order. Finally, after three hours on the phone with one of the account execs in his office, she discovered the problem: Mr. Takahara required only one qualification for the secretarial job—he wanted a blonde.

Japanese businessmen are notorious for their prejudice against women. As Barbara found out, there's a different side to the Japanese boss regarding women. When her boss continuously used the phrase *joshi jugyō-in* to denote all female employees in a company, Barbara decided to investigate. She discovered that the literal translation means "girl involved in schoolwork." Barbara began using a new Japanese phrase: *seku hara*—sexual harassment. Her Japanese boss got the message and has stopped using the offensive phrase.

Sexual discrimination and harassment are just as common in Japanese companies as in American firms, where sexual harassment in the workplace now makes up 20 percent of the caseload of complaints filed with the California Department of Fair Employment and Housing. When the National Organization for Women (NOW) surveyed American women in the workplace, 80 percent of those responding said that they had been sexually harassed. In a study by the Ministry of Labor of more than forty branches of Japanese-owned companies in the United States, 687 cases of sexual harrassment were reported in 1989 and 1990.

Kyosei Mutual Fire and Marine Insurance Company is trying to change this pattern with the release of a videotape (cost: $92) designed to warn Japanese businessmen in the United States of the hazards of sexual harassment.

As frustrated would-be salarywomen in Japan poured over the popular comic *Onna Gokoro* (stories of women trying to pursue both a career and marriage) during their tea breaks, a real-life drama even more dramatic was being played out in the courtroom. In 1990, for the first time in Japan, a Japanese court awarded damages in a sexual discrimination case to ten female workers in the amount of $640,000. Yet in April 1992 when a female member of the Kumamoto City Assembly filed a complaint of sexual harassment against a male member of the assembly for grabbing her breasts at a party and saying, "This is how to treat a woman," the District Prosecutor's Office decided not to indict him. According to their findings, the assemblyman was intoxicated at the time and had already been punished socially.

Japanese men have long believed that it is an integral ingredient of their macho image to boast about their relationships with geisha and bar hostesses and now, it seems, female office workers. This probably stems from the belief well entrenched in their psyche that women fall into two categories: those who bear children and those who give pleasure. It is ideas such as these that continue to hamper the progress of women in Japanese companies and have forced many Japanese women to open their own small businesses.

Women Entrepreneurs in the Japanese Workplace

They're young, they're intelligent, and they follow the motto of the Hanako Girl (the Japanese version of the Cosmo Girl): "Career and marriage alone aren't enough for me." They want not only to see the world but to be a part of it. They've had an opportunity to develop their individuality and initiative. Consequently, these women are turning to entrepreneurship as a way around the rigid structure of the Japanese old-boy network that exists on *both* sides of the Pacific.

Chihiro was proud of her golf score, which was in the low 90s. After all, she was still relatively new at the game and had little time to practice. But she was determined to make a good showing with her Japanese clients during tomorrow's game. Ever since she had come to the United States from Japan as a student to study finance, she had decided that America was the only place where she could start her own company and succeed. But that didn't mean she could ignore the traditions that still bound Japanese businessmen to their corporate ritual of doing business. Chihiro not only learned to play the game of golf, but also how to deal with the intricacies of talking shop while figuring out which club to use next. She knew that if she had stayed in Japan she would never have had this opportunity. First of all, she would never have been allowed on the same golf course with the men, while her competitors, who were all men, would have been able to establish their personal relationships with their clients while playing the game.

Although there are still relatively few role models in business for Japanese women to follow at home, in the United States the art of entrepreneurship is more open to women. According to the Small Business Administration's Office of Advocacy, women are starting small businesses twice as fast as men. One out of every twenty working women in the United States now works for herself. And that figure will continue to grow: women are expected to own half of all small businesses in the nation by the turn of the century. According to an eighteen-month study sponsored by the National Foundation for Women Business Owners, eleven million workers in the United States were employed by women-owned businesses in 1990 (women now own 5.4 million businesses, or about 28 percent of American firms). In California alone, women own more than 400,000 small businesses that generated more than $7 billion in sales in 1990. As more and more Japanese women travel to the United States and other countries, it stands to reason that they will become part of this growing phenomenon.

There is one Japanese company in the United States that *does* allow women to grow with the company and experience the positive side of Japanese management.

Shiseido: A Success Story for Women

As Erica arranged the display on her cosmetics counter, she was certain she'd make a lot of sales today. Her company was promoting their new line of color with a big ad campaign highlighting a "gift with purchase." However, as Erica handed out her promotional material to customers, she couldn't help but notice that many of the women merely put the material into their purses and headed for the Shiseido counter. She couldn't understand it: her cosmetics company had placed big signs all over the store promoting their free gift, not to mention all of the salespeople handing out blurbs about their new products. The Japanese company, on the other hand, had none of these things going on today and yet there was always a steady flow of customers at their counter. Erica couldn't figure it out. What was she doing wrong? What was their secret?

It wasn't long afterward that Erica was approached by a saleswoman from the Shiseido counter. She had been watching Erica for a couple of months and was impressed not only by her enthusiasm for selling, but also by the way she acted with the customers. Would she be interested in working for Shiseido? Erica jumped at the opportunity. Now she would find out the secret of their success.

Shiseido's philosophy is simple: they look for people who understand that respect for the customer is the most important thing in selling their products. They teach their employees to present their products with elegance and grace (for example, how to hold the cosmetic bottles), and provide extra services that will build a strong personal relationship between the salespeople and their customers (like free monthly facials).

The Shiseido motto: "Let the product speak for itself" also carries over into their management style: women are given promotions and responsibility on a timely basis, according to their strengths and talents. It's not surprising that many American women have built strong careers with the company, rising to management level. Shiseido's policy is to fill as many executive posts as possible with employees recruited at the local level. It is not unusual for female employees to stay with the company for twenty years or more. Shiseido serves thirty national markets worldwide (including a new joint venture with a Chinese cosmetics firm to sell skin-care and cosmetic products in Beijing in 1994). Of their 3,200 overseas employees, 98 percent are nationals of the host company.

An American Woman in Tokyo

Pauletta choked on her green tea when she saw the young Japanese model walk demurely into the showroom. On her the sample clothes Pauletta had brought from California looked like flour sacks. She smiled weakly at the Japanese businessman sitting across from her. Nothing had been going according to plan since she arrived in Tokyo to license her client's clothing styles with the Japanese manufacturer. The clothes hadn't fit any of the models— they were too big everywhere; even the color scheme seemed wrong. Pauletta could see her entire investment going out the window. Her fashion samples had been designed for Western figures and were not going over in Japan. She had heard that American women had a difficult time trying to crack the Japanese market, and now she believed it was true.

Back in her hotel room, Pauletta called her client in the States and told him the news: she hadn't gotten a no; worse, she had gotten no reaction at all. Pauletta now had two choices: go home and write off the entire trip or live on her credit cards and wait around to see what happened next. She sat around in her hotel room, waiting for the phone to ring. It never did.

At first Pauletta blamed her failure to make a deal with the Japanese on the fact that she was a woman, but she was wrong. Pauletta had made the mistake of many American business people trying to crack the Japanese market by not adapting her product for them. She decided to find out what it *would* take to get the Japanese account. She studied the experiences of other American women in Japan and found out that, on the whole, female Western executives are accepted as equals with their male counterparts. It was her business approach, and not her sex, that had prevented her from getting the account. She decided to start all over again.

Although Japanese department stores are usually stocked with Caucasian mannequins and Western-looking counter displays, the clothes and products themselves must be altered to fit the Japanese figure. Pauletta took the time to have her samples altered to fit the models, and since she was trying to license an unknown designer, she adapted a cacographic (meaning the incorrect spelling of a word or phrase) English name and saying, in order to attract attention. The Japanese are very status conscious, sometimes in ways strange to Westerners (for example, Japanese tourists proudly show off their sun*burns* not tans after a vacation in Hawaii).

Another way to engage the interest of the Japanese manufacturers was to rent a spacious showroom and fill it with nothing but models wearing her samples. Wasted space in Tokyo is considered to be very prestigious and would impress the Japanese.

On the day of her showing Pauletta couldn't write up the orders fast enough. She had learned that there is definitely a future for women working for the Japanese. It's all in how you play the game.

Is There a Future for Women in the Japanese Workplace?

Megumi had found it difficult to concentrate on her job all morning—her little boy had been ill before she left for work and she was worried. He was three years old and prone to allergies.

As the noon bell rang, she cleaned up her work station and then hurried across the courtyard of the industrial complex where she worked to check on him. She was relieved to find her little Tomoya smiling and laughing with the other children in the lunchroom. His stomachache was all gone. Megumi spent her lunch hour with him at the nursery school, then returned to work in the food company, not losing one minute away from her job. She was grateful to her company for providing the on-site nursery school for their female workers. She wouldn't have been able to return to the work force without it.

Megumi's company is not alone in providing child care for their female workers. Japanese companies realize that in order to combat the growing labor shortage, they must hire women workers. Women currently comprise at least 60 percent of the work force in many small Japanese manufacturing companies, and some women even change jobs to take advantage of this new trend for on-site child care. (As of 1990 there were 22,000 day-care centers in Japan.) The companies are aware that female workers are more inclined to become loyal employees if they know their children are receiving good care during the workday.

Japanese companies in the United States are also changing their view on child care. Union Bank in Los Angeles reported that since they installed an on-site child-care center their absenteeism has dropped, employee turnover has decreased, and maternity leaves have been shorter.

The future career track for women working for Japanese companies is not only improving in the area of child care, but also in recruiting. Sumitomo Bank has launched a program continuing over the next few years to hire women for approximately one-third of their new career-track recruits. Also, Asahi Breweries recently hired 110 women out of its 900 new hires and sent them out as account executives to liquor stores which have been primarily male territory in the past.

Many Japanese companies are doing their part to encourage women to enter the workplace, especially after the release of a survey in 1991 by the research institute of Rengo, Japan's largest labor union. According to the survey, 85.2 percent of the 1,150 women who responded said they felt discriminated against regarding office promotion, and 70 percent answered that discrimination existed on the issues of wages and job positions. Out of the 820 Japanese companies who participated in the survey, 70 percent said they are actively changing their work policies to meet the capabilities and desires of their female workers. Toyota Motor Corporation, for example, instituted a five-year program to boost the number of women on its production lines to five hundred, more than five times the current number. According to Toyota officials, these female workers will be paid a salary comparable to that of men doing the same job.

Nissan is already on the fast track with 560 female workers currently on their assembly lines, and the recent appointment of a woman, Ann M. Jennings, to be Nissan's new vice-president and general counsel in their U.S. headquarters shows their commitment. IBM Japan is a popular choice among Japanese women college graduates because of its active program to promote female managers.

The Japanese government is also trying to encourage women to climb the corporate ladder. They've even put out a video for companies showing them how to explore the job possibilities of their female employees, as well as how to deal with their most common complaints. And in April 1992, Shin Nihon Security Company's Cynderella Service was launched to protect women workers from being molested on the streets or on public transportation as they return home late at night.

In an unusual move, the Labor Ministry suggested that salary-men help their wives more at home, and the government also passed a bill enabling workers to take a year of maternity leave without pay.

Japanese companies in the United States are also becoming aware of the drastic changes in the work force. By the year 2000, 85 percent of new jobs in the United States are expected to be held by women and minorities. This can work to the benefit of women, especially in Japanese companies. Women have traditionally responded well to situations where cultural differences can create tension. They are often more flexible and sensitive to other people's needs. The Japanese realize that with a global shortage of talent, women can fill crucial management positions and do a good job.

Tips on How Women Can Make It to the Top in a Japanese Company

Jacqueline worked as a broker in precious metals for a Japanese firm. She had read every business book she could find on Japanese management and business practices, but she didn't understand how the Japanese businessman's mind really worked until she picked up a workbook specifically tailored to meet the needs of his everyday corporate life.

The workbook was divided into three sections: business strategy, habit and schedule, and diversion. There were work pages for client lists (including their bank account numbers and balances); a description list of clients (including a space to write down first impressions of each client, as well as a drawing of the face of the client to show what they looked like); gift lists (including gifts given and the value of each); a time sheet for the day divided into increments of six minutes from 9:00 A.M. to 8:54 P.M.; and, naturally, a list of golf courses. But the one thing that surprised her the most was a page devoted to the businessman's "Confidential Girl Friend," where such data as her bust size, lingerie brand, and girdle size could be recorded next to a sketch of a nude Western-looking girl, as well as her private, unlisted telephone number.

Jacqueline continued looking through the book and realized that the Japanese didn't have a page in their business workbook to deal with her. So she decided to teach them.

She didn't fret over the fact that behind those smiling faces she knew the Japanese businessmen suspected she wasn't as good as a man at her job and actually regarded her as something like a third sex. Instead, she improved her job skills and put her ideas into operation. She learned to place a high value on her ideas and opinions, and in return, got respect from her Japanese boss and co-workers. She began to develop interests outside the workplace that would benefit her on the job. At meetings she was very careful not to appear overly aggressive, yet not so quiet that they wondered what she was doing there in the first place.

Next, Jacqueline learned how to be visible in the workplace. She began wearing subtle and well-tailored suits and dresses with a sense of style. She adopted a darker more sophisticated color of lipstick. She also became more aware of keeping up her corporate image by not slouching around the office in casual shoes. Japanese men are used to seeing Office Ladies in Japanese companies wearing their fancy pumps to the office, then slipping into sloppy sandals at work. (They think of their company as "home" and act accordingly.) She wanted to make certain they viewed her as a serious businesswoman.

Jacqueline wanted to send out the right message not only by the way she dressed but by her actions as well. She wasn't shy about incorporating her personal successes into her marketing efforts and sharing information and power. She built personal relationships within the company, learned to take risks, sharpened her sales techniques, and, most important of all, learned to be flexible in her thinking and a visionary in her approach to dealing with her Japanese boss and co-workers. It wasn't long before she began to move up the corporate ladder in her Japanese company.

There's no denying that women have special talents in going to work for a Japanese company. Women are often good listeners and persistent yet quiet sellers, something the Japanese admire. Any businesswoman who is willing to work hard and take risks can get ahead working for a Japanese boss.

11

The Art of Business Dining Japanese Style

You get through to a man's soul at night.
—Popular saying
among Japanese businessmen

The Dos and Don'ts of Entertaining the Japanese

Tonight was to have been the highlight of Jason's career in international business management. Now it looked like the end. When he had been hired as the *komon,* or go-between, for the large American corporation and the Japanese government officials, Jason believed he had enough experience to handle any problem. The Japanese were interested in studying the products of the American company and had arranged to come to the United States for a formal meeting. *That* part had gone well, and the Japanese seemed very pleased with the company's products as well as with Jason's skills.

Then the Japanese asked him to arrange a formal dinner and a night of entertainment with the Americans. Jason decided to hold the dinner at a posh private club in an exclusive hotel, but when he arrived a few minutes late (unavoidable, traffic), he discovered that the Americans had already taken their seats—and one of the younger executives had unknowingly sat down in the *kami za,* or place of honor, reserved for the high-ranking Japanese official. After Jason straightened that out, there was a problem with introductions (the American manager was unaware of Japanese custom and introduced the highest ranking person last).

Things only got worse during dinner when the Japanese requested ashtrays on the tables and the hotel management refused to provide them, insisting that no one smoked in their dining room during meals. Another point of embarrassment arrived with the menus—all printed in English. There hadn't been enough time to have them translated. The Japanese said nothing and mumbled what sounded like *bifuteki* (beefsteak), but Jason could tell they were not pleased. Dinner conversation was strained as the Japanese asked about the history of the hotel, including the owner, architect, etc., and Jason could provide only scant details.

By the time dinner was over, Jason knew his career had gone downhill. Although the Japanese tend to eat quickly, they usually linger and drink tea, wine, or other liquor, then take off to a nightclub or bar. But not this night. When the Japanese officials stood up from the table and said, *Sayōnara,* they meant it.

Although his business skills during the day more than qualified him to work with the Japanese, Jason had not prepared for his evening with the Japanese as skillfully as he would have for an important meeting. The Japanese are known for their penchant for cultivating personal relationships and human relations (*ningen kankei*) before transacting *any* business, and these relationships are often cemented over a night of good food, liquor, and pretty girls. But even then you have to follow the rules. For example, when making introductions, the Japanese don't "save the best for last" as some Americans do, but always introduce the highest ranking official first. Also, there is *always* a seating arrangement, from the guest of honor or high-ranking official to the lowest executive. The seat of honor establishes rank and hierarchy, something the Japanese prize highly. In American business, the seat of honor is the one pulled out first from the table and usually has the best view or is the most comfortable. The Japanese are more concerned that it is the seat furthest away from the door (the lowest seat is the one closest to the door, providing a fast exit for undesirable guests) and facing something of beauty (e.g., a view, or flowers).

Many Japanese smoke constantly, even through dinner. If you suspect there may be a problem with the restaurant management, try to arrange for a private room away from other diners. Also, discuss the possibility of having the menus translated into Japanese in advance. This will save your guests, and you, embarrassment. Be prepared to know the history as well as interesting details about the establishment where you are dining. The Japanese like to know *everything* about where they are eating. Having this information at your fingertips also provides easy conversation and will help build trust between you and your Japanese boss or clients.

Customizing Your Dinner for Success: The Rules of Japanese Etiquette

Dining etiquette in Japan has enough rules attached to it to send even Emily Post into a dither. First, the easy part: after removing your shoes, place them together so they face the door you came in. Next comes one of the most difficult tasks: sitting for long periods of time at the low tables used in many Japanese restaurants, both in the United States and in Japan. Since you will be sitting with your legs tucked underneath you, be certain to wear comfortable clothing; women should wear skirts long enough to avoid any embarrassing moments. And if you're worried about your aching back, you can ask for a backrest, or *zaisu.*

Now that you're in position, *Hai, itadakimasu!* Let's eat! (Literal translation: Yes, I will take it.)

Suddenly you're faced with what appears to be one wooden chopstick. This is called *waribashi,* and the sticks are joined at one end to prove they've never been used before. Pull them apart into two chopsticks and you're ready to eat. Nearly everyone has tried using chopsticks at some time, but they still remain one of the most puzzling inventions from the Far East. Yet the Japanese have used them for 1,300 years, while the fork as we know it only became popular in the early seventeenth century.

While many puzzled Westerners try to figure out how they are going to cut up their meat when it arrives, not to worry: this is the chef's job, not yours. The food will arrive in bite-size pieces, perfectly prepared for chopstick use. (More than one Japanese businessman visiting a Japanese restaurant here in the United States that serves beefsteak has been known to pick up the whole steak between his chopsticks and eat it, bite by bite.)

Some of the more common taboos are: don't leave your chopsticks standing up in your rice bowl (this means death—a bowl of rice with chopsticks standing upright is offered to the dead in the family shrine). Lay them parallel on the chopstick holder or on the tip of your plate if a holder has not been provided. Also, don't scrape rice grains from your chopsticks, and be certain to finish the rice in your bowl—even if you're on a diet. Any sign of uneaten rice is taken as a nonverbal order for more rice and your bowl will be refilled until it is empty.

If you wish to select something from the serving plate, use the opposite ends of your chopsticks to help yourself. Dip your food quickly into the sauces. You may drink your soup from the bowl, using your chopsticks to pick up the fish, vegetables, or noodles. Slurping your soup loudly is not only allowed, but encouraged as a sign of appreciation, as is vigorous burping. This often confuses Westerners, who are not used to such sounds at the dinner table, and it is in direct contrast to the refined concept of the *oshibori*, or moistened white hand towel, that is offered to the diner to refresh himself. The *oshibori* is chilled in summer and heated in winter, and often dipped into scented water (jasmine, for example). The question of hand-towel sanitation has been the recent subject of several Japanese television commercial spots, since an average Japanese *oshibori* company circulates between 180,000 to 200,000 refreshing hand towels a day to banks, major corporations, soaplands, hostess bars, love hotels, even funeral parlors.

However, if wiping your face with a wet hand towel doesn't revive you (especially if you're wondering who used it before you), you can belly up to the oxygen bar in the cocktail lounge and order a round. For less than a dollar, you can breathe in a three-minute whiff of oxygen in four different scents. That should keep you awake long enough to get through the numerous rounds of toasts at a Japanese dinner, where protocol is still important.

It was nearly the end of the evening when Arthur lifted his glass and joined in with a loud *Kampai* (Cheers!) with his Japanese clients as they drank to everything from the Emperor's good health to their golf scores. Arthur had been sitting Japanese style for several hours drinking *sake,* but he was still sober enough to make certain that when he proposed a toast he remembered to recognize his Japanese host company first, and then thank the executives who had helped him in correct ranking order.

Traditional Japanese Food Like Mama-san Used to Make

Carolyn knew it was a great privilege to be invited to dinner at the home of one of her students. She had only been working with the teacher-exchange program in Japan for a few weeks, and she'd had little time to taste the local food specialties. She was especially eager to try *o-nigiri,* as her students called it, each proclaiming that *his* mother made the best.

As Carolyn sat down to dinner with her student and his parents, she subtly inquired about *o-nigiri.* The boy's mother looked astonished that the *gaijin* teacher wanted to try so humble a dish, but she didn't want to offend their guest so she brought out what appeared to be a handful of rice wrapped with seaweed. Carolyn tasted it and was surprised by the somewhat bland but salty taste. The boy's mother explained that a piece of salted fish or salted plum was usually placed in the middle. What made it so special to the Japanese was that, according to tradition, each mother formed the rice balls with salt-smeared palms in her own way and with her own sweat. Many adults still yearn for the *o-nigiri,* or rice balls, just like their mother made.

Westerners have long turned their noses up at the blandness of the Japanese diet that consists of vegetables, fruit, seafood, and various grains—especially rice. Yet, according to recent medical reports, the Japanese have long been enjoying a diet that contributes to long life and good health. Their longevity rates are now the highest in the world. (There were a record 3,625 Japanese centenarians as of September 1991.)

Rice is a staple at every meal, and a side dish of *tsukemono,* or pickled vegetables, usually accompanies a traditional meal, as do seaweed, fish, and soup. There are also grilled dishes, such as yaki-tori (chicken), tempura (batter-fried seafood or vegetables), shabu-shabu (stew), various kinds of noodles, and numerous uses for tofu (bean curd, which is low in calories, high in protein, and absorbs flavors when mixed with other food). But perhaps the most misunderstood Japanese food is sushi.

Sushi: It's More Than a Fish Story

Most Westerners have at least heard of sushi even if they prefer cheeseburgers to raw fish for lunch. In fact, a meal of sushi is eaten only at lunch and the name actually refers to the packed rice mixture; the term *sashimi* refers to the thin slices of raw fish used in making sushi.

The history of this popular snack food goes back a thousand years to when rice was used as a means of preserving fish and beef. (The non-meat-eating Buddhists later discarded the use of beef.) The acid produced by the rice during fermentation acted as a preservative until the Japanese found that adding vinegar to the rice was a quicker method of making sushi. Along the way, the Japanese discovered that the rice became more flavorful in the process— over the years the fish and rice changed positions in the hierarchy of importance. Now it is the fish that flavors the rice that is seasoned and packed, then topped with raw fish, egg omelette, vegetables, or seaweed. Sushi chefs are trained for years (in some areas, sushi apprentices are allowed to cook only the rice for the first five years, then it takes five more years before they are allowed to purchase the fish). Women were prevented from joining the profession of sushi-making until 1984, although they are still not encouraged to do so. It is believed that their warm blood and body temperature spoil the delicate taste of the raw fish.

The eating of sushi is just as important as the making. You can hold sushi between your first two fingers and thumb or you can use chopsticks. Next, dip the sushi fish-side down in soy sauce, then place it fish-side down on your tongue and eat it in one bite. If the chef is watching, don't use too much soy sauce or *wasabi* (Japanese horseradish) or you will insult him. Sushi is always served in twos so that the diner can fully appreciate the taste. Many Westerners find eating sushi to be an enjoyable experience—but there are some Japanese epicurean dishes that test the mettle of even the most adventurous of gourmands.

Frozen Whale, Live Squid, Fried Bees, and Other Delicacies

Charlie had heard of the Japanese fanaticism about fresh fish, but he never dreamed he would have the opportunity to experience it—that is, taste it—firsthand.

So far his sightseeing in Japan had been confined to his company's headquarters, but today his Japanese boss had promised him a rare treat. The only problem was that Charlie wished the treat—a plate of squid—wasn't staring him in the face. He had the feeling the squid was going to enjoy this more than he was. Although Charlie knew the squid had met its demise only minutes before being served, to him the seafood still appeared to be very much alive. Charlie picked up the squid between his chopsticks, opened his mouth and closed his eyes. As he felt it wiggling down his throat, he tried to smile—it was considered bad manners not to appear to be enjoying the ritual. When he finished, he grabbed a bottle of cold beer and gulped it down quickly. It was the best beer Charlie had ever tasted.

Westerners often find Japanese delicacies difficult to appreciate, as well as to eat. Much of the "liveliness" of the fish dishes served in Japan, however, relates more to the diner's imagination than to what is actually served on the plate. Returning businessmen and tourists love to recount how they watched the chef spear a fish in front of their eyes, then serve it immediately, although in actuality the fish is carefully prepared before it is served. For example, the term *odori ebi,* or dancing shrimp, actually refers to shrimp that were lively *before* they were cooked and, accordingly, are sweeter tasting. However, there is one dish that can do more than turn your stomach—it can kill you. *Fugu* is known as blowfish, balloon fish, or moon fish because it expands its body into a balloon-shape when caught. It can be eaten either raw or cooked and leaves the lips numb after eating. Its ovaries and liver contain a deadly poison (tetrodotoxin) that kills hundreds of Japanese each year when not removed properly. The thrill from eating it, according to Japanese businessmen, is knowing it could be your last meal, although the poison is fatal only around 60 percent of the time if consumed.

Unusual epicurean delights are by no means limited to seafood. Crimpled snake meat, fried bee grubs, sliced ovary of pig with mushrooms, even whale *sashimi* served at a near freezing temperature with a light ginger sauce, are considered to be taste treats. For dessert, you can indulge in pickled cherry blossoms and green-tea ice cream.

If you can't stomach smoked frogs, broiled sparrows, or shark fins swimming in your soup, Western fast-food has become almost a national mania in Japan in recent years, with such favorites as Kentucky Fried Chicken, McDonald's, Denny's, Arby's, and Pizza Hut now thriving in major Japanese cities. However, even here you may be in for a surprise: Pizza Hut in Japan has recently started serving seaweed pizza and Denny's latest Grand Slam meal features raw tuna.

It's not likely that unusual Japanese food will find its way into fast-food restaurants in the United States: a 1990 survey by the Japan Electric Industries Association found that although the majority of Tokyo housewives favored incorporating beefsteak, hamburger patties, and stews into their diets, 81.3 percent of the New York housewives surveyed said they didn't like the taste of Japanese food.

Formal Dining: The Japanese Way

As Kurt followed the kimono-clad waitress to his table in the Japanese restaurant, he paid little attention to the beautiful decor and the sound of a small brook running through the restaurant. He was starved. He hadn't eaten since breakfast, and even that had only been juice and coffee. As he sat down with his Japanese clients, he realized he was the only *gaijin* in the place. The Japanese restaurant was located in a major West Coast city, but you'd never know it by the clientele—they were all Japanese businessmen. But Kurt didn't let that bother him—he just wanted to order and enjoy his meal.

But the menu never came. What did follow was what seemed to be an endless array of special dishes, preceded by the serving of green tea to stimulate the appetite—this is a *cha-kaiseki,* an elegant, multicourse meal served with ceremonial tea. (Without the tea it is called *kaiseki,* and is even written with a different set of Japanese characters to clarify the meaning.) Carefully selected delicacies are brought to the table on square porcelain trays, bamboo platters, and lacquered bowls. The food is not chosen by the diner, but by the chef to compliment the mood of the season: for example, egg dishes are not served during the hot summer months because this is a difficult time for the chickens.

However, the diner's individual tastes are not completely ignored. For example, at one of Kyoto's famous *ryokan,* or retreats, the chef keeps meticulous records for each guest to avoid the embarrassment of serving the same dish twice. A *kaiseki* meal usually consists of ten or more courses on exquisite plates that are often hundreds of years old. (The same plate is never used twice for the same guest—although some companies, like Shiseido, have their own plates made for special dinners.)

Not only are the plates items of beauty: the chef takes great pains to transform the appearance of the food into a work of art for the eye as well as for the palate. Fish and vegetables are cut or carved in such a way as to suggest flowers, fruit, or even birds. Fried seaweed is often cut into thin strips and woven into small baskets. The Japanese believe that this artful approach to the senses (including the ear: the swishing sound of the meat gently cooking in a stew bouillon, for example) is also a way of controlling hunger so that the diner can take the time to enjoy the meal and savor the delicate flavorings.

All of this art, however, doesn't come cheaply: at the famous *kaiseki* houses in Kyoto, dinner starts at $500 per person. But that's just small change in the land of limitless business expense accounts.

The Expense Account Tribe: Japanese Executives

Bill had never seen anything like it. He and his Japanese boss had been entertaining a supplier for the company at a hostess bar when the tab arrived. Bill couldn't resist taking a look at it. Even with his limited understanding of Japanese, he could read the figures:

¥100,000—nearly $800. Four small flasks of unusual *sake* had cost more than $100 alone. He wondered how much the bowl of popcorn and peanuts had cost. He knew that the company had a high entertainment budget and he had heard rumors that his boss's expense account was more than his salary. Now he believed it. His boss gave the hostess his business card and the matter was settled.

This is not unusual—in fact, it's expected. Large companies can handle whatever amount is needed to nurture the good-old-boy network, but for a small company entertainment expenses can make up 20–30 percent of all their projected costs. Japan's expense-account tribe of businessmen spends about $123 million a day on corporate entertaining, or about $45 billion a year, according to 1991 figures (up from a record $36.6 billion in 1990, and was more than the $42.5 billion Japan budgeted for education in 1992). This includes tipping (*chippu*) even though the Japanese don't tip in the same way we do and may even be insulted if a tip is offered for performing a service. Tipping implies to them that they are not doing their job and must be bribed to do it. However, a service charge of 10 to 15 percent is usually added to hotel, restaurant, and bar bills and is later shared among the employees. This eliminates individual competition, so that the employees work equally as hard to provide the best service possible for their guests.

Extravagant entertaining is not just limited to company executives, who are expected to entertain clients several nights a week at restaurants and bars. Most companies consider it to be just as important for department heads to entertain their subordinates, not only to ensure their loyalty to the company, but to keep any interpersonal friction to a minimum. The Japanese care more about their emotional ties and obligations to one another than about their pocketbooks. Their entire business system depends on this, and it is important to be flexible in your own schedule, as Harvey discovered.

Harvey's meetings with his Japanese boss and visitors from the home office had gone very well, but after a long day Harvey begged off going out with them after work. He didn't speak Japanese and decided he didn't want to spend his evening trying to understand their English. The next day the Japanese conducted the entire meeting in Japanese as if he wasn't there. What Harvey hadn't understood was that if the Japanese are pleased with the progress made during the day, they will often decide on the spur of the moment to continue their business at night. This doesn't always mean that actual business will be discussed, but that the business of cementing a personal relationship is often more important than the final outcome of the deal. These relationships, however, can be expensive: dinner for four at an elegant Kyoto restaurant can cost around $6,900—complete with geisha.

The Flower and Willow World of the Geisha

Chiaki hugged her small suitcase close to her as she walked down the cross-hatched alleyway and then through the covered passageway leading into the Asakusa District of Tokyo. She mustn't be late for her first day at school. She hurried down a tiny street filled with paper lanterns until she came to the teahouse. She hesitated. For a moment she was frightened, but there was no turning back. Chiaki was only nineteen, but she had decided to commit her life to being a geisha.

Her parents hadn't been happy about her decision (there are only a few thousand women who still engage in the profession now, compared to eighty thousand at the height of its popularity in the 1920s), and they had insisted she spend at least a year in college before making her final decision. But Chiaki had not changed her mind. After all, she argued, as a *maiko* (apprentice) she would be paid a salary of $16,000 a year, which was the same as she would make as an OL (Office Lady) after graduating from college. She believed she would have more opportunity for advancement as a geisha than as an OL, as well as the glamour and tradition that were part of the job. A geisha was an integral part of the business world, while an OL was considered to be a *hisho,* or gofer.

Although it was once a form of indentured labor, the glamour and mystique of geisha still prevails with a new generation of young women, like Chiaki, who are choosing the profession. And age is not a factor in the length of her career. Many Japanese businessmen have said that a geisha hasn't truly blossomed until she reaches forty.

The geisha plays an important role by allowing the businessman to unwind and take charge of his own needs after spending his day dealing with the demands of his company and employees.

Although we consider a teahouse or nightclub to be a place of entertainment, to the Japanese it is the frontline where the *real* business of doing business takes place; that is, the ongoing and often imperious ritual of building a personal relationship with your Japanese boss or client.

Even though business is rarely discussed, many corporate executives have finalized a deal while listening to the mournful ballads and witty stories of the geisha.

What makes these women so attractive? Perhaps it is the silent understanding between the businessman and the geisha that only two rules are to be followed by the geisha: never take any flattery to heart, and, most important, never repeat anything a client says about his business.

There is another type of geisha, often called the "plain man's geisha," and you'll find her in the *karaoke* club.

Karaoke: Singing for Your Supper to Make the Deal

Tonight Ralph was a happy—and prosperous—man, and he owed it all to the Japanese. When his bar business had dropped off dramatically because of the recession, he had decided to take his savings and invest it in a $5,000 *karaoke* system to help bring in business. At that time he didn't even know that *karaoke* meant "empty orchestra." To him it now meant big bucks. His place was busy seven nights a week with everyone from workers at the local plant to a few Japanese tourists who occasionally wandered in and sang a couple of songs. Business was so good Ralph was even thinking of expanding.

Karaoke clubs are a $3.5 billion business in Japan. Their popularity in Tokyo now surpasses sumo wrestling: according to a survey taken in 1991, 87 percent of workers say that *karaoke* is their favorite entertainment, while only 61 percent answered sumo matches. These bars in Japan are called *snakku* (snack bar), and the hostesses are often Thai or Filipino women who will light your cigarette, flatter you, and ply you with drinks before pushing the *karaoke* mike into your hand. (Japanese businessmen find this is often their only mode of emotional expression and usually sing sentimental songs.)

The success of your relationship with your Japanese boss or client could be riding on your ability to get through a couple of numbers. It's easy to get in on the fun. Pick songs you're familiar with (most laser-disc player systems have 2,000 songs to choose from). Lyrics are provided (they're color-coded, instructing you exactly when to begin each word). Relax and don't scream into the microphone, and don't get carried away and wander all over the club. You may not get back in time to read the next line. If you need a couple of drinks to help loosen you up, be careful with your alcoholic intake. With the Japanese, however, this is often easier said than done.

Sake: The Nectar of the Gods

Marc had never dreamed that working for the Japanese would be so uplifting: as in the number of bottles of beer he had already consumed at the "Welcome Party" for the new hires in the company. (The Japanese also celebrate with farewell, job-transfer, forget-the-old-year, let-your-hair-down, even cherry-blossom-viewing parties.) The liquor hadn't stopped flowing since someone thrust a bottle of beer into his hand as he walked through the door. Everyone was having a good time, and so was Marc. He discovered that the Japanese become very uninhibited and often act childish when they've had too much to drink. He didn't realize that indulging in beer, *sake,* and other alcoholic drinks is one of the few social activities where the Japanese allow themselves to relax. He was surprised, however, to hear his new co-workers criticizing the boss and some of the company policies. The next day he was just as surprised to discover these same co-workers working diligently and voicing no criticism of anything.

What Marc had witnessed was the use of alcohol to excuse or buffer criticism of their problems at work without their having to shoulder the responsibility afterward. It is accepted among Japanese employees that anything said during a drinking session is not to be repeated or taken seriously; the session is an opportunity for them to vent their frustrations. They view their drinking ability as a badge of merit with a godlike reverence. And why not? For centuries the Japanese have believed that the Shinto gods who created their islands were exceedingly fond of liquor. Their religious traditions are steeped in rites involving ceremonial alcohol, from a baby's birth to marriage vows to funerals. The most popular alcoholic beverage for this purpose is *sake.*

Sake has an alcoholic content of 16 percent, but warm *sake* is absorbed quickly into the bloodstream. Warming the *sake* enhances the flavor—but when served in larger cups it cools too quickly, spawning the tradition of drinking *sake* in *sakazuki,* or thimble-sized cups. Tradition dictates that you never fill your own cup, causing many Japanese businessmen to lose count of how many *sakazuki* they've consumed during an evening's revelry. More than 60 percent of Japanese corporate executives and managers drink more than four days a week according to a report by the Leisure Development Center in Tokyo, adding that "drinking has become part of their work." However, there are only 2.2 million problem drinkers in Japan (out of a population of 124 million). Alcoholics Anonymous has a mere three thousand members at last count, stemming from the cultural aversion of the Japanese to admitting there is a problem, rather than from the actual number of existing alcoholics in Japanese society.

Although two-thirds of the alcohol consumed in Japan is beer (the Japanese drank a record average of 37.7 standard-size bottles of beer per adult between June and August in the summer of 1991), the newest trend is toward light wines with low alcoholic content. These wines contain about 6–7 percent alcohol and some are mixed with soda. One of the most popular is Summer Wine (*Natu-no-Wine*), but mixed beer drinks are also gaining followers. You can order a Dog's Nose (beer with gin), a Panache (beer with lemon juice), or a White Velvet (beer with champagne).

None of these so-called fad drinks, however, will ever replace *ocha,* or tea, in the heart of the Japanese.

Tea: The Japanese Panacea

Karen focused her eyes on the low black lacquered table—it was so shiny she could see her reflection in it as she sat with her legs tucked under her on the floor. She looked younger, she thought, more relaxed than she had in years. Was it because of the clean mountain air? Or the peaceful surroundings of the secluded four-hundred-year-old Buddhist monastery? Or was it the strange aroma of incense blending with the steamy sweetness of the thick green tea beside her? She sipped the tea and smiled. Now she knew why the Japanese considered tea to be the core of relaxation, hospitality, and consolation—and also the way to enlightenment. This was the Japan she has dreamed about—not the hustle of the city, the towering new skyscrapers, the crowded subways. When it's all said and done, Karen thought, pouring the tea over her rice in Japanese fashion, it all begins and ends with tea.

The first tea shrubs were grown from seeds brought back from China by a monk named Saicho in 801 A.D., but tea reached its spiritual and cultural height in the sixteenth century when Rikyu, the greatest of all tea masters, instituted the first independent tearoom. Although the tea ceremony dictates rigid rules, there is no set recipe for preparing the leaves, allowing for that one great moment in Japanese life where individuality can reign supreme, where each person is his own master. No wonder the Japanese proclaim tea can take you out of the present world and into one where peace is the ultimate emotion.

Tea remains an integral part of Japanese life, even down to their everyday expressions: *nichijō sahanji*, which means "a usual tea-and-rice thing." According to a new study, tea also has a positive effect on Japanese health. The drinking of green tea has been suggested as the reason why many Japanese men can smoke incessantly yet are less likely to get cancer than Western men.

Tea has become part of their business life as well. Tea breaks at ten o'clock in the morning and at three o'clock in the afternoon are de rigueur in every office. Japanese businessmen often conduct informal meetings at *Kissaten*, or teahouses, where many a corporate deal has been signed over tea.

Even though the business of Japan is business, it is important to understand and observe their after-hours rules of etiquette. Only then will you be able to move easily through their corporate maneuvering, which can take you everywhere from the peace and quiet of a teahouse to a noisy *karaoke* bar.

12

Seven Strategies for Success

The surest way not to fail is to determine to succeed.
—Richard Brinsley Sheridan

The Secrets You Must Know to Work for a Japanese Boss

The Japanese have long viewed business as a war, while we treat it as an enterprise. They will go to great lengths to set up strategies, and one company in particular has been rumored to have a five-hundred-year game plan. At times you may feel that Japanese companies are more concerned with your strategy than anything else. Strategy is very important in doing business with the Japanese, as Konoskuke Matsushita wrote in his autobiography: "Business is like sword fighting in the traditional Japanese way. You cannot back out and you cannot let the other side win or you are a dead man."

You can be certain of winning with the Japanese by following my Seven Strategies for Success. We'll examine each one separately, giving you different situations as examples, then showing you how to apply that strategy. Knowing these strategies will not only help you in the workplace, but will also make you indispensable to your Japanese boss.

189

One: The Boss Must Not Lose Face

One of the biggest problems Western employees confront is that Japanese bosses often do not take on the responsibility of making the final decision or of admitting when there is a mistake or problem in the company because they don't want to lose face. Let's take a look at some situations where this is likely to happen.

SITUATION: You are in charge of a major account at a Japanese advertising agency when your Japanese boss gives you some copy he has translated from Japanese into English. Although he speaks English well, your boss's interpretation and translation of the ad copy are incorrect and could prove to be embarrassing to both him and the company if presented that way at the meeting with the client. Why didn't he ask you for help?

STRATEGY: A Japanese professional will go to great lengths to protect his face. He believes that if no errors are pointed out there is nothing wrong, and no face is lost. He cannot admit ignorance or inability without suffering a serious loss of self-image. It would be considered impolite to point out any mistakes in front of others at a meeting. Your strategy is to quietly correct the material before the meeting to avoid any embarrassment, and then approach him in private to get his approval before the meeting. Leave the corrected material on his desk with the request that he look it over before the meeting to make sure that you have presented his material in a correct manner. If he has any questions about the changes you've made, he will send back the material and ask for an explanation. If everything is okay, he will say nothing. Proceed at the meeting with your corrected material.

SITUATION: You are working for a small Japanese company when you discover that although your sales are up, the company is losing money. You find out that your cash flow is being crippled by several outstanding accounts receivable that have not been paid. Your Japanese boss ignores the situation. What should you do?

STRATEGY: The Japanese schedule their accounts payable on a long-term basis of six months to a year and are not accustomed to asking for money on a thirty-to-sixty-day period. It is up to you to take the responsibility of collecting from the overdue accounts to eliminate the possibility of your boss having to make that decision and losing face. The Japanese are averse to making *any* kind of decision on their own when working with Westerners. They prefer to have you as a go-between to make the endorsement so that they are not responsible for the outcome. Many Japanese bosses follow an old *shōgun* credo: "Do not move, as mountain does not. Stay quiet, as forest is always so."

SITUATION: It is Friday afternoon. You and your staff are working on a project for your Japanese boss when he tells you he wants it finished by Monday. What do you do?

STRATEGY: In Japan, executives are expected to give up weekends for the company, and clerical staff members are also willing to make such sacrifices. Japanese managers expect the same kind of work ethic from their American subsidiaries. You and your staff should complete the assignment over the weekend. This will help to build your relationship with your boss and gain his trust, which is one of the most important strategies in working with the Japanese.

SITUATION: Your Japanese manager is reluctant to make any changes in your company policies, even though certain ones need to be changed. Why is this?

STRATEGY: As a rule, Japanese managers come to the United States for three to five years and are reluctant to make any major changes during that time. The reason is because when they return to Japan, if something went wrong *here,* they will lose face there, even if they weren't here at the time. This could mean the loss of promotions for them. You will have to institute any changes on your own.

SITUATION: You have just arrived in Japan after a long, difficult flight and are invited to dine with your Japanese client. You are exhausted and tell them that you will see them tomorrow at the morning meeting.

STRATEGY: It would be bad form not to accept the invitation, causing your Japanese client to lose face. You do not want to be branded as *tsukiai ga warui,* no good at fellowship. This is probably the worst thing that can be said about a businessman in Japan. Also, do not try to finalize the deal during this first formal meeting. The Japanese never say no in public and this could also lead to loss of face if you pressure your Japanese client for an answer at dinner. Instead, pay more attention to developing your relationship with the Japanese. Your subsequent meetings will go more smoothly and you'll finalize the deal more quickly once you have established a rapport with them.

Two: Learn About Japanese Customs and Culture

Little things can make or break you during negotiations with the Japanese, whether you are on your home territory or in Japan. Knowing *and* understanding their culture and customs is as important as having a quality product.

SITUATION: You arrive in Japan eager to do business, but are confused when the first thing you are offered is tea, not a contract. What is the importance of the tea?

STRATEGY: More than one Western businessman has nearly blown the whole deal by refusing to drink the bitter green tea offered to him. This is the first step in establishing your relationship with the Japanese. Refusing this simple ritual can throw off the pace of the meeting. Contracts often depend on your conduct. Besides understanding their cultural differences and customs (such as the importance of the tea-drinking), it is vital to do your homework on the background of the Japanese company—know their key people, latest sales figures, company standing in the industry, etc. The Japanese have done their homework—they probably even know your golfing handicap. Learn everything about the company, including the hierarchial order of the businessmen you'll be meeting. Also, talk to other American businessmen who have done business with them. Leave your jokes back in the locker room and stick to safe subjects, such as your family. Let your host guide the conversation and at the proper time he will get around to discussing business.

SITUATION: You are a nonsmoker, but you have heard that the Japanese smoke constantly, especially during meetings. How do you handle this?

STRATEGY: The Japanese smoke more than we do—60.5 percent of Japanese men smoked as of 1990 and the number of women smokers in Japan jumped from 1.6 percent to 14.3 percent of the female population. However, it is not their custom to ask if they may smoke in your presence or to offer you a cigarette. They consider that a personal decision. Also, the Japanese will not make any comment when you sneeze, but it is considered rude to blow your nose in public. However, it is acceptable to spit, slurp soup, or stare openly at foreigners.

SITUATION: Every time you ask your Japanese boss a question—whether you're on the production floor or in a meeting—you never get a direct answer. Why is this?

STRATEGY: It is part of the culture to avoid giving a direct answer, so the Japanese have devised a catchall phrase in response: "That would be difficult . . ." (*"Sā, chotto muzukashii desu ne . . ."*). They leave the rest for you to fill in with whatever answer you want to hear.

SITUATION: You have just been promoted to manager in a Japanese company. As a woman, you have heard that you can expect to encounter some cultural differences. What are they and how do you cope with them?

STRATEGY: Your Japanese co-workers may experience a kind of culture shock having a woman in charge. You may feel they are not following your instructions or even acknowledging you. The Japanese men are not avoiding you on purpose, but are merely acting Japanese. In the Japanese culture there is no code of chivalry toward women. Men lead and women follow. This is a cultural difference that Japanese women have accepted for centuries, and it is carried over into the workplace. It is the duty of the female worker to help her boss on and off with his coat, brew his tea, etc. Your best strategy in this, and in any situation, is to secure their trust and respect: incorporate them into your business philosophy and vision of the company. Be flexible and keep your sense of humor. Socialize with them and employ consensus decision making.

SITUATION: Your job requires that you entertain Japanese customers frequently. You have some idea about the cultural differences, but you are concerned that if you make a mistake it could cost your company business. What are some of the important customs you should know?

STRATEGY: Learn to anticipate the needs of others. When dining with Japanese customers or co-workers, fill the glasses of others, but never your own. Slurping and loud swallowing are expected, and always show gratitude for any favor done, no matter how small. When dining at a restaurant, the meal is made up of lots of little tastes with rice, or *gohan,* as the center of the meal. The Japanese believe that the longer the list of food items served, the better the meal. Use hesitancy as a strength the way the Japanese do, and avoid noisy and boisterous behavior in public. Speak in respectful tones and carefully watch what the Japanese do when you are in an unfamiliar situation (this avoids asking them a direct question and getting an embarrassed laugh or no response at all). Do not talk business over dinner. Japanese businessmen are not won over by discount price incentives and free options—they care more about establishing a personal relationship with you. Once he trusts you and knows you will give him a fair deal, the Japanese will probably not even ask you what the terms are or look at the contract.

Three: Be Aware That the Japanese Are a Vertical Society (*Tate Shakai*)

In the world of Japanese business everything is done according to rank, often in ways so subtle you may not even be aware they are occurring. Here are a few examples of the vertical society at work.

SITUATION: You have found a Japanese buyer for your company who speaks English, knows Western ways, and has experience running a similar kind of company. Then, without warning, he backs off. What happened? What do you do next?

STRATEGY: It is important to be patient and not try to rush the deal. Give the situation enough time for the wheels of Japanese business to turn. Many Japanese businesses are still controlled by a senior officer back in Japan. Your Westernized buyer probably does not have the authority to finalize a major acquisition and must present the deal to the old guard back in Japan. This can still work to your advantage: it is easier to market your business through a Westernized Japanese buyer, but you may have to wait longer than you anticipated for the deal to be finalized.

SITUATION: You are working for a Japanese company but your immediate manager is an American. He gives you an assignment but it is changed by a Japanese manager with the company. Who is really in charge?

STRATEGY: In the majority of the situations, the real power is wielded by the Japanese managers. The American managers may have important-sounding titles but they are usually responsible to the next person in the chain of command on the hierarchical ladder. In Japan, members of the board of directors merely wait their turn to reach the top of the hierarchy (due to lifetime employment and promotion by seniority). Americans are promoted by local Japanese managers, but many times they are not given the power that goes along with the title. However, this system is slowly changing as Japanese companies in the United States continue to Americanize—the longer a Japanese company has been in the United States, the more likely it is the American manager has assumed real power and can make high-level decisions. Until this shift of power reverts to the American manager in your company, you must learn to accept the situation. In the long run, it is your good work, loyalty to the company, and understanding of the Japanese business style that can speed up the process, and even put *you* into that position of power.

SITUATION: You have been assigned the job of planning a social evening for your Japanese bosses and your American co-workers. Will it be difficult for them to mix socially?

STRATEGY: The Japanese regard social drinking as a stress breaker that offers a solution to the cultural conflicts facing them everyday. According to a report by the Leisure Development Center in Tokyo, "Alcohol levels the ground, crumbling the rank and hierarchy of Japan's vertical society." Any problems between the bosses and employees that exist have a way of coming out into the open for discussion after they've had a few drinks. This could be a good time not only for frank conversations, but for both bosses and employees to develop better personal relationships with each other.

SITUATION: You have always worked in a union shop with a clear-cut structure, but now you've taken a job with a Japanese-owned company in the United States. You are concerned about whether or not they have unions in the company, and how they differ from their American counterparts.

STRATEGY: In Japan both white-collar and blue-collar workers belong to the same union within the company. Japanese unions are structured within the corporation to propel the interests of the company forward rather than to identify with the individual needs of craft- or job-related unions. In the U.S. subsidiary of a Japanese company you are automatically included in the company union. Within this corporate union there is a specific hierarchy. Your position on that ladder determines how you are accepted by management, other co-workers, and clients.

SITUATION: During negotiations with your Japanese clients you direct most of your attention to the one who speaks English. Is he the senior member of the team?

STRATEGY: Do not show favoritism to any one person. Although this can be difficult if only one member of the Japanese team speaks English, you don't want to alienate the others and lose your perception of who is the most important. When you exchange business cards before the meeting, study the individual cards of your Japanese clients to determine their rank and level. Then proceed accordingly during the negotiations. Also, if the Japanese begin to argue among themselves during the meeting, chances are that the Japanese have broken rank within their rigid, vertical

structure. This could be an opportune moment to gain concessions otherwise not possible. The Japanese like to keep every stage
of the work process moving on a vertical scale, otherwise they see
this as an imbalance, resulting in waste. They will be more likely to
concede rather than to upset harmony.

Four: Practice Team Effort

The driving force in a Japanese company is the common belief that
both management and employees work together as a tightly knit
unit. The Japanese equate organized teamwork as being the most
important aspect of the workplace. Team effort means identifying
the needs of your Japanese boss and co-workers in varying situations and working together toward a common goal.

SITUATION: You believe in the Japanese concept of using teams
in the workplace but you would like to have a more thorough
understanding of how it works.

STRATEGY: One of the major differences between the Western
and Japanese workplace is that 90 percent of the Japanese believe
and accept the fact that they belong to the middle class. This idea
of homogeneity creates an atmosphere in which class conflicts do
not exist, and workers and management nurture a relationship
that is both trusting and cooperative. This is enhanced by the lack
of private offices where the average worker can often feel
excluded. Lack of verbal abuse by management helps raise the
workers' self-esteem, and bosses often wear the same uniform as
their employees. Labor issues are discussed during frequent
across-the-table consultations between employers and employees
during which the ideas and aspirations, as well as the problems of
the workers are presented, and then acted upon to a satisfactory
conclusion for both sides.

SITUATION: You are trying to have a part made for a new
machine in your Japanese company, but you must have an
approval sheet signed by everyone involved before work can begin.
What is the reasoning behind this?

STRATEGY: The Japanese consider communication and consulting with each other to be the very essence of their jobs. From problem-solving to developing new products, they believe that foolproof, coordinated plans of action are generated through teamwork decisions. Secure approvals from everyone on the team, beginning at the lower levels and working your way up to upper-level management. Instead of a signature, everyone will affix a personal seal, or *hanko*, to the paper. The seal is carved on the end of a piece of wood and is stamped in bright orange ink. (The number of papers sealed by your *hanko* signifies the amount of your responsibility.) If they want further modification on the part, you must go through the ranks again. Once approved, the decision will go into immediate and coordinated application.

SITUATION: You are working to meet a deadline for your Japanese boss, but you have not received all the vital information you need from a Japanese co-worker. How do you approach him?

STRATEGY: Never reprimand a Japanese worker in front of other employees. Face is lost on both sides and the relationship will never be the same. The Japanese avoid confrontations and arguments so no one loses face, even if it means delaying or cancelling a decision. They work by consensus and not on an individual basis, so it is better to discuss the general issue and what the goals of the team are rather than those of the individual. Call a meeting of the entire team and describe what information you need. Then wait. As a group Japanese employees usually know each other well and are accustomed to interpreting nuances of behavior among themselves. They often have an understanding of the strengths and weaknesses of each worker on the team. More than likely they will be able to establish who has the missing information and will work it out among themselves to secure the information you need to help you meet your deadline.

SITUATION: You are working for a Japanese company and their decision-making system done by consensus often seems to take up your whole day. What is behind this?

STRATEGY: Japanese managers and employees view themselves as all moving in the same direction with equal effort and prefer to make decisions within a structured organization. This idea stems from their social system where harmony is most important. They are accustomed to *dantai*, or group members from the same source, where no one mixes with outsiders. Japanese companies train and nurture their employees by encouraging numerous group activities during which the workers can bond together in similar units. This is often a source of friction between Americans and Japanese when American workers see their own individualism as being the most important thing instead of dedication to the group. Japanese managers believe this display of individuality shows lack of loyalty and commitment. The Japanese reserve their individuality for their innermost personal selves, where they believe it is more important. You must accept the fact that business is done differently in a Japanese company and that you have to be able to change your way of thinking. What you perceive as wasting a whole day having small meetings is not a waste at all in the eyes of the Japanese. By getting everyone's consensus on a project before the main meeting, no time is lost at the meeting because everyone knows where the others stand on the issue. Also, it is very important to Japanese employees to get to know one another on a personal basis, and this is accomplished by frequent discussions during the day.

SITUATION: You have been invited out for an evening on the town with your company team. What is the Japanese view of group drinking?

STRATEGY: The Japanese consider after-hours socializing and drinking to be an extension of their work environment. (The Japanese have a saying, "It's okay to cross against a red light, as long as we do it together.") There are no worries about repercussions for making a commotion when they are drinking together as a group. A joint U.S.-Japanese study on the drinking habits in both countries revealed there is a more generous attitude toward drinking in Japan except in two areas: drinking and driving (drunk-driving accidents account for a mere 1.1 percent of traffic accidents in Japan), and drinking on the job. The latter violates their spirit of team effort in the workplace, but at night raucous behavior is off-the-record.

Five: Learn to Use Nonverbal Communication

What isn't said is often more important to the Japanese than anything spoken. "Words separate, silence bonds." They respect the art of silence and you can learn to use nonverbal communication to your advantage in working for a Japanese boss.

SITUATION: You are assigned to a new job in your Japanese company. You ask your Japanese boss questions about the procedures in his department but you receive the silent treatment. What can you do to find out what you need to know?

STRATEGY: Although we consider asking questions to be a healthy sign of curiosity as well as intelligence, it is considered insulting to your Japanese boss to ask him questions. It is also considered impolite by your supervisor to explain too much. A new employee is expected to watch what his supervisor does, then follow him, learning the job in the process. When you want to ask a question, observe the Japanese way by asking an indirect question: "Excuse me, but . . ." then indicate with a look or shrug of your shoulder what it is you are having difficulty with, whether it's how to operate a piece of machinery or where to file some paperwork. The Japanese will understand that you need help and come to your assistance. Also, watch other employees and learn to use the company library to research information needed for your job.

SITUATION: You are in the middle of negotiations during a meeting with your Japanese client when everything stops and there is dead silence. What happened?

STRATEGY: When you've said something that the Japanese client doesn't like there is often immediate silence. They use that silence to either think about what you have said or to disagree with it. This type of silence can be interpreted as the "long maybe." It is often impossible to know what they are thinking. They expect you to feel it. They prefer a suggestion to a direct statement, and will talk around a subject rather than making points on that subject since that could result in someone losing face. When you realize you've hit a snag in the conversation, don't go into a long detailed explanation and make excuses like, "Well, at my old company we did things this way . . ." That will stop the entire process completely, and the Japanese will probably not say anything meaningful for the rest of the meeting. Instead, sit quietly, and wait. The Japanese will speak when he's ready. He will probably not directly state what the problem is until his last statement. Once you know where you've gone wrong, you can say something like, "Yes, I see," and then cautiously agree with what he's said before making your argument. If you want him to change his mind, present your argument in an indirect way and explain that although this idea may be wrong, he may encounter it and he must at least understand it. You will usually not change his mind immediately, but like many differences in doing business with the Japanese, the most important thing is patience.

SITUATION: You are sitting in a meeting with a Japanese businessman and you notice that he is making funny movements with his head. What's happening?

STRATEGY: Read his body language. When you see the Japanese stiffen up and tilt his head as if to say, Huh? then you know that something is wrong and it is time to make adjustments in your tactics. Be aware that the Japanese businessman will normally speak only Japanese and use his interpreter during the meeting. But if there's something he doesn't like, he will use silence as a strategy to put you off guard, then he may ask you a question in English to accentuate the fact that he was not pleased (many times this is the first indication you have that he *does* speak English). He may even exaggerate the problem (a common Japanese tactic) to bring about the changes he wants. Also, make sure you speak slowly and clearly. Otherwise he will use that as an excuse and say he didn't understand you.

SITUATION: You are in the middle of a meeting with your Japanese client and everything is going well until he makes a statement that is so totally out of line with what you are doing that you can feel your self-control slipping away. How do you tell him without losing the deal?

STRATEGY: First, do not lose your temper and begin yelling, banging your fists on the table, etc. This type of verbal communication is also a form of nonverbal communication—to the Japanese it is considered a sign of weakness and is extremely bad manners. No matter what you say or do after that, you have lost the deal. Never show any sign of emotion. Instead, use their favorite form of communication—silence. It can work just as well for you to get your feelings of disapproval across to him.

SITUATION: You've been on the job a few weeks but find it very difficult to get to know your Japanese co-workers. If human relations (*ningen kankei*) are so important, why is it so difficult to get to know your Japanese co-workers?

STRATEGY: On the average Japanese co-workers are so used to working together they can anticipate each other's needs without verbal communication. They have a shared history with the company (they spend more time there than at home) and know what to expect from their co-workers. Although many Americans say that the Japanese inclination toward silence is the underlying cause for their problems in the workplace, the Japanese insist silence is a medium of communication for them. For example, the Japanese will often say something in an indirect way, while the American believes he's merely asking him a question. Problems ensue when the Japanese is waiting for the job to be done and the American is waiting for more direct instructions. The Japanese may also nod his head up and down while you are speaking. However, this doesn't mean that he understands what you are saying—he is merely acknowledging that he hears you. Do not be offended by his silence. You may soon find yourself communicating with him in the same way.

Six: Think Japanese

Many Westerners spend a lot of time and effort trying to understand the Japanese. However, there are times when the only way to do that is to think Japanese. Here are a few examples.

SITUATION: You have been hired as an executive for a Japanese company. However, you soon realize that the Japanese managers in the company vacillate between having delusions of grandeur and an inferiority complex. Why is this?

STRATEGY: The Japanese often suffer from what they call their *shimaguni konjo*, or island-nation mentality. They believe they are different and if they are different, are they superior or inferior? The majority of the time they hold to a sense of racial supremacy in the eyes of the world. At the same time, the Japanese inherently believe that Westerners are lazy and show a lack of devotion to their company. Because of this they often have a problem dealing with American executives who come to work for them. You can overcome their prejudice against American workers by proving to them that as an executive you are working for the good of the company and not just to achieve wealth and power. For example, learn the company song and sing it, know the company philosophy and your company's ranking in your industry, and wear the company smock designated for your position.

SITUATION: You want to work for a Japanese company but are unsure of how to apply for a job. What is the first step?

STRATEGY: When a worker goes to a Japanese company for an interview, he doesn't apply for any particular job. His intent is to first be accepted as part of the company, then go into its training program, and after training, be assigned to the department where the management team feels he will best serve the company. Many Americans who want to work for the Japanese, however, don't understand their way of thinking and become too aggressive during the interview—demanding to know what job they will be offered. (The word "aggressive" in Japanese is derived from two words: *kōgeki-teki na*—*kōgeki*, which means attack or assault, and *teki*, which means enemy or foe.) Appear confident during the interview and show your interviewers that you are willing to apply your talents wherever you are needed in the company.

SITUATION: You are being sent to your home office in Japan for training. What can you expect from the Japanese there?

STRATEGY: The Japanese see themselves as diplomats when foreigners come to their country. They strive to create a good impression and enhance the prestige of their country in the eyes of the world. When you meet your Japanese counterparts in Japan, they will probably acquiesce to you constantly, complimenting you on your knowledge of this and that. Don't be fooled. Even if they know more about something than you do (especially company business), they will never show it. Be humble and you will get more respect.

SITUATION: You made a mistake that caused embarrassment to your Japanese company. What should you do?

STRATEGY: Although Japan is often called the country of the mask, where you can get away with anything if you are discreet, if there is a public embarrassment, you should make a formal apology to everyone in the company. The Japanese way of thinking is that if you have broken a rule or made a mistake, your boss or co-workers have lost face because they did not check your work. To regain face, your Japanese boss and co-workers expect you to humble yourself to them. This must be an honest effort and a sincere one. Do not shout and protest that it wasn't your fault. Apologize profusely and/or write a letter of apology and make certain it is read by everyone involved.

SITUATION: You are trying to break into the Japanese market with a quality product but you're getting nowhere. What could be the problem?

STRATEGY: One often-overlooked aspect of successfully breaking into the Japanese market is packaging. Do as the Japanese do: observe and take notes, then figure out what you can do to make your product more appealing. The average Japanese spends at least $2,000 a year on social and business gifts and they are obsessed with the appearance of those gifts. A carefully wrapped, perfectly shaped, blemish-free melon is given with as much ceremony as an expensive pearl necklace. Chocolate chip cookies are individually wrapped in fancy tissue before being carefully assembled into a gift box. In a country where a uniform attitude usually prevails, how you package your product is the exception. Make certain your product is packaged in a way that represents prestige and quality, as well as artistic endeavor. Nothing cheap or shoddy will do. The addition of a trendy English name (even if it has no relationship to your product) can give an added boost to its appeal. Stay away from black-and-white color schemes (these colors remind the Japanese of funerals), while their flag colors of red and white are always popular. Also, check your pricing. The bottom- and top-end products sell very well, but there is little potential for middle-priced items in Japan.

Seven: Do Not Try to Become Japanese

In the Japanese culture, ego-suppression is a way of life and has prevented the growth of creativity and individualism that they need to succeed in the global marketplace. The Japanese would like to establish a common ground between our two societies where Western employees can learn to understand the ways of Jap- anese business, yet be themselves. We should recognize that there are certain situations when it is more important *not* to try to become Japanese to succeed.

SITUATION: You have found a Japanese company that offers the challenge and benefits you've been looking for. With your past experience, you more than qualify for the job. Should you apply, or are they looking only for a Japanese worker?

STRATEGY: Even though they are now a major player in the global economy, Japan's biggest challenge as we head toward the twenty-first century is not money or products, it's people. When the Japanese open a plant in the United States they realize it is to their advantage to hire more American managers to westernize their operations. The Japanese are looking for qualified Ameri- cans who can grow with them.

SITUATION: You have been hired to train new American employ- ees for a Japanese company. Should you implement only Japanese training methods in your classes?

STRATEGY: Although it is a common consensus among Japanese businessmen that Americans should act more like them, there are many cultural and historical reasons why Americans cannot and should not try to become Japanese. However, all companies can profit by adopting Japanese training methods and business practices concerning such issues as quality control, on-time delivery schedule, competitive cost and pricing, and customer service. *Not* being Japanese can open doors in many Japanese companies because *gaijin,* or foreigners, are given preferential treatment. For example, Shiseido, the international Japanese cosmetics company, instructs their sales personnel *not* to look Asian, but American in every way—from the way they apply their makeup to their style of dress.

SITUATION: You enjoy working for the Japanese, but their group thinking is a constant frustration to you. Should you consider leaving your job or go all the way and give up your individuality?

STRATEGY: The Japanese do not regard individualism as an asset to have in their own group structure but it is much admired and even expected from a foreigner. Your American ideas and know-how can take you a long way with the Japanese. It is important to remember that you have to be an individual in the first place to be able to exist between both cultures. For example, Americans rarely read technical manuals through to conclusion. We stop at about page three and try to put the thing together. Naturally, this causes a lot of tinkering and dumb moves, but we get a feel for whatever the object is. Putting it together wrong also stimulates thinking. We learn more and gain mastery faster than if we always played by the rules. This essence of taking chances and not avoiding risk is what new products and technology are made of. Be part of the group when necessary, but never forget who you are.

SITUATION: You have just completed a course in the Japanese language—are you ready to conduct your first meeting in Japanese with your Japanese clients?

STRATEGY: You should be aware of the pitfalls and possible loss of face even if you speak Japanese fluently. Many times the Japanese will stare at you as if they haven't understood what you said. In their minds, they haven't. They often can't accept the idea of a foreigner, or *gaijin,* being able to penetrate the language barrier they have erected around themselves. They fear they might have to reveal the real person underneath and this would be difficult for them to do. (The Japanese are taught from childhood to hide their true feelings.) Because the Japanese language is filled with so many hints at and nuances of what is being said (it has been noted by Japanese linguistics professors that most Japanese only understand each other about 85 percent of the time), it is a good idea to have an experienced interpreter on hand to deal with any questions, even when you think you understand what was said. Then you won't be tempted to break the silence and make concessions that are not necessary. Learn to enjoy their enigmatic silences and subtle manners so you can concentrate on your language ability and gain the best advantage.

SITUATION: You have invited your Japanese boss or client to lunch. Should you take him to a Japanese restaurant?

STRATEGY: Japanese businessmen usually do not interrupt their workday to sit down to a long meal at lunch and discuss business (it is anathema to them to eat and talk at the same time). Many Japanese are used to eating a simple lunch in the plant cafeteria or a bowl of noodles at their desk. Even Japanese executives usually have cold fish, pickles, and rice for their noonday meal. The American business lunch, however, is slowly gaining popularity as Japanese businessmen in the United States become more Westernized. These businessmen usually prefer not to go to a Japanese restaurant. The current rage is French and Italian food (one Japanese version of a popular Italian dish is called *supageti sando,* a spaghetti sandwich with meat sauce and noodles stuffed inside a split French roll.) Have a glass of wine or a beer with your Japanese client and *bon appetit!*

13

Hitch Your Star to the Rising Sun

[Japan] is what our future is all about.
—Ned McWherter
Governor of Tennessee

How to Get a Rewarding Job Working for a Japanese Boss

Rob knew his company had been having trouble since they lost a big contract, but he wasn't worried about his management job. His last performance reviews were excellent and he had just received a raise a few months ago. There were a few things about his job he would like to change—working for a public company often stifled his entrepreneurial instincts—but he was comfortable where he was. He had embarked on his career in management right after graduate school, changed jobs only once since that time, and had proven himself to be a loyal, steady worker. At forty, he was in his prime, confident, and ready to continue moving up the corporate ladder.

Then, without warning, Rob found himself in the unemployment line, along with thousands of other corporate middle managers who were victims of layoffs, downsizing, and budget cuts. (In many companies there had been no union layoffs, only management cuts.) Rob discovered that the workplace had changed since he was a young man. Finding another job seemed almost impossible. According to the U.S. Bureau of Labor Statistics, in the 1970s the job market grew at an annual rate of 26.9 percent, while in the 1990s that rate has decreased to only a 12.1 percent growth. The number of jobs created in 1970 was 20.9 million compared to only 14.9 million in 1990. Rob also discovered he had a lot of competition on the career track: by the year 2000, one-fifth of the work force will be between the ages of forty-five and fifty-four, the age when Rob expected to move up into a top management position.

Rob began to consider a career change as part of his strategy to find another job. He wasn't alone. Nearly ten million Americans change jobs each year, and the Department of Labor is predicting that as we approach the twenty-first century, the average worker will not only continue to change jobs, but change *careers* at least two times. (According to experts, the work life of the average American worker is 10,000 days long, although the average stay with a company is only 5.3 years, often through no fault of the employee.)

Rob embarked on a grueling job search that required sharpening old skills and learning new ones. Six months later he not only found a new job, but a new career as well. The company offered the benefits he wanted, as well as the opportunity for long-term career advancement without the confinement of a conservative corporate culture. He believed he would have enough influence in the company to make a difference without layers of middle management to stifle him. His new job also offered the chance for travel, freedom to try out new ideas, and the opportunity to compete on a global level—and to promote better understanding between the two leading economies of the world.

Rob is now working for the Japanese.

The American Job Market as We Approach the Year 2000

Bruce had seen the layoffs coming and decided to pursue a new career with a Japanese company *before* he received a pink slip. For the past few years he had watched the American job market go through a painful metamorphosis. As the pressure for companies to slash costs as well as employees escalated, Bruce knew that these layoffs were not the short-term ups and downs experienced by American business over previous years, but instead represented a new shift in the global economy.

What happened to the American Dream in the 1980s? Most experts agree that deregulation and the shrinking defense budget have been major causes for the downsizing of America. The costly debacles of financial institutions and the heavy debt loads of the real-estate market have also taken their toll on the economy. According to a survey by the American Management Association, in 1991 alone more than half of U.S. companies cut jobs. Many cuts were permanent, especially in middle management. Fifty-five percent of the firms surveyed trimmed their managerial staffs, the highest level since the mid-1980s. The auto industry has laid off 350,000 workers since 1979, and in Southern California more than 41,000 aerospace employees found themselves without jobs in 1991. Nearly half of the workers who lost their jobs in the late 1980s changed careers or industries, and more than 40 percent of them returned to work for lower pay.

The competition for the remaining jobs in the American marketplace will only get tougher. According to the Institute for Educational Leadership the labor force will bulge with an influx of another 20 million workers by the year 2000—83 percent of them will be women and minorities. The majority of new jobs will be low-paying service jobs (for every computer programmer job, for example, there will be twelve cashier jobs available) as jobs in corporate middle management continue to disappear.

As job security becomes more myth than reality, more Americans are going to work for the Japanese—not because they provide lifetime employment (some Japanese companies now require American employees to sign a contract stating that they understand they are *not* being offered lifetime employment), but because the Japanese companies are leading in technological advances, consumer trends, and customer satisfaction. The Japanese also offer their employees additional computer literacy and communication training—two skills experts maintain are mandatory as we head into the twenty-first century.

When Bruce decided to go to work for the Japanese, he knew that the only job security a worker has in *any* company in the current marketplace is the experience, knowledge, and skills that he brings to the job. Building your own job security begins with picking the Japanese company that's right for you.

The Japanese Job Search

Donna had worked her way up out of the secretarial pool to executive assistant and finally to a management job when her company was forced to cut back personnel. For Donna, beginning a job search was a new and painful experience. She answered ads in the newspaper, left her resumé at personnel offices, and checked the unemployment-office listings. But after three months without results, she realized she was at a dead end. What was wrong? She had worked her way up from the bottom of the company to a responsible job, but when it came to looking for a new job, she realized she needed help.

Donna is not alone. Most of us spend more time planning the family vacation than looking for a job. In conducting a job search, first evaluate your skills *and* your expectations, taking into consideration salary, security, growth, challenge, and family obligations.

Next, plan a strategy. Begin by researching the company where you want to work. Donna had come into contact with sales reps from a Japanese company on her previous job and had been impressed with their attitudes about their jobs as well as with the quality of their product. She went to the library and, using its database system, researched the background of the Japanese company she was interested in. Using the information she acquired from such periodicals as the *Japan Trade Journal,* she obtained press kits and quarterly or annual reports of not only one Japanese company, but several others on the target list she had created. She researched each company, finding out if people were promoted from within the company structure, what the company benefits were, and if additional training was available to their employees.

She also contacted the Japan External Trade Organization (JETRO), the Consulate General of Japan (these organizations have offices in most major U.S. cities), and other pertinent Japanese groups, such as the Japan America Society, for employment information.

Donna also realized that education was an important factor in determining her strategy for a career change. The latest Department of Labor statistics reflect an enormous gap in salary earnings based on education: $18,902 median annual income for high school graduates compared to $31,209 for college graduates.

Her next step was to catalog what *she* had to offer the company by drawing up a plan that highlighted her experience and skills, and also showcased what she could do for the company to enhance their product and corporate image.

Finally, Donna renewed her contacts with the people she knew within the company and made new contacts by finding out the names of the hiring sources in the other companies on her list. (Most experts suggest that job-seekers make at least ten contacts a day to gain three interviews per week. This kind of schedule should bring about a potential job offer in less than two months.)

Donna was ready to put her job-search plan into action, except for one thing: her resumé. Like many job seekers, hers was not only outdated but outmoded.

Your Resumé: Can It Get You Through the Door of a Japanese Company?

The average resumé receives no more than a thirty-second consideration when it is being filtered through the system. When you submit your resumé to a Japanese company, it's more important than ever that it serves as your calling card and is representative of not only what you've done, but *what you can do* for the company. Make yours stand out. Highlight your skills and achievements rather than simply reporting your job description. List your most salable points that will pique the interest of the company and invite an interview. The Japanese are not only interested in what skills and knowledge you can bring to their organization, but in whether or not you can bridge the differences between the two cultures in the workplace. Your education is also important, although in Japan some companies are changing their rules. For example, beginning in 1992 Sony in Japan will no longer require a prestigious university name on their job applications, although academic achievements and talent will continue to be deciding factors in the hiring process.

The standard resumé is one page long. Check for any grammatical, spelling, or typing errors. No gimmicks: clean, white or buff bond paper is preferred. Choose either a chronological or functional resumé—whichever highlights your achievements best. It is important to enter a Japanese company at the highest level—so if you have a contact in management, mention that person in your cover letter. Japanese companies prefer to hire a worker who has established a personal relationship with someone they know who is reliable—some Japanese companies also require a guarantor, or personal reference, who can be held responsible for you (sometimes financially) if something goes wrong once you have been hired.

Remember, whether you do it yourself or pay a career counselor $500 to write your resumé, it will only get you through the door. Getting the job is up to you.

What Makes a Good Job Interview?

Lauren felt apprehensive as she approached the hotel suite, but it was too late to turn back now. The directors of the Japanese company were waiting to interview her regarding a job she had applied for. Lauren took a deep breath before knocking on the door. She'd had no idea when she answered the single-line want ad in the newspaper that she would have to go through a long screening process over several weeks before being selected for a final interview with *three* Japanese bosses.

Lauren's mind was filled with questions as she walked into the room. Would they speak to her in English? Should she bow? Take off her shoes? What if they asked her if she spoke Japanese? Did they expect her to drink tea?

Lauren had already made one mistake: instead of focusing all of her attention on trying to figure out what the Japanese might do differently during an interview, she also should have directed her energies to understanding how she could succeed at *any* job interview.

Confidence is your most important interview tool. However, like most skills, it comes only with practice. Learn how to stand comfortably with your hands at your sides, not in your pockets. Take your seat with assurance and don't slouch. (Be aware that the Japanese always have a seating arrangement—wait to be shown where you should sit.) Use a tape recorder to practice your answers to some of the more obvious questions that you'll be asked. A video recorder is also a valuable way to study your gestures, facial expressions, and body language. (Keep in mind that while we believe that anyone who does not make eye contact may be deceitful or shy, the Japanese consider direct eye contact to be impolite.) If possible, use a coach, someone who will point out any disturbing vocal speech patterns (answering "Yeah" repeatedly to questions or saying "Um" between sentences) as well as any annoying habits you may not be aware of (tapping your fingers on the table, for instance). Remember, how you speak is just as important as what you say and how you say it. Practice keeping conversation flowing evenly between you and the interviewer(s). In Japan it is not uncommon for interviewers to ask if you have any questions about the company. Even if you have only one or two questions, it is generally considered best to ask *three* questions to make the interviewer feel at ease.

You should not initially ask about salary or benefits, but concentrate your questions on what the interviewer would like to see accomplished in the company in the future. Even if you don't have the direct experience they're looking for, be prepared to parallel what the job requires with your own skills and experience, as well as with the results of what you have done in the past. Let the interviewers know you did your homework and are familiar with the background of their company. Address your interviewer by name (check the pronunciation of the names of the people interviewing you ahead of time: the romanized spelling of Japanese names can often mislead Western speakers.)

Be careful, however, of illegal questions like age and ethnic background—and if you are a woman, your child-care arrangements. You are not legally obligated to answer the first two, and regarding the last question, you can tell the interviewer that you have already arranged adequate child care and then go on to the next subject.

Also, be prepared with your answers to typical questions like: What are your weaknesses? Why have you had so many job changes? Tell me about yourself. Why did you leave your last job? You may be overqualified.

Final points: maintain a good mental attitude during the interview and practice good listening skills (take notes if necessary). Dress accordingly (never dress down—some experts suggest that you dress for the job next up the ladder). Keep your responses brief but with enough detail to give meaningful answers.

Now that you've done your job search, prepared your resumé, and practiced your interview skills, you're ready for the next step to finding a rewarding job with a Japanese boss.

You *Can* Find the Job You Want: It's Not Classified Information

Colby skimmed through the want ads in the classified section. Nothing again today. It was very frustrating. He was interested in working for a Japanese company, but there was nothing in the classifieds that fit his experience and skills. The jobs offered by the Japanese companies in the newspapers included everything from a senior brand manager with an MBA, to a national advertising director with five years experience in a foreign market, to a senior secretary job at a large Japanese computer company that required fluency in Japanese.

Colby decided to give up his dream of working for the Japanese. They probably wouldn't be interested in him anyway.

Colby was wrong. He had a college degree, experience in middle management, and a strong desire to learn more about the Japanese culture and management style. He was the *perfect* candidate to work for the Japanese. He just wasn't looking in the right places. While many newspapers do run ads for major Japanese corporations with subsidiaries in the United States, they may not reflect positions that are obtainable for job seekers who are at entry level or middle management. You have to venture further than the usual method of looking through the want ads. Instead, start with the phone book. Look up the services and companies listed under your specific job experience or talent: computers, advertising, cameras, video, travel, automobiles, etc. If you live in an area where there are stores that carry Japanese periodicals or books, get a copy of your local Japanese Yellow Pages (printed in both English and Japanese). It's filled with useful information about Japanese companies and services. Check with your local universities and colleges, Chamber of Commerce, and business organizations about seminars on working for the Japanese. They can sometimes offer specific help in answering vital questions, whether you're already in the Japanese market or looking to start up operations.

There are several employment agencies that specialize in both permanent and temporary jobs in Japanese companies. They can help you find work in such diverse fields as banking and finance, international trade and sales, bookkeeping and accounting, office design, mechanical design engineering, software engineering, marketing, teaching, and import/exporting. Also, some Japanese companies, like Sony, are registered with computerized recruiting services. For a reasonable fee, you can be cataloged in the service on a yearly basis. Remember, there are all kinds of jobs related directly or indirectly to trade with Japan: high-tech manufacturing, construction, tourism, law, distribution, and research, to name a few.

Many jobs with Japanese companies can be found in California, for example, where more than 80,000 jobs have been created in the state by the influx of 500 Japanese corporations and 246 Japanese plants (the highest number in the United States). At least 280,000 other workers in the state, from truckers to lawyers, earn their living from transpacific trade, most of it from Japan. Florida is also a good center for international commerce and trade and is expected to have a diverse economy throughout the 1990s. (There are presently eleven Japanese manufacturing plants in Florida.) Texas, Ohio, and southeastern states such as Tennessee, Georgia, and Kentucky will continue to win factories and other industrial facilities from Japanese investors through the decade. But if you want to see how a Japanese company operates on the home front, then you might want to take a job overseas.

Working in Japan: Is It Right for You?

As Francine pulled the blanket tighter around her, she watched a huge cockroach, or *gokiburi,* slither across her cold *tatami* floor. She didn't pay any attention to it. She was used to the little creatures showing up in her small apartment. As she tried to keep the heat going in her *kotatsu* (a sunken fireplace used to hold charcoal or heated electrically), the evening express train went by, shaking her second-floor apartment like an earthquake. *That* she'd never get used to. Or would she? Sometimes she felt like packing up and leaving Japan, but something always stopped her. Was it the breathtaking beauty of the countryside after a gentle rain? Or the warm smiles and friendliness of the people? Maybe the living conditions weren't what she had expected, but she never got tired of watching the sunset from the balcony of her *danchi,* or company apartment.

And there was more. She loved the early morning smells and sights at the Tokyo fish market as well as the wild, vibrating sounds of the discos at night in the Roppongi district. And she loved her job with the Japanese trading company. Her Japanese boss and co-workers made every effort to help her understand the company's setup, and her Japanese was improving every day. She was just starting to read company memos, faxes, and signs printed in Japanese characters. She still wasn't used to the crowded office area that she shared with her Japanese co-workers, but she'd never forget the night they brought the house down in the *karaoke* bar singing their rendition of "Stop in the Name of Love." She didn't always understand her Japanese co-workers, but she treasured the hand-painted lacquered bowls one of them had given her for helping her with her English lessons.

Working in Japan was not easy, but Francine discovered that the secret of working abroad is to treat it as a challenge on *all* fronts, not just in the workplace.

If you work for a Japanese company, you may want to take an

overseas assignment to further your career. Some companies require it: a tour of duty in Japan is considered essential for IBM executives, as well as other American companies trying to catch up in the global marketplace. They know they have to strengthen their strategies and their work force in order to deal with the Japanese competition.

You can also benefit financially from overseas duty: more than 75 percent of companies with overseas operations pay a foreign-service-premium to encourage an employee to relocate. This is usually about 15 percent of their salary, although it costs the company an average of five times the worker's annual salary to move and maintain that employee in Japan.

If you are married, your spouse may encounter difficulty overseas finding employment. Only about 10 percent of employers compensate for the lost wages of a spouse by paying married employees higher salaries or a bonus. Women expatriates are still in the minority (only about 5 percent) and the majority of them are single—54 percent, compared with 15 percent of the men. However, finding a job in Japan once you're there is not impossible. The job market is good. According to the Ministry of Labor, in 1986 there were 375,000 new job openings—by 1990 that figure had swollen to 650,000. Besides the electronics and computer industries, as well as teaching English to both adults and children, sport and fitness is a growing $2.5-billion business and the leisure market is now a $450-billion industry. (The Japanese are building numerous theme parks in their country that are expected to generate $75 million in revenue in 1991 for U.S. companies.) However, you will need a work/employment visa to work in Japan and this may take some time to secure (a temporary visitor visa is valid for a ninety-day stay or less). Check with your closest consulate general of Japan *before* you leave regarding the specific visa requirements for the job you want.

Speaking Japanese: Just How Important Is It?

When Monte and Gayle went to work for a Japanese boss, neither one of them could speak Japanese. Monte was a top-notch salesman whose job description dictated that he spend his time working with American customers. He had no need to learn Japanese. Gayle, however, had daily contact with the home office and was just able to get by with the limited knowledge of the language she acquired on the job. What both Gayle and Monte didn't realize was that their restricted knowledge of Japanese was not only slowing up their productivity on the job, but hurting their chances for advancement. When their Japanese company started a language school in-house, they both decided to take advantage of the opportunity.

Monte signed up for the class and loved it, but admitted it would be difficult to learn to speak Japanese fluently. The important thing was that he learned about the culture and subtle nuances of the Japanese people simply by being exposed to their language. He could then understand their management style better and this would definitely help him advance in his job.

Gayle, on the other hand, was placed in an advanced class to sharpen her speaking and writing skills. Her new training earned her a temporary assignment in the home office in Tokyo where she would be groomed for a future management position. Then she could use her language skills to increase her ability to compete on a global scale.

Both Gayle and Monte are part of a new generation of American workers who realize how important languages are to American management as we approach the twenty-first century. As the world markets compete more and more for global business, American managers who are not proficient in another language may find themselves out of the mainstream. It is important to remember that nine-tenths of the world's population does not speak English. In a 1991 survey by Dunhill Personnel System, only 25 percent of the American managers surveyed claimed fluency in a foreign language, and most lacked sufficient cultural understanding of that language.

Recent business school graduates with fluency in Japanese have found many doors open to them that were closed a few years ago. Trade experts have been especially critical of American executives who deal with the Japanese and can't speak their language. They believe that this is a handicap that needs to be corrected. In order for an executive to be on top of his job, he must be able to communicate directly with employees, customers, and vendors. More and more international companies are pushing to hire bilingual employees, bringing about a new sense of awareness of the importance of learning Japanese. Enrollment in Japanese language classes in American schools is up sharply—in California alone the number of students taking such classes has quadrupled in the past few years. Japanese is a difficult language to master, and experts from the U.S. Defense Department estimate that it takes five times as many class hours to gain basic fluency in Japanese as in Spanish or French. Interest in learning Japanese has created the need for new academic testing procedures. The National Endowment for Humanities has awarded $400,000 to a project to develop a Japanese-language test to measure proficiency for college admission.

Japanese companies are actively looking for bilingual employees to do business both with Japanese transplants here and with their affiliates in Japan, but Japanese language skills are only one factor in the equation.

Telephone Etiquette When Dealing With the Japanese

Kathy was very excited about her new receptionist's job at the investment company. Besides having a designer office and a fancy phone system, she enjoyed answering calls from overseas, especially from Japan. She knew how important those calls were to her boss so she always answered with a big "Hi!" and "Sure thing, Mr. Tanaka. Yeah, just one sec and I'll put ya through—gotcha!" When her boss said it was very important he talk to Mr. Tanaka in Tokyo, Kathy would call his office at least ten times a day until she got through. Kathy had no idea she was losing business for her boss. What should she have done?

Instead of answering overseas calls with a curt, colloquial "Hi!" Kathy should have said, "Hello," and then the name of her company in a positive, upbeat voice. "Yeah" instead of "Yes" is also bad form, and a simple "Thank you" and "Please" go a long way with Japanese callers on the other end. Also, avoid calling a Japanese client everyday once you have already left a message. The quickest way to lose a deal with the Japanese is by being too aggressive. They will get back to you at the proper time. They also shy away from taking cold calls and prefer introductions and personal contacts instead.

Work out some telephone-answering techniques with your boss and co-workers that you feel comfortable with. Even if the expressions sound a little stiff to you, they will give your company that little extra touch of elegance and formality prized by the Japanese. It also demonstrates the willingness to take the extra time and effort needed to show them respect, which indicates to the Japanese this is also the way your company does business. If you have a regional accent that is difficult to understand, work on your pronunciation and diction so that you are not misunderstood. Finally, the word *arigatō*, thank you, is the most beloved word in the Japanese language. Use it often.

What Japanese Bosses Want: Do You Have the Right Stuff?

Mr. Oshida put down his pen and took off his glasses. His eyes were so tired the names on his worksheet were beginning to blur: Dawson, Simon, Rivera, Washington, Brown—such strange-sounding names these Americans had. He had been appointed section chief at the Japanese transplant almost six months ago and he still had trouble pronouncing his employees' names. But he'd had little trouble with their work. He had discovered that with encouragement and a little time, the Americans did very well working as a team and were flexible in a wide variety of jobs. They showed both good technical and general management skills, and some of his workers were already speaking some Japanese. He also admired their willingness to learn something new, then improve upon it. They were enthusiastic about their work and had responded well to training on the job. He had also been impressed by the number of employees who spent much of their own time learning about *his* customs and went out of their way to break down their cultural differences.

"Mr. Oshida, you want to go out and have a beer?" one of his men called from the doorway. Mr. Oshida smiled. Suddenly he wasn't tired anymore. Yes, he thought, grabbing his coat, the Americans were the best workers he'd ever had.

Working for a Japanese company requires more than excellent job skills. You must also understand the Japanese mind. Ask yourself these questions: Can you work as part of a team? (More and more American companies are incorporating teams into their companies and have discovered that they not only improve quality, but worker morale as well.) Are your communication skills good? (Most American workers, even if they can't speak Japanese, should become accustomed to nonverbal communications, such as lack of direct instructions on a project. Also, English writing skills are very important to the Japanese.) Can you adapt to different management styles easily? (For example, you must learn to understand and appreciate their group decision-making process.) Are you reliable? (The Japanese are reluctant to hire anyone without having established a personal relationship with them: having a good attendance record and being on time to work, as well as meeting deadlines, can prove your reliability.) Do you show initiative in your work? (Learn basic computer skills for whatever job you do.) Are you creative? (The Japanese need people with innovative ideas. The Japanese system of consensus decision making is too widespread in their culture to allow individual creativity.) Are you people-oriented? (Interpersonal skills, such as a good customer service aptitude, are very desirable to the Japanese.) Do you understand their different sales techniques? (Know who is the right person to make your pitch to in a Japanese company: visit the person in charge first. That person will be the one recommending your product to the company executives.) And most important of all, can you make the transition between two cultures for the benefit of the company? (It is important to make a commitment to the Japanese culture as well as to the job, including interpersonal sensitivity and flexibility with your Japanese boss and co-workers. Most Japanese companies operating in the United States would like to become Americanized, but without a total loss of their identity.)

Finally, whatever field you're working in with the Japanese, don't think of yourself as strictly American or Japanese, but as a company person.

Joint Ventures With the Japanese: A Marriage Made in Heaven?

Drew grabbed his surfboard and headed down to the beach, ready to catch one of those killer waves he had heard about from the locals. It was mid-August, the time of year in Japan when the big swells sent wild reef breaks at Kaifu climbing off the scale. He hoped the surf was cranking and going off today. He only had time to catch a few waves before an important meeting with his new Japanese business partner.

"*Yosenami wa donna kanji desu ka?*" Drew asked a friendly looking surfer in Japanese. ("How's the surf today?") Drew didn't need an answer. He could see what he wanted to know in the big smile on the other surfer's face. As Drew paddled out into the water, he still couldn't believe his luck. Who would ever have thought that he would not only be catching some of the best waves of his life in Japan, but that he was involved in a new joint venture with the Japanese. He had just signed an agreement with a licensing company to market his surfwear in Japan—he and his Japanese partner estimated that they would generate over $3 million in sales during the first six months of business.

Drew is just one of many American entrepreneurs who have discovered how profitable it can be to hook up with a Japanese company in a joint venture. Americans are going into every type of business with the Japanese from scaled-down furniture to flying to the moon. From used jeans made by American companies such as Levi Strauss and Wrangler (vintage 1950s and 1960s jeans sell for as high as $1,400 a pair), to restored World War II jeeps, Americana is big business in Japan. Even Elvis is turning Japanese: managers from the Graceland estate and Japanese investors are considering entering into a partnership to build an $80-million 1950s and 1960s theme park in Tokyo.

You don't have to be a big furniture concern or an aerospace company to have a Japanese partner. Several American entrepreneurs have become part of the international marketplace with items as diverse as antique cars, memorabilia from America's past (neon signs, unopened Coke bottles, knickknacks, etc.), and personal accessories like hats and jewelry.

Here are a few tips to help you operate a joint venture with the Japanese. Join up with a quality partner. Look for Japanese companies or individuals with products that complement yours—this makes it easier to "piggyback" distribution. Discuss your long-term goals at length with your partner. Americans often want to grow more quickly than their Japanese business partners, so make sure you agree on where the relationship is headed. Negotiations will probably take longer than you are accustomed to, and when it comes to doing business with the Japanese, always expect the unexpected at anytime. Don't take it for granted that if the Japanese speak English, they understand how to market your product effectively in Japan. Check out language interpreters carefully, especially if you are marketing your product with videos, and make certain that nothing about your product has been lost or misinterpreted in the translation.

Contact your local U.S. Department of Commerce office and the Japan Information Service Industry Association for information regarding seminars and trade fairs in Japan. The U.S. Department of Commerce also helps small businesses and franchises find established representatives in Japan, conducts market research about your product, and can help you put together a list of potential customers (they started a five-year Japan Corporate Program in 1991 to help American companies export their products to Japan). With programs like this and more planned for the future, now is the time to enter the Japanese market.

Working for a Japanese Boss: What the Future Holds for You

James looked out of his office window at the Manhattan skyline from the sixty-eighth floor of the Japanese-owned building. His company was Japanese, he worked for a Japanese boss, and he was drinking Japanese tea during his break. But he had the best of both worlds. He was paid a good salary, enjoyed good benefits, traveled for the company, and, best of all, liked his job. Sometimes he wondered why he had waited so long to make the change. Sure, he'd heard all the stories, memorized a lot of statistics, and learned about the management style of the Japanese before going to work for them. He had also learned to be more flexible, more democratic, and personally involved with his team of workers.

And now the Japanese were changing their managerial methods to comply with American standards. For example, James had recently been promoted to his job as manager based on his work performance and initiative, instead of on his seniority with the company, the traditional Japanese way.

With the balance of power changing in the business world, James knew his future was working with the Japanese where he could still enjoy the benefits of being an American and help the United States maintain its place in the world economy.

The Japanese are very much aware that the United States will continue to serve as the center of international commerce well into the future. Tokyo's inflated cost of living prevents it from taking over that position. (Office space in Tokyo is three times more expensive than in Manhattan, having risen 160 percent since 1987. All land in Japan is currently valued at over $13 trillion, compared to $3.5 trillion for the entire United States. However, Japan has only 4 percent as much land as the United States.) Consequently, the Japanese have invested heavily in the United States as a sign of confidence in the future and have made many concessions in their management style to instill that confidence in their American transplants. A recent survey of 245 white-collar American workers who work for Japanese companies substantiates that fact: 74 percent of them said they were happy with their jobs.

American companies are also reaping the benefits of working with the Japanese—out of a group of one hundred midsized corporations, those with operations in Japan rebounded 30 percent faster from the round of layoffs in the early 1990s than those without them. American companies have also responded to Japanese competition by making better quality products and promoting more responsive management. In addition, the Japanese have successfully introduced incentive bonuses, company training for their employees, and the concept of work teams to the American workplace. They are also hiring more Americans in managerial positions in their U.S. subsidiaries as fewer Japanese are being sent abroad and more Americans are being sent to Japan on the office-exchange program.

The Japanese are committed to the advancement of Americanization in their companies abroad. They realize this is not only important to their future, but to that of the world economy as they continue to increase their significant role in global business.

We are on the threshhold of a new era of progress for the American worker where your future can be assured working for a Japanese boss. By combining their Eastern technology and management skills with our Western marketing expertise and innovation, we can create a new concept in the workplace that will make both countries stronger and unite us in a common goal. The Japanese will continue to move forward in their search for global prosperity. We must do the same. We must work that much harder to keep up with the Japanese and make the year 2000 the dawn of the Pacific-American century.

Glossary of Japanese Terms

Business and Cultural Terms:

aidentiti a key management concept among Japanese executives that refers to both corporate and personal identity; derived from the English word *identity*.

amae practice of self-discipline—the ability to fit into the spirit of the group within the company structure.

arigatō thank you (polite form: *domō arigatō;* even more polite and usually used by women: *domō arigatō gozaimashita*); one of the most important words you can use in doing business with the Japanese.

bōnenkai a "let-your-hair-down" party given at the end of the year by most Japanese companies where office workers can air their grievances and mend problems with fellow workers.

buchō general manager in a Japanese company.

Bushidō way of the warrior or samurai, designating traditional Japanese ideals of conduct—code still followed today by many Japanese businessmen in their approach to doing business with the West.

danchi a Japanese company apartment.

dango bid rigging—business practice used by Japanese construction companies who meet in secret to secure winning bids for their companies; one of the biggest gripes of American companies doing business with the Japanese.

gaman-zuyoi strong perseverance, referring to a senior salaryman who has been with his company at least thirty-five years.

gaiatsu foreign pressure—favorite strategy used by Japanese businessmen to make a change in a business practice, but without having to shoulder the responsibility.

ganbare phrase used by Japanese businessmen that means: "Hang in there!"

gimu one of the required debts in the life of every Japanese, stemming from the emperor, parents, or ancestors.

giri also a required debt, which means duty to one's name and company.

gyōsei shidō traditional guidance given to a Japanese company by the Japanese government in support of research and development.

hai often interpreted by Westerners to mean "yes" but more often than not it means, "I understand or hear you." It is often used as a way of allowing the listener to indicate in a polite way that he acknowledges what's been said without having to give an answer.

hanko personal seal used instead of a signature in Japanese business (carved on the end of a piece of wood and used with bright orange ink).

hansei the idea of promising to reflect on nefarious deeds to presumably reform; practiced routinely by Japanese businessmen and politicians.

hara o gaguru "to look someone in the stomach," not the eye—Japanese businessmen say this when they are probing your real motives.

haragei "words from the stomach"—the art of communicating by suggesting your meaning in the fewest possible words.

hisho Japanese secretary, but the term refers more to the duties of a gofer.

honne honest voice or real intentions—what the Japanese are really thinking and what is not being said.

insaida derived from the English word *insider* with similar meaning in regard to business practices.

ippan shoku term meaning general-office work—usually applied to women workers and denoting less pay, regular hours, and short-term expectations on the part of the employer.

jichinsai ancient Japanese ground-blessing ritual performed by a Shinto priest for Japanese corporations both in Japan and the United States.

joshi jugyō-in term that refers to all female employees in a company, but literally translated means "girl(s) involved in schoolwork."

ka section or department in a Japanese company.

kachō section chief in a Japanese company.

kaigi meeting(s) held during the business day.

kaizen continuous improvement system used in quality control.

kakushi gei hidden talent expected of every Japanese worker, usually only put on display at company parties or during evenings out on the town.

kami za   place of honor—at meetings, dinner, etc. Literally means: "place of the gods."

kanban   "just-in-time" manufacturing system developed by Taiichi Ohno that relies on "lean production" for its success.

kao   face—the unspoken yet always present status of every Japanese in the eyes of the people he meets. He will go to any length to protect his "face."

kao ga hiroi   "a person who has a broad face"—in business this means he has many contacts.

kao o kashite   "lend me your face"—expression used when Japanese businessman wants to talk to you.

kao o tatette kudasai   "please save my face"—used by Japanese business-man when his face is on the line.

kao o tsunagu   "tying up your face"—a Japanese businessman who must continuously work hard to keep up his contacts.

karaoke   "empty orchestra"—a singalong machine that provides both the words and the music—you provide the voice. Popular in nightclubs both in Japan and in the United States with employees of Japanese companies.

karoshi   death from overwork—the salaryman disease of the 1990s.

Keidanren   the Federation of Economic Organizations founded in the late 1940s that helps direct business development and ensures support from the Japanese government by controlling business donations to political parties.

keigo   rank distinction of a Japanese businessman.

keiretsu   business conglomerates with a parent company and numerous subsidiary businesses that are all linked together.

keiyaku   written business contract, usually only a few pages long.

kiken   dangerous—part of the "3 K's" in the Japanese workplace.

kiken na dokubana   literally, "Dangerous Poison Flowers"—a union for prostitutes, actually called the National Federation of Special Restau-rant Workers.

kitanai   dirty—part of the "3 K's" in the Japanese workplace.

kitsui   hard—part of the "3 K's" in the Japanese workplace.

kohai   term used to describe the junior worker in the *senpai/kohai* rela-tionship (see *senpai*).

kojinshugi   individualism—the war cry of Japan's young generation as they seek to break the ties with their traditional past.

komon   a go-between who makes introductions between Japanese and Western businessmen.

mado no hito   "window people"—refers to a worker who has passed the age of retirement and wants to stay in the company, or a worker who for whatever reason will never be promoted—they are given a desk by a window with nothing to do.

meishi   business card(s) that is as important to the Japanese businessman as his blue suit—you can't do business without them in Japan.

moh kete imasu ka   "Are you making any money?"—the favorite greeting of Japanese businessmen from Osaka.

nemawashi   "attending to roots"—the preparation of the business plan by involving all concerned workers before the plan is put into action.

nenko joretsu-sei   age seniority system that determines the pay of workers in Japanese companies—very unpopular in American subsidiaries.

ningen kankei   human relations—doing business with the Japanese is nearly impossible without that important personal relationship.

noren   originally the "split curtains" that hung in front of a small business; today it refers to the company "face" or symbol of pride; logo.

on   debt in the life of the Japanese received from his family, teacher, emperor, or anyone else imparting an incurred obligation to be fulfilled. This is used in the business world by Japanese businessmen who will often give gifts to incur *on* or debt.

Onna Gokoro   Japanese comic book catering to women with stories about women trying to pursue both a career and marriage.

Onna no Jidai   the Era of Women—term penned by the Japanese media to describe the 1990s regarding women's issues in Japan.

puraibashii   derived from the English word *privacy*—this is a new concept to the Japanese that is not yet fully understood by them.

Rengo   Japan's largest labor union, representing two-thirds of their organized work force.

ringi-sho   the practice of circulating written proposals to everyone involved in the consensus decision-making process.

ryō   company dorms for single male employees.

sabisu   customer service—the Japanese have based their economic stronghold on their quality goods that have the best customer service records in the world.

san   suffix added to last name to add honorific meaning—you never add *san* to your own name, but you always use it at the end of the name of your Japanese boss, client, or co-worker.

seifuku   company uniform or smock.

seiketsu   cleanliness—one of the four elementary points of the quality-control system in a Japanese company.

seiri   arrangement—second of the four elementary points of quality-control system in a Japanese company.

seiso cleaning—third of the four elementary points of quality-control system in a Japanese company.

seiton order—fourth of the four elementary points of quality-control system in a Japanese company.

seku hara Japanese interpretation of sexual harassment in the workplace.

senpai term used to describe the senior worker in the *senpai-kohai* relationship—this form of mentor-student relationship is very important to the integral workings of Japanese companies.

sensei term of respect used in place of *san* when added to the last name of a teacher, doctor, or politician.

shataku low-rent company housing provided for employees by the employer.

shokai-jo written letter or instructions given to Japanese businessman from a colleague of the same rank that serves as an introduction for a Western businessperson.

Shunto "spring offensive" by Japan's labor unions for better wages and working conditions for their workers—meetings are held with major corporations to determine what changes are needed in the workplace.

tate shakai the vertical society—how the Japanese do business, make decisions, etc. according to rank and hierarchy.

tatemae face or facade—the outer appearance that the Japanese show to the world.

tsukin jigoku "commuting hell"—the Japanese transit system.

wa social harmony, comes from the ancient word meaning circle.

washo! washo! war cry (Go! Go!) heard in the streets during the spring and fall offensives, calling the workers to join in the traditional meetings for better wages and benefits.

Yuaikai Friendly Love Society—Japan's first labor union founded at the turn of the century.

Zenchu Japan's rice farmers' union.

Other Japanese Words Used in This Book:

aiso the art of smiling and being courteous, even in times of personal embarrassment or tragedy.

awa-odori soap dance, a sexual ritual performed in a bathhouse by a naked woman as she massages her male customer with soapsuds.

beiju age of rice (eighty-eight years of age)

bēsu-bōru transliteration of the Japanese spelling of baseball.

bifuteki Japanese interpretation of the American word *beefsteak*.

buraku　community or hamlet—a district in a village.

burakumin　literally means "hamlet people" and refers to Japan's untouchables—originally they were the butchers, tanners, and undertakers of society, and were thought to be unclean, according to Buddhist beliefs.

cha-kaiseki　a formal Japanese dinner consisting of a multitude of courses served with ceremonial green tea.

chan　suffix used to make diminutive form of names—used only among children or young lovers.

chaya　teahouse

chikan　mashers on Japanese train system.

chippu　Japanese interpretation of the word *tip*—a custom practically nonexistent in Japan.

chūgen　midyear gifts

dantai　group members from the same source (company, family, neighborhood, etc.) where no one mixes with outsiders.

ero-manga　Japanese erotic comic books.

eta　"much filth"—Japanese word previously used to describe the *burakumin*.

fugu　blowfish that contains deadly poison in its ovaries and liver; eating it can be fatal if it is not prepared properly.

futon　padded quilts spread on the floor in a Japanese home and used as a mattress and covers.

gaijin　foreigner or outside person, originally from the word *gaikokujin*.

geisha or *geiko* (in Kyoto)　literally means "art person" and refers to women who cater to businessmen with conversation, dance, and music in expensive teahouses.

genki desu ka　"How are you?"—Japanese greeting.

geta　wooden clogs—worn today mostly by young geisha apprentices.

gohan　rice (refers to boiled or steamed rice eaten at meals).

gokiburi　a Japanese cockroach.

hakujin　white man, race—foreigner, meaning Occidental.

hakko ichiu　Japanese pre-World War II military plan to cover the world under one Japanese roof.

han　squad of school children.

hara　stomach—the center of the Japanese soul.

hara ga ōkii　"big stomach"—means that someone is big-hearted.

hibakusha　survivors of the A-bombings in August, 1945—most of whom still suffer from the effects of radiation poisoning.

hiragana　the Japanese system of writing that encompasses the fifty-one characters of the Japanese alphabet.

ichi ban   number one.

ikebana   ancient art of Japanese flower arranging—often done in conjunction with the tea ceremony.

itadakimasu   literally, "I will receive it." Expression used when beginning to eat a Japanese meal.

itto   first class, especially when referring to a status item, such as a watch or automobile.

Japayuki-san   "Miss Going-to-Japan"—women flown to Japan from other parts of Asia to become prostitutes.

Jiyi Gakuen   Freedom School—alternative school where Japanese students are taught nontraditional ways such as self-expression and assertiveness.

juko   cram school.

kaiseki   Japanese formal dinner served with a multitude of courses, but *without* the ceremonial green tea.

kami   Shinto term for Japanese gods or divine beings; also means the head or source of something.

kamikaze   "divine wind"—refers to the typhoon winds which once saved the islands of Japan from being overrun by Kublai Khan's armada in the thirteenth century; name given to World War II suicide pilots.

kampai   traditional Japanese drinking toast.

kappa   flat-headed *sake*-loving mythological creature who preyed on virgins to impregnate them.

katakana   system of writing employing different Japanese characters that is used only for foreign words and official documents.

kenbei   hatred of the United States.

kissaten   Japanese teahouses that are more like salons where businessmen can conduct business rather than taking a client to their home; also popular places for Japanese to come and relax with tea and a good book.

kodomo no hi   children's day celebrated on May 5.

kōgeki-teki na   aggressive.

koseki   official family register—every Japanese citizen has one.

kotatsu   sunken fireplace in the middle of the floor in the main room of the Japanese home and covered with a quilt—charcoal was previously used, now it is more likely to be electricity that provides the warmth.

kun   suffix added to names instead of *san* when used between young men.

ma   space used in speech pattern meaning interval or pause; these enigmatic pauses in speech during negotiations by Japanese businessmen often cause much friction with Westerners.

maiko   apprentice geisha—differentiated by her flowing kimono sleeves and trailing sash, or *obi*, in back.

manga   Japanese comic books.

mikudari-han   Japanese method of divorce before World War II—a short letter of intent three-and-a-half lines long was written by a Japanese man when he wanted to divorce his wife.

minshuku   country inn, not as expensive as a *ryokan*.

mu   nothingness, the ability to see possibilities in a void.

Natu-no-wine   Summer Wine—popular low-alcoholic wine.

nichijō sahanji   a popular Japanese expression meaning "a usual tea and rice thing."

nigo-san   Japanese slang for mistress means "Miss Number Two."

Nisei   first generation Japanese-American, born in the United States.

nudo gekijo   Japanese striptease theaters.

obāsan   grandmother.

ocha   Japanese green tea, derived from the Chinese word for tea, *ch'a*.

odori ebi   "dancing" shrimp dish, referring to the lively state of the shrimp before they were cooked.

ofuro   the Japanese version of a hot tub or bath, sometimes located out of doors, but always used for relaxation, never cleansing.

okotoba   "August words," referring to the speech given by Emperor Akihito to South Korean President Roh Tae Woo in 1990 as a statement of regret for Japan's treatment of Korea.

o-nigiri   hand-made rice balls with a salted plum or fish inside—a traditional favorite Japanese snack food.

oshibori   a damp, moistened hand towel served hot in winter, cool in summer in Japanese restaurants.

pachinko   pinball machine game first introduced to Japan after World War II and now a billion-dollar-a-year industry—patrons sit for hours playing and win only small prizes, like soap and candy.

rori-kon   Lolita complex.

ryokan   Japanese inn or retreat with outstanding service and food.

Sā, chotto muzukashii desu ne. . . .   "That would be difficult" is a catch-all phrase used by the Japanese to avoid giving a direct answer.

sakazuki   traditional thimble-sized cups used to drink *sake*.

sake   Japanese rice wine, sometimes spelled *saki* or *osake*.

sashimi   thin slices of raw fish used in making *sushi*.

sayōnara   goodbye.

seibo   year-end gifts.

shabu shabu   Japanese stew made with beef, fish, and vegetables.

shi   the number four; also means death.

shikata   way of doing things.

shikata ga nai   "it can't be helped"—favorite expression of Japan's elderly.

shimaguni konjo   island-nation mentality—expression used by the Japanese to describe why they believe they are different from the rest of the world.

shimon   fingerprinting—required of all aliens, and until recently, of all Japanese-born people of Korean descent.

shinjinrui   literally, "new breed"—term used to describe Japanese young people who have broken with tradition, often used by older Japanese in contemptuous manner.

shōgun   military leaders invested by the Emperor during Japan's time of isolation from the rest of the world in the pre-Meiji Era (before 1868).

shōji   a sliding screen with a wood frame and translucent paper panels—used as a room divider or door in Japanese homes.

snakku   Japanese snack bars.

sonnojoi   "revere the Emperor and expel the barbarians"—popular slogan among subservient groups in the late nineteenth century.

sumo   Japanese wrestling.

supageti sando   Japanese version of spaghetti sandwich.

sushi   packed rice mixture topped with fish, vegetables, egg omelette, or seaweed and wrapped in seaweed.

tabi   Japanese socks with separated division between the big toe and other toes to be worn with thong sandals.

tachishōben   act of urinating in public.

taichiai   "Charge!"—yell given at sumo wrestling games.

take   bamboo.

takobeya   sweatshops—literally, octopus rooms.

tanitsu kokka, tanitsu minzoku   Japan is "one nation, one race."

tatami   thick rush mat(s) measuring about six feet by three feet used to cover floors in Japanese houses; also the way that rooms are measured regarding space (a two-*tatami* room, three-*tatami* room, etc.).

taue   rice transplanting—the oldest Japanese work ethic that was the beginning of the concept of teamwork.

tempura   batter-fried seafood or vegetables.

tofu   bean curd.

tsubame   swallow—name given to Japanese gigolos.

tsukemono   side dish of pickled vegetables served at Japanese meals.

tsukiai ga warui   "no good at fellowship"—just about the worst thing that can be said about a businessman in Japan.

uchikake   elaborate white kimono overcoat worn only at weddings.

uki-yo "floating world,"—usually used to refer to the historical Japan of geisha and prostitutes.

usagi goya literally, "rabbit hutch(es)"—slang term used by the Japanese to describe the size of their tiny, cramped apartments.

waribashi wooden chopsticks joined at one end—they are broken apart for use and used only once; served in restaurants.

wasabi Japanese horseradish.

yaki-tori grilled chicken, usually served on a wooden skewer.

yakuza Japan's version of gangsters, usually kept under control by the National Police Agency, known for their flamboyant style of clothing and decorative body tattoos.

yoseba Japan's illegal labor market.

zaisu a backrest that can be used when sitting on *tatami* mats.

Bibliography

The following are sources and references that I have found to be informative and enjoyable:

Aguayo, Rafael. *Dr. Deming: The American Who Taught the Japanese About Quality.* Secaucus, N.J.: Carol Publishing Group, 1990.

Alston, Jon P. *The Intelligent Businessman's Guide to Japan.* Rutland, Vt., and Tokyo: Tuttle, 1990.

Axtell, Roger E. ed. *Do's and Taboos Around the World.* New York: Wiley, 1990.

Benedict, Ruth. *The Chrysanthemum and the Sword.* Rutland, Vt., and Tokyo: Tuttle, 1946.

Brockman, Terry. *The Job Hunter's Guide to Japan.* Tokyo and New York: Kodansha, 1990.

Condon, John C. *With Respect to the Japanese: A Guide for Americans.* Yarmouth, Maine: Intercultural Press Inc., 1984.

Copeland, Lennie and Griggs, Lewis. *Going International: How to Make Friends and Deal Effectively in the Global Marketplace.* New York: Random House, 1985.

DeMente, Boye. *Japanese Etiquette and Ethics in Business.* Lincolnwood, Il.: Passport Books/National Textbook, 1986.

DeMente, Boye. *P's & Cues for Travelers in Japan.* San Francisco: Shufunotomo Co., Ltd. Japan Publications Trading Co. Inc., 1974.

Friedman, George and LeBard, Meredith. *The Coming War With Japan.* New York: St. Martin's Press, 1991.

Ishihara, Shintaro. *The Japan That Can Say No.* New York: Simon and Schuster, 1990.

Kakuzo, Okakura. *The Book of Tea.* Rutland, Vt., and Tokyo: Tuttle, 1956.

Katzenstein, Gary. *Funny Business: An Outsider's Year in Japan.* Tokyo: Soho Press, 1989.

Kinoshita, June and Palevsky, Nicholas. *Gateway to Japan.* Tokyo and New York: Kodansha, 1990.

Lanier, Alison R. *The Rising Sun on Main Street: Working With the Japanese.* Morrisville, Pa.: International Information Associates, Yardley, 1990.

Maraini, Fosco. *Meeting With Japan.* New York: Viking, 1959.

Morgan, James C. and Morgan, Jeffrey J. *Cracking the Japanese Market.* New York: Free Press, 1991.

Rowland, Diana. *Japanese Business Etiquette: A Practical Guide to Success With the Japanese.* New York: Morrow, 1985.

Van Wolferen, Karel. *The Enigma of Japanese Power.* New York: Knopf, 1989.

Vogel, Ezra. *Japan as No. 1: Lessons for America.* Cambridge and London: Harper and Row, 1980.

Welty, Paul Thomas. *The Asians: Their Heritage and Their Destiny.* New York: Lippincott, 1976.

Appendix

Addresses of Japanese Organizations and Institutions

Consulate General of Japan
250 East 1st Street
Suite # 1507
Los Angeles, CA 90012
(213) 624-8305

Consulate General of Japan
280 Park Avenue
New York, NY 10017
(212) 986-1600

Consulate General of Japan
2520 Massachusetts, N.W.
Washington, D.C. 20008
(202) 234-2266

Consulate General of Japan
625 N. Michigan Avenue
Chicago, IL 60611
(312) 280-0400

Consulate General of Japan
1601 Post St.
San Francisco, CA 94115
(415) 921-8000

Japan America Society of
    Southern California
ARCO Plaza
505 South Flower Street, Level C
Los Angeles, CA 90071
(213) 627-6217

Japan America Society Inc.
333 East 47th Street
New York, NY 10017
(212) 832-1155

Japan America Society of
Washington, Inc.
Bacon House Mews
606 18th Street, N.W.
Washington D.C. 20006
(202) 289-8290

Japan-American Society of
Chicago, Inc.
40 North Dearborn, Suite 910
Chicago, IL 60602
(312) 263-3049

Japan Society of Northern
California
350 Sansome Street, Suite 630
San Francisco, CA 94104
(415) 986-4383

JBA (Japan Business Association
of Southern California)
345 Figueroa Street, Suite 206
Los Angeles, CA 90017
(213) 485-0160

Japan Development Bank
575 Fifth Avenue, 28th Floor
New York, NY 10017
(212) 949-7550

Japan Development Bank
601 Figueroa Street, Suite 4450
Los Angeles, CA 90017
(213) 362-2980

JETRO (Japan External Trade
Organization)
1221 Avenue of the Americas
New York, NY 10020
(212) 997-0400

JETRO (Japan External Trade
Organization)
725 South Figueroa Street
Los Angeles, CA 90017
(213) 624-8855

Ministry of International Trade
and Industry
1221 Avenue of the Americas,
44th Floor
New York, NY 10020
(212) 819-7770

Office of Japan w/n ITA
(International Trade Association)
14th and Constitution NW
Room 2318
Washington D.C. 20230
(202) 377-2425

President's Export Council
Room 3215
Washington D.C. 20230
(202) 377-1125

U.S. Department of Commerce
Fourteenth Street between
Constitution Avenue and E
Street NW
Washington D.C. 20230
(202) 377-2000

Index

241